THE REVELS PLAYS

Former editors
Clifford Leech 1958–71
F. David Hoeniger 1970–85

General editors
David Bevington, E. A. Honigmann, J. R. Mulryne
and Eugene M. Waith

THE STAPLE OF NEWS

MANCHESTER
UNIVERSITY PRESS

A
TRVE RELATION
OF THE NEVVES OF
this prefent VVeeke.

Containing thefe particulars :

A late great ouerthrow giuen by *Bethlem Gabor* to the Emperour.

With his other Proceedings and Defignes.

The feuerall Ambaffages lately fent into *Germany,* whereby many braue Refolutions are manifefted.

The Mutinies of many Imperiall Souldiers in feuerall parts, many of them running ouer to ferue the Proteftant Princes and States, as *Bethlem Gabor, The States of the Vnited Prouinces, The Marquis of Durlack, Count Mansfield,* and others.

L A S T L Y,
It difcouereth many good tidings and notable paffages lately hapning in the *Empire, France, Poland,* the *Low Countries,* and many other parts of . Chriftendome.

L O N D O N,
Printed for *Nathanael Butter,* and
Nicholas Bourne. 1624.

Title-page to one of the numbered and dated newsbooks which started to appear in 1622.

THE REVELS PLAYS

THE STAPLE OF NEWS

BEN JONSON

edited by Anthony Parr

MANCHESTER
UNIVERSITY PRESS
Manchester and New York

*distributed exclusively in the USA
by* St. Martin's Press

Introduction, critical apparatus, etc.
© Anthony Parr 1988

Reprinted 1999

The right of Anthony Parr to be identified as the editor of this work has
been asserted by him in accordance with the Copyright, Designs and
Patents Act 1988.

First published by Manchester University Press 1988

This edition published by Manchester University Press
Oxford Road, Manchester M13 9NR, UK
and Room 400, 175 Fifth Avenue, New York, NY 10010, USA
http://www.man.ac.uk/mup

Distributed exclusively in the USA by
St. Martin's Press, Inc., 175 Fifth Avenue, New York,
NY 10010, USA

Distributed exclusively in Canada by
UBC Press, University of British Columbia, 6344 Memorial Road,
Vancouver, BC, Canada V6T 1Z2

British Library Cataloguing-in-Publication Data
A catalogue record for this book is available from the British Library

Library of Congress Cataloging-in-Publication Data applied for

ISBN 0 7190 5906 2 *paperback*

07 06 05 04 03 02 01 00   10 9 8 7 6 5 4 3 2 1

Typeset in Hong Kong
by Best-set Typesetter Ltd
Printed in Great Britain
by Bell & Bain Ltd, Glasgow

TO MY PARENTS

THE REVELS PLAYS

BEAUMONT *The Knight of the Burning Pestle*

CHAPMAN *Bussy d'Ambois*

CHAPMAN, JONSON, MARSTON *Eastward Ho*

DEKKER *The Shoemaker's Holiday*

FORD *'Tis Pity She's a Whore*

JONSON *The Alchemist The Devil Is an Ass Poetaster Sejanus: His Fall
The Magnetic Lady The Staple of News*

LYLY *Campaspe* and *Sappho and Phao Endymion Galatea* and *Midas*

MARLOWE *Doctor Faustus Edward the Second The Jew of Malta
Tamburlaine the Great*

MARSTON *Antonio's Revenge The Malcontent*

MIDDLETON *A Game at Chess Women Beware Women Michaelmas Term*

MIDDLETON AND DEKKER *The Changeling The Roaring Girl*

WEBSTER *The Duchess of Malfi The White Devil*

Contents

Illustrations

General Editors' Preface

Clifford Leech conceived of the Revels Plays as a series in the mid-1950s, modelling the project on the New Arden Shakespeare. The aim, as he wrote in 1958, was 'to apply to Shakespeare's predecessors, contemporaries and successors the methods that are now used in Shakespeare's editing'. The plays chosen were to include well-known works from the early Tudor period to about 1700, as well as others less familiar but of literary and theatrical merit: 'the plays included', Leech wrote, 'should be such as to deserve and indeed demand performance'. We owe it to Clifford Leech that the idea became reality. He set the high standards of the series, ensuring that editors of individual volumes produced work of lasting merit, equally useful for teachers and students, theatre directors and actors. Clifford Leech remained General Editor until 1971, and was succeeded by F. David Hoeniger, who retired in 1985.

The Revels Plays are now under the direction of four General Editors, David Bevington, E. A. J. Honigmann, J. R. Mulryne and E. M. Waith. Published originally by Methuen, the series is now published by Manchester University Press, embodying essentially the same format, scholarly character and high editorial standards of the series as first conceived. The series concentrates on plays from the period 1558–1642, and includes a small number of non-dramatic works of interest to students of drama. Some slight changes have been made: for example, in editions from 1978, notes to the introduction are placed together at the end, not at the foot of the page. Collation and commentary notes continue, however, to appear on the relevant pages.

The text of each Revels play, in accordance with established practice in the series, is edited afresh from the original text of best authority (in a few instances, texts), but spelling and punctuation are modernised and speech headings are silently made consistent. Elisions in the original are also silently regularised, except where metre would be affected by the change; since 1968 the '-ed' form is used for non-syllabic terminations in past tenses and past participles ('-'d' earlier), and '-èd' for syllabic ('-ed' earlier). The editor emends, as distinct from modernises, the original only in instances where error is patent, or at least very probable, and correction persuasive. Act divisions are given only if they appear in the original or if the structure of the play clearly points to them. Those act and scene divisions not in the original are provided in small type. Square brackets are also used for any other additions to or changes in the stage directions of the original.

Revels Plays do not provide a variorum collation, but only those variants which require the critical attention of serious textual students. All departures of substance from 'copy-text' are listed, including any relineation and those changes in punctuation which involve to any degree a decision between alternative interpretations; but not such accidentals as turned letters, nor necessary additions to stage directions whose editorial nature is already made clear by the use of brackets. Press corrections in the 'copy-text' are likewise collated. Of later emendations of the text, only those are given which as alternative readings still deserve attention.

One of the hallmarks of the Revels Plays is the thoroughness of their annotations. Besides explaining the meaning of difficult words and passages, the editor provides comments on customs or usage, text or stage-business – indeed, on anything judged pertinent and helpful. Each volume contains an Index to the Commentary, in which particular attention is drawn to meanings for words not listed in *OED*, and (starting in 1996) an indexing of proper names and topics in the Introduction and Commentary.

The introduction to a Revels play assesses the authority of the 'copy-text' on which it is based, and discusses the editorial methods employed in dealing with it; the editor also considers the play's date and (where relevant) sources, together with its place in the work of the author and in the theatre of its time. Stage history is offered, and in the case of a play by an author not previously represented in the series a brief biography is given.

It is our hope that plays edited in this fashion will promote further scholarly and theatrical investigation of one of the richest periods in theatrical history.

DAVID BEVINGTON
E. A. J. HONIGMANN
J. R. MULRYNE
E. M. WAITH

Preface

This edition started life as a doctoral thesis at the University of Toronto, and my first debt is to that institution for the award of a Connaught fellowship in 1981–84. Toronto has more than its fair share of Jonsonians, and to many there I am grateful, including John Astington, William Blissett, Alexander Leggatt, and especially Brian Parker, whose close scrutiny of my work saved me from numerous follies and errors. I am similarly indebted to G. R. Hibbard for many saving suggestions; and, at a later stage, to Eugene M. Waith, whose attentiveness as General Editor has been exemplary. For remaining blemishes I am of course responsible.

Two friends, Catharine Lawrence and Paul Yachnin, have been an ever-ready source of stimulus and encouragement; and Ruth Versfeld lent invaluable support when it was most needed. My greatest debt is to David Hoeniger, who as supervisor gave unstintingly of his long experience with the Revels – and much else besides – and has been throughout a rigorous and sympathetic guide.

I was encouraged at various stages of this project by D. F. McKenzie, whose own work on Jonson and the history of the book trade has been an inspiration and a challenge. I would also like to acknowledge the help I have received from librarians at the British Library, the Bodleian, the Humanities Research Center at Austin, Texas, and the Robarts and Victoria College libraries in Toronto. Finally, all Revels editors are fortunate to have John Banks at the helm: to him and his colleagues at Manchester University Press, my thanks.

A. N. Parr
King's College London
1987

Abbreviations

A REFERENCE WORKS AND JOURNALS

Bentley   G. E. Bentley, *The Jacobean and Caroline Stage*, 7 vols (Oxford, 1941–68).

Cotgrave   Randle Cotgrave, *A Dictionarie of the French and English Tongues* (London, 1611).

Dahl   Folke Dahl, *A Bibliography of English Corantos and Periodical Newsbooks 1620–42* (London, 1952).

E.L.N.   *English Language Notes.*

E.L.R.   *English Language Review.*

E.&S.   *Essays and Studies.*

E.S.   *English Studies.*

Florio   *Queen Anna's New World of Words* (London, 1611).

H.L.Q.   *Huntington Library Quarterly.*

J.E.G.P.   *Journal of English and Germanic Philology.*

J.H.I.   *Journal of the History of Ideas.*

J.I.H.   *Journal of Interdisciplinary History.*

Linthicum   M. Channing Linthicum, *Costume in the Drama of Shakespeare and his Contemporaries* (Oxford, 1936).

M.L.N.   *Modern Language Notes.*

M.L.R.   *Modern Language Review.*

N.&Q.   *Notes & Queries.*

Nares   Robert Nares, *A Glossary . . . of Words, Phrases, Names, and Allusions . . . in the Works of English Authors.* Ed. Halliwell and Wright (London, 1888).

P.&P.   *Past & Present.*

P.B.A.   *Proceedings of the British Academy.*

P.B.S.A.   *Papers of the Bibliographical Society of America.*

P.M.L.A.   *Publications of the Modern Language Society of America.*

P.Q.   *Philological Quarterly.*

Partridge   A. C. Partridge, *The Accidence of Ben Jonson's Plays, Masques, and Entertainments*, (Cambridge, 1953).

R.D.   *Renaissance Drama.*

S.B.   *Studies in Bibliography*

S.E.L.   *Studies in English Literature.*

S.P.   *Studies in Philology.*

S.T.C.   *A Short-Title Catalogue of Books printed in England ... and of English Books Printed abroad* (to 1640). Compiled by A. W. Pollard and G. R. Redgrave, 2nd ed., rev. & enlarged by W. A. Jackson, F. S. Ferguson and K. F. Pantzer (London, 1976–86).
T.L.S.   *Times Literary Supplement.*
Tilley   M. P. Tilley, *A Dictionary of the Proverbs in England in the Sixteenth and Seventeenth Centuries* (Ann Arbor, 1950).
Wing   *A Short-Title Catalogue of Books Printed in England ... and of English Books Printed in Other Countries, 1641–1700.* Compiled by Donald Wing. 3 vols (New York, 1972).
Y.E.S.   *Yearbook of English Studies.*

B WORKS BY JONSON

Alch.   *The Alchemist*
B.F.   *Bartholomew Fair*
C.A.   *The Case is Altered*
C.R.   *Cynthia's Revels*
Cat.   *Catiline*
Conv. Drum.   *Conversations with Drummond*
D.A.   *The Devil is an Ass*
Disc.   *Discoveries*
E.H.   *Eastward Ho*
E.M.I.   *Every Man In His Humour*
E.M.O.   *Every Man Out of His Humour*
Ep.   *Epigrams*
M.L.   *The Magnetic Lady*
N.I.   *The New Inn*
N.N.W.   *News from the New World*
N.T.   *Neptune's Triumph*
Poet.   *Poetaster*
S.S.   *The Sad Shepherd*
Staple   *The Staple of News*
S.W.   *Epicoene, or, The Silent Woman*
Sej.   *Sejanus*
T.T.   *The Tale of a Tub*
U.V.   *Ungathered Verse*
Und.   *Underwoods*
Volp.   *Volpone*

C EDITIONS

B.&F.   *The Dramatic Works in the Beaumont & Fletcher Canon.* Gen.
ed. Fredson Bowers (Cambridge, 1966–   ).

Bond   *The Complete Works of John Lyly.* Ed. R. Warwick Bond. 3
vols (Oxford, 1902).

Bowers   *The Dramatic Works of Thomas Dekker.* Ed. Fredson
Bowers. 4 vols (Cambridge, 1953–61).

Bullen   *The Works of Thomas Middleton.* Ed. A. H. Bullen (1840). 8
vols rpt. (New York, 1964).

Cunningham   Francis Cunningham's revision of Gifford's edition of
Jonson's *Works.* 3 vols (London, 1871).

de Winter   *The Staple of News.* Ed. de Winter (New York, 1905).

Dodsley   *A Select Collection of Old English Plays.* Originally published by Robert Dodsley. Ed. W. Carew Hazlitt. 15 vols
(London, 1874–6).

E.&G.   *The Plays and Poems of Philip Massinger.* Ed. Philip
Edwards and Colin Gibson. 5 vols (Oxford, 1976).

F   *The Workes of Benjamin Jonson. The Second Volume* (London,
1640).

F3   *The Works of Ben Jonson* (London, 1692).

Gifford   *The Works of Ben Jonson.* Ed. William Gifford. 9 vols
(London, 1816).

Grosart   *The Non-Dramatic Works of Thomas Dekker.* Ed. A. B.
Grosart (1884–6). 5 vols rpt. (New York, 1963).

H.&S.   *Ben Jonson.* Ed. C. H. Herford & Percy and Evelyn
Simpson. 11 vols (Oxford, 1925–52).

Holaday   *The Plays of George Chapman: The Comedies.* Gen. ed.
Allan Holaday (Urbana, 1970).

Kifer   *The Staple of News.* Ed. Devra Rowland Kifer. Regents
Renaissance Drama Series (London, 1975).

Lucas   *The Complete Works of John Webster.* Ed. F. L. Lucas (1927).
4 vols rpt. (New York, 1966).

McKerrow   *The Works of Thomas Nashe.* Ed. R. B. McKerrow
(1904–10). 5 vols rpt. (Oxford, 1966).

Whalley   *The Works of Ben Jonson.* Ed. Peter Whalley. 7 vols
(London, 1756).

Wilkes   *The Complete Plays of Ben Jonson.* Ed. G. A. Wilkes. 4 vols
(Oxford, 1982).

1716   *The Workes of Ben Jonson.* 6 vols (London, 1716).

The titles of Shakespeare's plays are abbreviated as in C. T. Onions, *A Shakespeare Glossary*, p. x; the text used is that of the Arden edition. Reference to Jonson's plays and masques is to Herford and Simpson, except where a title has been published in The Revels Plays. For Jonson's poetry I have used the edition of the *Poems* by Ian Donaldson (London, 1975).

Quotations from pre-eighteenth-century sources in the Commentary and Introduction are given in the original spelling, unless taken from modernised editions; but I have silently normalised i/j, u/v, and the long 's'. The only exceptions to this occur in the discussion of technical bibliography in section I of the Introduction, and in collation of the text. I have also expanded archaic contractions, such as y^e for 'the' or *invēted* for 'invented', without comment.

A word should be said about the use of brackets in the text. All added stage directions (i.e., those not found in *F*, either in the text or headnotes or in the margin) are placed in square brackets, and attributed in the collation. Directions taken from marginal notes in *F* and which do not occupy a line or lines to themselves are placed within round brackets, to avoid confusion with the spoken text.

Introduction

Stationers' Register

The Staple of News was entered on the Stationers' Register for John Waterson in 1626, a few weeks after its first performance by the King's Men:[1]

> John Waterson Entred for his Copie vnder the handes of
> Master Doctor WORRALL and Master Islip warden
> A booke Called *The Staple of Newes* being
> A Comedie./ . . . . vj^d

This entry seems to mark a new initiative on Jonson's part. He had not published any of his plays for ten years; moreover, none had appeared separately (reprints apart) since the quarto edition of *The Alchemist* in 1612. His two previous efforts for the stage, *Bartholomew Fair* (1614) and *The Devil is an Ass* (1616), had not been entered on the Stationers' Register and were not included in the 1616 Folio of Jonson's *Workes*. In the event, however, *The Staple* did not get into print before these two plays. No quarto edition was apparently forthcoming, and we next hear of the play on 7 September 1631, when John Waterson's rights in it were transferred to Robert Allot.[2]

The 1631–40 Folio

Jonson had suffered a stroke in 1628, and was probably in no position then to seek publication of his later output. But it seems that in 1631 he and Allot planned a companion volume to the 1616 Folio (*F*), and to that end *Bartholomew Fair*, *The Devil is an Ass* and *The Staple of News* were printed in folio, each with its own title-page bearing the imprint: 'I.B. [John Beale] for ROBERT ALLOT . . . . . 1631'.[3] We know that Jonson distributed copies of the plays to various patrons and friends,[4] and Greg speculates that a few bound-up volumes 'were allowed to go out at the time of printing as a supplement to the collection of 1616'.[5] None the less, no second volume of Jonson's *Workes* was formally published until 1640, when the three plays were issued with their original title-pages but with the blank leaf (A1) preceding *Bartholomew Fair* imprinted thus on the recto:

THE/VVORKES/OF/*BENJAMIN JONSON.*/The second Volume./
CONTAINING/THESE PLAYES,/*Viz.*/ 1 Bartholomew Fayre.
                              2 The Staple of Newes.
                              3 The Divell is an Asse.
                              [Device: McKerrow 339]/
    LONDON,/Printed for RICHARD MEIGHEN,/1640.

This nine-year gap between printing and issue contains one of the
most complex series of transactions over publishing rights known to
us from this period. Simpson called it a 'record of muddle, evasion
and dishonesty',[6] and its details have occupied a number of biblio-
graphers, most recently W. P. Williams, who has thoroughly in-
vestigated the legal wrangles and conflicting initiatives which led
eventually to publication in 1640–1.[7] I shall briefly summarise the
main developments.

The 1631 project was soon abandoned: it was presumably to have
included Jonson's later masques, and perhaps *The New Inn* (acted in
1629).[8] But Jonson had no time for the 'lewd Printer', as he called
John Beale,[9] and infirmity must have hindered his attempts to see the
book through the press. In any event, the plays printed up to that
point were left on Allot's hands; Jonson may well have forbidden their
publication. Allot died in 1635, and the following year his widow
transferred his rights to John Legatt and Andrew Crooke (who had
been Allot's apprentice).[10] Their freedom to publish was however
limited by an agreement with Allot's widow and her new husband
Philip Chetwin, under which the latter had a controlling interest
in Allot's copyrights and existing stock, which included the 1631
sheets. Crooke's various attempts to evade the terms of this agreement
involved him in a lengthy legal battle with Chetwin (1637–9), one
which failed however to give Legatt and Crooke the control they
sought over the Jonson copyright.[11]

Meanwhile there were developments on other fronts. In 1640
Crooke brought out a new edition (*F2*) of the 1616 Folio, printed by
Richard Bishop; and he then entered into a dispute with Thomas
Walkley, another stationer, over Jonson's remaining unpublished
works (excluding the 1631 plays). Walkley had been given the right
to publish these by Jonson's literary executor, Sir Kenelm Digby,
and been supplied with 'true & perfect copies';[12] but Crooke and
an associate called John Benson managed to acquire copies of their
own and registered them (something Walkley had neglected to do
with his own copies), whereupon Benson brought out two small
volumes of mainly non-dramatic pieces by Jonson. Walkley sought a

warrant to restrain their activities, but Benson and Crooke counter-attacked and succeeded in having Walkley's stock seized on a debt charge.

To this development we owe the emergence in 1640 of the volume containing just the three plays printed in 1631. It is probable that prior to the dispute with Crooke and Benson Walkley had approached Chetwin with a view to bringing out a Jonson volume combining the 1631 plays with the unpublished works received from Digby. But when the scheme was delayed by Walkley's legal troubles, Chetwin apparently went ahead in association with Richard Meighen (who had been involved in selling the 1616 Folio) and put out the 1631 plays on their own. It was only the following year that, Walkley's petition to the Chancery Court for restoration of his stock apparently being successful, the way was open for publication of the larger volume – the one which constitutes the real Volume Two of the First Folio of Jonson's *Workes*, though it lacks a general title-page.[13]

We should note, however, that this volume is also the natural companion to the 1640 (*F2*) reprint of the 1616 Folio, as the practice of calling the 1692 one-volume edition of Jonson '*F3*' indicates. Students of the later plays (all those not printed in 1616) are compelled by convention to talk of their first and second editions as *F* and *F3*, and this may further confuse an already cloudy situation. For our purposes, however, what matters is that *The Staple of News*, like *Bartholomew Fair*, was printed once only before the Restoration, but issued probably no fewer than four times: in 1631 at the time of printing, in 1640 with Meighen's title-page, in the following year without the title-page but with a 1641 reprint of *The Devil is an Ass*, and finally in 1641 again in the combined volume.[14]

The printing of the play
In many copies of *F* the 1631 plays are ordered to agree with Meighen's title-page, which for some unaccountable reason puts *The Staple* in front of *The Devil is an Ass*. This clearly violated Beale's (and no doubt Jonson's) intentions, although the printer's haphazard methods invited subsequent confusion.

Examination of the rules used in the skeleton formes in 1631 confirms that the three plays were printed consecutively and in chronological order, using basically the same furniture.[15] *Bartholomew Fair* was printed A-M4 (pp. 1–88) behind its own title-page; *The Devil* runs N-Y4 (pp. 91–170). These two plays Jonson mentions having sent (separately) to the Earl of Newcastle, in an undated letter in which he also complains about Beale's 'delayes and vexation' and apologises for not being able to send *The Staple of News*.[16] We do not know the length of this delay, nor the reason for it, but it may help to explain why when the play finally emerged its continuity with the rest of the book was precarious. It is initially signed Aa, as we might expect (the printer eschewing sig. z at the start of a new play); but the double-letter signature lapses into single at C3, and the pages are numbered from the beginning, [1, title-page], 2–75, [76, Epilogue], instead of following those of *The Devil*.

The Staple occupies nineteen sheets in folio, and collates Aa-Bb4, cc1–2, c3–4, d–H4, 1–16; the title-page, unusually, is signed Aa1, and its verso carries The Persons of the Play. Aa2 (recto and verso) has The Induction, Aa3 The Prologue for the Stage, and Aa3*v* The Prologue for the Court. The play was printed mainly in two skeleton formes (A & B), with some recourse to a third (c).[17] There is some irregularity of distribution in the early quires and in the last, but much of the time skeletons A & B (one or other occasionally replaced by c) are routinely assigned to the machining of inner and outer formes, though they tend to swap around between signatures. In the absence of information about procedures in Beale's shop it is difficult to know whether the use of three skeletons implies the use of more than one press, but since the appearance of c always allows either A or B to drop out of sight for several pages it does not appear that a third skeleton was introduced to speed up the work. On the contrary, it may be a sign of interruptions in printing which led to A or B not being ready to hand when work resumed.

The text was set by formes. This can be deduced from the recurrence of individual type-pieces in the first five pages of a gathering (something which cannot happen in *seriatim* setting where five pages must be in type simultaneously before printing can commence). Yet conclusive evidence for setting by formes is slender; there are very few places where one can feel wholly confident that type recurs. This could be because Beale's compositor worked (it seems) from a generous fount of type and was embarrassed only by an occasional shortage of upper-case W (common among printers at this time, and more noticeable in *Bartholomew Fair*).[18] There is virtually no use of italic for roman or *vice versa*, in a play where Jonson makes considerable call on italic, both in the text and in marginal notes; badly broken pieces quickly disappear, and those that remain exhibiting distinctive damage tend to recur at fair intervals (rarely within a single signature).[19]

John Beale has rightly been censured for his careless printing of this volume.[20] To begin with, there are in *The Staple* numerous trivial misprints like 'miny' for 'mine' (I.i.19), 'hec' for 'hee' (I.Int.77), 'Sit' for 'Sir' (III.ii.59 & 78), or 'Centleman' (IV.ii.157). Single letters are omitted: 'Exhange' (I.ii.71), 'abou' (III.ii.199), 'Stawberries' (IV.ii.54); or added: 'sprove' for 'prove' (IV.iv.3), 'Hawkes' for 'Hawke' (V.v.57). Words and letters are occasionally transposed: *'my in mouth'* (III.Int.19), and 'ti' for 'it' (IV.iv.17). A number of speeches are misassigned (see, for example, the crop at IV.ii.121–7), and Acts and scenes are misnumbered (I.ii, V.v). These errors are less excusable in view of the fact that, as G. R. Hibbard points out in connection with *Bartholomew Fair*,[21] Beale was almost certainly printing from a scrupulously prepared manuscript in Jonson's own hand. This is evident from such features as the massed entries at the start of each scene (which Jonson borrowed from humanist editions of the classics), the elaborate marginal notes, and his use of a rhetorical punctuation for the actor's guidance in speaking the lines. This method of pointing to indicate the length of pauses seems not to have been understood by the printer; it survives intact in instances like III.ii.116–22, where Jonson's manuscript was clearly followed with care (as Herford and Simpson point out). But the opening scene of the play shows how easily his system is vitiated by inexpert setting (for instance, the comma at the end of line 19 in *F* should probably have been a period or semicolon, and in line 26 the colon after 'longings' in *F* wrecks the balance of the line).

It is abundantly clear from all this that the 1631 volume lacked the kind of authorial supervision which it is still agreed was given to the 1616 Folio. Indeed, it is hard to imagine that so many patent errors in printing would have survived the scrutiny of a reasonably competent proof-reader in Beale's shop. Yet there is evidence of quite specific intervention in limited parts of the text, namely sheets 4, 6, 11, 12 and 19, during the course of printing. Of a total of ten alterations, seven are confined to two sheets (11 & 19). Some of these changes are simply to correct type derangement or obvious errors in setting, but four adjustments – at III.ii.118, III.iv.27 & 49, and V.v.5 – prompt the reflection, as the Oxford editors put it: 'This is scanty evidence of proof-reading by Jonson, but would Beale or his compositor have troubled to make such changes?'[22]

This edition
The present edition is based on a collation of thirteen copies of the Folio text: four in the British Library, two in the Bodleian, and seven in the Humanities Research Center at the University of Texas at

Austin. Of these, only the British Library copies are known to have been collated by Herford and Simpson. None the less, what emerges from this examination differs little from earlier reports on Jonson's text. Only two further variants have been discovered; a fresh collation establishes, moreover, that the number of genuine variants is even fewer than Herford and Simpson supposed.[23] Disappearing commas and apostrophes to which they draw attention are almost invariably the result of poor inking (including 'paths,' at III.iv.32), and an apparent substitution of exclamation for question mark next to '*iealous*' at IV.Int.18 (since the sense is not interrogatory) turns out to be a progressive fracturing during printing of what Jonson called the 'admiration' point.

In this edition Jonson's original scene-divisions are retained, but *F*'s mass entries at the start of each scene are redistributed to agree with the entries of individual characters. These original scene-headings are recorded in the apparatus, as are the side-notes in *F* not incorporated into the text as stage directions. A word needs to be said about the side-notes. It was Jonson's practice, in preparing his plays for publication, to supply marginal comments and directions for the guidance of the reader; but in the 1631 volume he went further than before and included a great many notes which simply restate or summarise the action and dialogue. These glosses are unevenly distributed through the text, but they seem intended to give it the general appearance of a substantial literary work (though there is no attempt to parade Jonson's learning as in the marginalia to his Roman tragedies). Their modern usefulness is confined to the provision of a few stage directions, the remainder being relegated to the collation.

At the same time, I have included a number of stage directions of my own devising (placed within square brackets, of course, like other additions to *F* such as individual entrances and the speech heading for the first speaker in a scene). One aim in this edition has been to bring out the theatrical life of a play which has rarely been tested in performance, and although some of my suggestions are speculative, they may complement Jonson's own attempts to prepare the play for readers by focusing attention on dramatic detail and movement.

No attempt at an historical collation has been made, although all significant later editions have been examined, some of their emendations and stage directions adopted, and others recorded in the apparatus. *F3* (1692) I have treated on an equal footing with other editions.

Obvious printing errors have been silently corrected, and likewise –

unless there is real doubt about the sense of a passage – the vagaries of punctuation that were habitual in Beale's shop. Spelling has been modernised throughout, except in a few instances where this would obscure the original meaning or mask a significant play on words, or where the modern form violates Jonson's metre. A number of distinctive spellings are preserved in the collation. Jonson's punctuation has been replaced by a system intelligible to a non-specialist reader, although I have tried not to sacrifice the rhetorical shape and movement of the verse, and to this end have adopted a slightly heavier pointing than is favoured in many modern editions of Jonson.

A special problem is posed by the use of metrical apostrophe, placed in *F* 'between two unelided but lightly sounded syllables to indicate they are metrically equivalent to one syllable' (*H.&S.* IX 50). It seems that Jonson wished to distinguish 'apostrophus' from elision, preserving an extra-metrical syllable lightly sounded (though his discussion of this in *The English Grammar*, Bk.II, ch.1 is less than clear); a good example of the practice is V.i.9: 'Methinks I should be'on every side saluted'. It does not however seem consistent to preserve this pointing in a modernised text. The real difficulty comes in deciding what to do with cases where elision is possible, as in II.v.60: 'My curious eyes, by which alone I'am happy'. Here a hint of anapaestic rhythm in the first half of the line seems to be echoed in the second (*I'am happy*), and elision may disturb this balance and create an unwanted abruptness. On the other hand, to ignore the apostrophe altogether is often to lose the benefit of a subtle metrical discipline, in which strict iambic consorts with lighter and more playful rhythms, as in this line from the Epilogue: 'If so, we'are sorry that have so misspent / Our time and tackle' (11–12). After some hesitation, I have followed R. B. Parker's procedure in the Revels *Volpone* (see p. 8) as the least unsatisfactory solution to the problem. The metrical apostrophe is represented in the text only if an elision is possible in modern usage (e.g. *I'd* for *I'had* at I.ii.144). Otherwise it is recorded in the apparatus as follows: if the apostrophe seems anachronistic but true to Jonson's practice, it appears immediately after the siglum (e.g. III.iii.10. *they were*] they'were *F*). But where it is suspected that the apostrophe has been omitted by the printer (perhaps because he failed to understand Jonson's markings) the collation reads: IV.ii.33. *He has*] *F;* He'has *conj. this ed.*

An imaginative reconstruction of the interior of the Blackfriars playhouse, reproduced from Irwin Smith, *Shakespeare's Blackfriars Playhouse: Its History and its Design* (New York University Press, 1964).

2. CAREER AND DATE

The Staple of News marks Jonson's return to the stage after an interval of nine years, a period which Herford calls 'the heyday of his personal dictatorship in the literary world'.[24] The year 1616 had seen not only the production of *The Devil is an Ass* but also the publication of his *Workes*, and in the years that followed Jonson turned his attention to many other kinds of writing, including a translation of Horace's *Ars Poetica*, his English Grammar, work in history and divinity, as well as a great deal of verse. The splendid masques also produced in these years are only one part of a rich literary maturity too often overlooked in the conventional account of Jonson's 'decline' after *Bartholomew Fair*; and our play, which may be said to consummate this phase of his career, offers abundant evidence of fresh creative energy and diverse interests put at the service of a confident artistic design. It may well be true that prior to *The Staple* 'his withdrawal from active concern with the stage ... contributed to confirm his prestige',[25] by allowing Jonson to assume the role of literary elder statesman and avoid the (for him) delicately balanced task of writing for the popular stage. But we should not infer that he was simply shirking this challenge or that his comeback was a reluctant one, forced upon him by the drying-up of commissions from the Caroline court. The evidence, such as it is, permits the conjecture that Jonson was incubating *The Staple of News* from the beginning of the 1620s, and may even have drafted portions of an earlier version by the autumn of 1623.

In 1620 Jonson scored a major success with his masque *News from the New World*, which, almost without precedent for entertainments of this kind, received at least nine performances during the pre-Lenten period of that year.[26] It is in this masque that the main idea for *The Staple* is broached, when the Factor declares that

> I have hope to erect a Staple for newes ere long,
> whether all shall be brought, and thence againe
> vented under the name of Staple-newes ...   (45-7)

A vigorous debate between the various newsmongers forms the anti-masque; the news that is discussed largely represents the communications network of the upper class: newsletters, chronicle records, diplomatic gossip, sophisticated speculation, all carefully distinguished from the 'printed Conundrums' which tickle the curiosity of the lower orders. All these enterprises, however, are opposed to 'the neat and cleane power of Poetrie' which is the true 'Mistris of all discovery' (102–4). Despite this characteristic stress, Jonson appears in 1620 to have found news an occasion for elegant and fantastic parody rather than purposeful satire; but the fact that he re-used material from the masque in the later play shows that his mind was already running upon concerns which, largely as a result of developments in the news trade itself, were to demand a more comprehensive treatment.

In his poem 'An Execration upon Vulcan' (*Und.* 43), commemorating the fire which ravaged his library in November 1623, Jonson reveals that among the perished manuscripts were 'parcels of a play' (43). There has been speculation that these comprised an incomplete early version of *The Staple of News*,[27] and it is not unlikely that, with the success of a masque about news behind him, and provoked by the advent of regular newsbook journalism in 1622, Jonson began to meditate a stage play to deal with this expanding phenomenon. If so, there may be special point to his chiding of Vulcan for devouring his own careful labours rather than ephemera like 'Captain Pamphlet's horse and foot, that sally / Upon the Exchange . . . / The weekly *Courants*, with Paul's seal' (79–81). But such a comparison would come naturally to Jonson in any case, and there is nothing specifically to link the play with a date earlier than 1625. The news peddled by the Staple is essentially consistent with what was being reported during that year, though since the newsbooks faithfully reflect the stalemate of the Thirty Years War in the endless recurrence of military names and indistinguishable campaigns, not too much weight can be placed on this. He took some care, though, to make his play up to date in early 1626. The references to Spinola, for instance, put his much-reported siege of Breda in the past – it ended in June 1625 – and allude to the more recent threat of invasion across the Channel (see notes to III.ii.48–9 and 87–9); and given Jonson's usually slow rate of composition it seems likely that references to Charles I's coronation on 2 February and the death of William Rowley a few days later (III.ii.205–6, 298–301) were interpolated for the first performance shortly afterwards.

The ending of the play suggests that it was completed in late 1625, a jubilee year which Pennyboy Senior acknowledges by returning Pecunia's women with the words 'It is their year and day of jubilee'; although Jonson might have been thinking in Old Style dates which carried that year up to March 1626. As far as the earlier limits of its composition are concerned, an important part of the play's design, that embodied in the character of Lickfinger and his views on poetry and cooking, is borrowed from Jonson's unperformed masque *Neptune's Triumph*, which was originally to have been given at Court on Twelfth Night 1624. In sum, then, *The Staple* was probably conceived in its present form during 1624 or early 1625 (perhaps after the destruction of an earlier version), and was largely or entirely written during 1625, being completed close to the occasion of its first performance in February 1626.

3. SOURCES AND TRADITIONS

As so often with Jonson, the 'sources' of *The Staple of News* are manifold, and past attempts to identify them have generally revealed how unprofitable it is to seek an individual inspiration for the whole or part of the play. In one sense, its origins are nothing less than Jonson's entire reading and previous literary endeavour, for the play images and defends a cultural perspective that is shaped by a life's work as scholar and working dramatist. On an elementary level this can be seen in the patchwork of literary allusion, mainly but not exclusively to the classics, which enriches the poetic structure and provides a kind of running commentary on the contemporary life of the play – a feature admired by Richard James in his lines on the occasion of its first performance, commending Jonson on 'Your rich Mosaique workes, inled by arte / And curious industrie with everie parte / And choice of all the Auncients'.[28] There is also the fact that *The Staple* comes late in a consciously shaped career, so that Jonson is already aware of approaching 'the close, or shutting up of his Circle',[29] recapitulating old concerns, and drawing on his own past work for fresh inspiration. None the less, the play is not simply a re-hash of earlier, better efforts (though much criticism has implied this); nor is it without firm antecedents in the 'old way' of morality literature and drama. Jonson's attempt to renew familiar conventions and tropes and make them serve his mature concerns is the real subject of 'source' study here; and two such efforts at recreation in particular need to be discussed: the tradition of the prodigal play and the personification of wealth.

The prodigal play

Jonson's previous essays at the prodigal play, apart from the early *Cynthia's Revels*, had on the whole dealt playfully and sceptically with a *genre* which by the early seventeenth century only distantly reflected its original inspiration in the parable of the Prodigal Son. The typical prodigal play insisted on the citizen virtues of thrift, industry and respect for elders, and is memorably burlesqued in *Eastward Ho* (1605); one of the authors' targets in the writing of this play may have been *The London Prodigal*, an anonymous public theatre comedy combining romantic intrigue with the prodigal plot which had been acted by the King's Men, Jonson's own company, probably in 1604. If so, it could explain why traces of this play have been detected in *The Staple of News*.[30] In *Every Man In His Humour* (1598), Jonson had used a standard device of the prodigal play, that of the disguised father spying on his errant son, but in doing so he turned the convention upside down, with Old Knowell being outwitted by his son Edward and forced to acknowledge that his subterfuge was ill-considered, an 'impertinent search' in view of the innocuous nature of Edward's recreation. We may choose to take this as an early Jonsonian comment on the sententious moralising of many prodigal plays; and he was to use a similar device, in Justice Overdo's cloaked pursuit of enormities at Bartholomew Fair, to expose the ineffectuality of authority figures who fail to co-operate with the realities of daily life. Nevertheless, the excesses of the prodigal Cokes and his friends are not vindicated in *Bartholomew Fair*; they simply go uncorrected, and while this is important for the communal harmony and spirit of tolerance prevailing at the end of the play, it does not imply a rejection of the conservative values enshrined in the original parable. It comes as no surprise, then, that Jonson's last engagement with the story in *The Staple* should be a sophisticated but wholly unironic retelling, one which keeps its distance from the bourgeois concerns of citizen plays and cuts much deeper in its analysis of the social contract, but which is equally at odds with the parodic treatments of the prodigal story which became fashionable at coterie theatres in the later Jacobean period.[31]

Jonson's method is illustrated by his use of disguise not for purposes of intrigue but to shape the educative design of Pennyboy Canter, who is reported dead but is actually masquerading as a beggar to observe his son's misleadings. By transferring the biblical reference to one who 'was dead, and is alive againe' (Luke xv.24, 32) from the son to the father, Jonson is able to dramatise the resurrection of values which transform both the prodigal and the miser into liberal men;[32] it is probable that he was seeking to restore the emphasis of the parable story on the triumph of the elder generation, renewing society through an act of wise forgiveness. This message is softened or obscured in many plays of the period which variously indulge the prodigal's excesses; and indeed, an overriding interest in the energetic folly of youth was always latent in the dramatic tradition which combined the biblical paradigm with the plot mechanics of Terentian New Comedy, letting the story gather theatrical vigour from the intrigues and innovations of the young. But *The Staple*, like Shakespeare's last comedies, keeps the challenge of the new generation firmly within bounds, not allowing their success to distract from the more important affirmation of a past redeemed and traditional assumptions made new.

The story of the Prodigal Son in its pure form is of course a narrative, a rake's progress, and Jonson seems to have found it useful because it offers a linear movement which is able to reveal interior connections between the several concerns of his play. The prodigal's customary riot of spending, his pursuit of courtesans, the dissipation in a tavern, followed by his reduction to penury – all elements traditional to the story – in *The Staple* become a logical sequence connecting Pennyboy Junior's blindness to the proper use of wealth, his flaunting of Pecunia before the confidence men of the news office, the abuse of language and decorum by the jeerers at the feast, and the climactic folly (which precipitates his ruin) of the proposal to found a Canters' College. In this respect, the play differs from several of Jonson's major comedies where a single location provides the focus for most or all of the action. It is relevant to note this here because the News Staple is often likened to Subtle's laboratory in *The Alchemist*, another dream factory whose pretensions are exploded at the moment of maximum complication in the plot.[33] In some ways, clearly, Jonson allowed the alchemist's lair to shape his conception of an office where rumour is turned into gold. But we should also note that he avoids investing all his dramatic resources in the news office, and one consequence of this is that the theme of money and its abuse is not limited to the intrigues of greedy tricksters and their gulls. In recent years critics have started to perceive that the play is not really about cupidity and avarice in the same way that (say) *Volpone* is; but the extent to which Jonson has shifted from a single satiric focus in earlier plays to exploration of a series of related trends has not been fully appreciated.[34]

The play's organisation reveals other debts to the past. The triadic structure which Jonson places on the story – that of the liberal mean flanked by avarice on the one hand and prodigality on the other – derives ultimately from the first chapter of Book IV of the *Nicomachean Ethics*, where Aristotle discusses liberality 'as a disposition

to observe the mean in dealing with material goods',[35] and carefully
defines the deviations from this ideal use of wealth. These concepts
were common coin in the Renaissance, of course, but it appears that
Jonson was concerned to observe the Aristotelian distinctions more
exactly than some of his contemporaries in the theatre. In particular,
he seems to have grasped Aristotle's insistence that prodigality 'does
not imply the possession of more than one vice, that of squandering
one's means'.[36] The point is cheerfully ignored in many plays which
seize the opportunity to dwell on the prodigal's whoring, drinking
and dicing, but in The Staple the basic idea that 'to exhaust one's
means is much the same as ruining oneself, because our "means"
are our means of living'[37] remains clear and prominent, arguably at
the loss of some dramatic colour. Thus Pennyboy Junior's pursuit
of Lady Pecunia is not allowed to lose its conceptual focus; and his
eventual reform is prepared in the play not by encouraging the audience to enjoy his escapades and will his deliverance from disgrace,
but by an unsentimental demonstration that prodigality is capable of
being moderated into liberal virtue.

The personification of wealth
A good deal of attention has been paid to two Greek satires on the
abuse of wealth as putative sources for The Staple.[38] Jonson certainly
knew both Aristophanes' Ploutos and Lucian's dialogue Timon, the
latter apparently influenced by the former in its depiction of wealth as
a blind figure threatened with imprisonment by misers and searching
for a good and moderate man who will not abuse him. The idea of the
golden mean in the handling of wealth is nominally advanced in both
works through the female figure of Poverty (representing frugal
moderation rather than beggary), who brings Timon comfort and
sanity before he rediscovers gold, and who in Ploutos demonstrates
to Chremylos her superiority over Wealth. But there is a subtle difference between this emphasis on plain living and the larger question
of the right use of wealth. Even Timon, which is arguably a more
complex treatment of the theme than Ploutos, tends to undercut
its realistic advocacy of the mean by insisting rather crudely on the
superfluity and vanity of riches. Lucian's Wealth is a bejewelled
temptation, his 'beauty is just paint and powder',[39] redundant in
a life stripped to essentials. It is a view which was to appeal more
to the advocates of *contemptus mundi* than to Jonson – who, for all
his sense of the corrupting power of extravagance, understood that
the concept of a just sufficiency must in a society like his own be

G 2

Woodcuts showing Lady Pecunia in contemporary dress. From *The Roxburghe Ballads* (1880).

expressed in terms of practical aims and goals if it was to have any guiding effect.[40]

The point can be refined by examining Jonson's relation to Horace, whose Epistle 'To Numicius' satirises the omnipotence of 'regina Pecunia' in Roman society. 'Nil admirari', says Horace, and asks the crucial question: 'quid censes munera terrae, / quid maris extremos Arabas ditantis et Indos?'[41] One seventeenth-century translation of these lines significantly alters the emphasis, conjuring 'Silver, Gold, and pretious jems, with which / Both *Indies* do the rest o'th'world enrich':[42] the image of a powerful and expanding Europe drawing the two Indies into its sphere replaces Horace's temperate notion of a Rome set off from well-heeled barbarism; and Jonson's own portrayal of wealth in *The Staple* is also poised between an exotic and commercial East and a new world in the West. Pecunia is a loadstone, a creature of magnetic allure who becomes in Jonson's scheme a complex embodiment of value, an object of conflicting desires, and a measure of a society's capacity for civilised and decorous behaviour.

For Horace, the idea of riches waiting to be discovered induces a sense of *carpe diem*: 'quidquid sub terra est, in apricum proferet ætas, defodiet condetque nitentia ' – 'Time will bring into the light whatever is under the earth; it will bury deep and hide what now shines bright.'[43] But the sentiment seems to play no part in Jonson's resonant conceit of the 'Infanta of the Mines'.

One way in which Jonson explores this distinction between the proper use of wealth and the renunciation of it is to place traditional assumptions in a theatrical context which challenges and even undermines them. In Act III, for instance, Cymbal visits Pennyboy Senior in order to secure the investment of Pecunia in his News Staple, and is met by a rant from the usurer:

> What need hath Nature
> Of silver dishes or gold chamber pots,
> Of perfumed napkins, or a numerous family
> To see her eat? Poor and wise, she requires
> Meat only; hunger is not ambitious.
> Say that you were the emperor of pleasures,
> The great dictator of fashions for all Europe,
> And had the pomp of all the courts and kingdoms
> Laid forth unto the show, to make yourself
> Gazed and admired at? You must go to bed
> And take your natural rest; then all this vanisheth.
> Your bravery was but shown; 'twas not possessed ...   (III.iv.52–63)

This speech, derived from Seneca, has sometimes been cited as evidence of Jonson's characteristic attitude to worldly wealth,[44] and obviously it has its place in the play's critique of contemporary indulgence. But Cymbal's bemused asides ('This man hath healthful lungs', 'He has the monopoly of sole speaking') are only one of the ways in which the miser is undercut by his context. The sentiments he expresses, conventionally admirable in themselves, here become associated with the spirit of parsimony that he embodies in the play as a whole. What is remarkable is that, even though this scene follows closely upon the exploitation of Pecunia at the news office, and the self-indulgent chatter of the jeerers, Pennyboy Senior's speech fails to crystallise our objections to any of the abuses we have witnessed. We can see how subtly Jonson is working here if we compare the method of a play which is virtually a prototype for *The Staple* in some ways, the late morality play *The Contention between Liberality and Prodigality* (published in 1602, but probably a reworking of an older play).[45] In a dialogue that is pivotal to the action, the character of Virtue makes the point that wealth is an important concept in itself, a measure of human purpose and well-being, and is trivialised by novelty and fashion: 'Man's sense so dulled is, so all things come to pass, / Above the massy gold t'esteem the brittle glass'.[46] Prodigality, representative of this folly, is arraigned and condemned at the end of the play, but reprieved after he repents: 'I find the brittle stay of trustless Fortune's state . . .'.[47] The verbal echo ('brittle') reinforces an earlier insistence that Fortune is the natural ally of money's unplanned waste: in Act II she had given Money to Prodigality on the grounds that she 'dealeth not by merit but by chance'. But the perils of *laissez faire* economics are matched by the rigid controls of Tenacity, who by subsequently confining Money causes him to fall into a consumption. Jonson may have got from this the idea for Lady Argurion's similar collapse in *Cynthia's Revels* (though there it is caused by prodigal fickleness), and the details of Money's imprisonment and eventual deliverance by Liberality anticipate the later scenes in Act IV of *The Staple*. The overall difference, however, is that whereas *The Contention* relies upon simple exposition to separate the intrinsic idea of wealth from the miser's obsessions, Jonson does it by dramatising Pennyboy Senior's paradoxical inability to grasp the full significance of 'massy gold', symbolised in the resplendent Lady Pecunia.

A key factor in Jonson's more theatrical treatment is clearly his replacement of the rather colourless 'money' figures in plays like *The Contention* or *All for Money* with a dramatic creation capable of acting as a complex image of desire. But in availing himself of the device of female personification and turning it to his own use, he is working within a long-standing though somewhat unstable native tradition, one which reflects a perennial ambivalence about wealth's relation to the good life and the demands of morality. In the anonymous play *The Trial of Treasure* (1567), for example, there seems to be a more than casual connection between the cautionary nature of the morality and the fact that Treasure is a lady. The basic opposition in the play is between the figures of Just and Lust; and Treasure, defying all good advice, elects to remain with the latter. Subsequently the two lovers are converted by Time into 'a similitude of dust and rust',[48] though in view of the emphasis upon mutability it is not clear how far such dissolution is a result of their sin. The ambiguity of the play's message is evident in the words of God's Visitation, who at the end counsels 'men in all things to keep a measure, / Especially in love to uncertainty of treasure'.[49] Yet the lines are an apt gloss on the ancient trope of money as a lady, Dea Moneta, for in this figure can be expressed the bounty and fulfilment which flow from riches properly used, and also the lurking doubt about whether it is not in the very nature of money to destroy its holder. Female personification turns the money figure from a neutral agent into one of dangerous promise. She bears the marks of an antifeminist tradition (Jonson's own Lady Argurion is 'A *Nymph* of a most wandring and giddy disposition')[50] and is responsible for men's downfall; but she can also become a kind of indispensable mascot, a symbol of virtuous power. This sort of versatility produces, at one extreme, the startling alignment of Lady Pecunia with the highest of national causes:

> And as the Coyne, she [i.e., Queen Elizabeth] hath repurifyde,
> From baser substance, to the purest Mettals:
> Religion so, hath shee refinde beside,
> From Papistrie, to Truth . . .[51]

At the other extreme we have the specious Lady Munera, savagely disposed of by Artegall in Book V of *The Faerie Queene*, or the unequivocal villainy of Lady Lucre in Robert Wilson's play *The Three Ladies of London* (1584). But if these portraits borrow their tone and emphasis from the conventional misogyny of the age (or its regular mirror image in the cult of Cynthia and the ubiquitous 'Lady' figures of moral allegory), their lack of consistency seems to reflect a more fundamental problem of response. The portrait of Lady Meed drawn by Langland in *Piers Plowman* is intensely ambivalent, but it is also coherent and tough-minded, insisting on the need to understand what she represents. By comparison, what Raymond Southall has called 'the coronation of Lady Money'[52] in the materialistic imagery of much Elizabethan verse often seems relatively frivolous, with much strained analogy and colourful assertion, and a tendency to oscillate between adoration and disgust.

A ready illustration of the latter can be found in *The Three Lords and Ladies of London* (c. 1590), a direct sequel to *The Three Ladies* mentioned above. Here, the outright condemnation of Lucre and her associates at the end of the earlier play is suddenly and inexplicably reversed, when Policy tells Judge Nemo (who sentenced them all to prison in the first place) that he 'can from thence redeem them all'.[53] It is not clear what kind of weight the word 'redeem' is meant to bear here; at any rate, it is a thoroughly theatrical rescue. Lady Lucre is married off to Pomp, for (we are reminded) 'London's Lucre may not be separated from London's Pomp', and Policy imposes tight controls on Fraud and Usury. We are recognisably in a world of city pageants and the thrifty celebration of London's growing wealth, and we can only admire the efficient rationalisation of Lucre's role in it all. The allegory is designed to serve emphatically bourgeois ends, and the demonstration of the right use of wealth is untroubled by moral ambiguities. On occasion, however, this 'civic' mode could be put to more questioning purpose, as in Thomas Dekker's 1609 pamphlet *Worke for Armorours*, in which Queen Money and Poverty are at war, fighting for control of London. Money is (as usual) apostrophised by Parsimony, but on this occasion is not his prisoner, matching him in indifference to Poverty's cause. Dekker encompasses the hard facts of city life here, but can propose no answer to the problems he raises; the conflict ends in stalemate, and the two sides prudently declare 'a perpetuall truce', agreeing 'league and confederacy', so that throughout England 'the one should have as much to do as the other . . . it was impossible to sever them'. However, Dekker cannot resist a Utopian flourish at the end: 'A law was presently enacted, that Fortune should no longer be blinde . . . that she maight see those upon whom shee bestowes her blessings because fooles are served at her deale with riches which they know not how to use, and wise men are sent away like beggers from a misers gate with empty wallets'.[54] It is an ironic coda, of course, implicitly acknowledging what really goes on; but at the same time it is an attempt to give the work a moral dimension, to convey beyond its documentary function a sense of how things ought to be. In his own very different way, this is also to be Jonson's endeavour in *The Staple*, and it is instructive to compare his somewhat abstract allegory of wealth with popular literature's attempt to deal with the same problems.

One such attempt forms a close analogue to *The Staple of News*, illuminating better than all other suggested 'sources' the tradition within which Jonson conceives his play. This is a verse pamphlet by Thomas Andrewe entitled *The Massacre of Money*, published in 1602, which describes the exploitation of wealth by human beings in terms of a familiar hybrid mythology, part-classical, part-Elizabethan. The poem opens with a disquisition on the Golden Age, when the 'ground disdain'd the plowes uncivill touch'. With the coming of the Iron Age, however, men 'In the deepe entralls of the earth gan digge: / When (as amaz'd they stood) unto their sight / Appear'd a woman all in silver dight'. Pecunia (for so it is) bids farewell to the 'tonguelesse cavernes of the earth', and Avarus, the leader of the miners, calls his men to recognise that 'This is a Queene, behold her majestie, / Nay more, a goddesse, see her deitie'. Prodigus praises her beauty in extravagant terms, tempting her with travel and fame if she will join him; but Liberalis steps in to warn her that 'Though in thy selfe lyes no disaster crosse, / Yet in thy usage stands or good, or losse'. Avarus renews his suit, and after further argument Pecunia is convinced and throws in her lot with him, begging him to 'Encrease my heapes by thy assiduall toile'. Prodigus tries to kill Avarus, but three goddesses step in, Fortune, Vice and Virtue. Fortune embraces Avarus as the 'first and primate of my schoole', and after a lengthy contention she, on behalf of herself and Vice, challenges Virtue to battle. On the latter's insistence, they repair to England for the fight. Jove and Pallas intervene on Virtue's part, Venus on Vice's; Jove's thunderbolt decides the issue. Virtue devotes herself to Eliza, at whose court 'Pecunia is disposed thriftily', and the poem ends with a conventional eulogy of the Queen.

Shortly before this poem was written, Jonson had contrived a not dissimilar conclusion for *Cynthia's Revels*, in which the prodigal Asotus, having previously abused Lady Argurion, is reconciled to the ideal monarch Cynthia (in lieu of the father's traditional forgiveness in the parable). Jonson is more interested here in the prodigal plot than in the personification of Money, who fades from the play after Act IV, but the point made is the same: the golden mean is figured in the civilised splendour and decorum of the court. *The Staple of News* creates a less exalted world, remote from Elizabethan affirmations; but by the 1620s Jonson had found an answer to contemporary uncertainty and decay in the language of court masque, which does much to shape the figure of Lady Pecunia and to endorse her proclamation of the golden mean at the end of the play.

A Miracle, of Miracles.

As fearefull as euer was feene or heard of in the
memorie of M A N.

Which lately happened at *Dichet* in Sommerfetfhire, and fent
by diuers credible witneffes to be publifhed in L ON D ON.

Alfo a Prophefie reuealed by a poore Countrey Maide, who being dead the
firft of October laft, 1613. 24. houres, reuiued againe, and lay fiue
dayes weeping, and continued prophefying of ftrange euents to
come, and fo died the 5 day following.

Witneffed by M. *Nicholas Faber*, Parfon of the Towne, and diuers
worthy Gentlemen of the fame countrey. 1613,

Withall, Lincolnefhire.Teares. For a great deluge, in which fiue Villages
were lamentably drowned this prefent month.

At London printed for *Iohn Trundle*: and are to be fould
at Chrift Church gate. 1614.

Title-page to a traditional 'book of news', describing a visitation of the Devil
as a headless bear. Such pamphlets were very common in Elizabethan and
Jacobean publishing, and continued long after the trade in foreign political
news became established.

4. JONSON AND THE NEWS TRADE

''Tis no *Curranto*-News I undertake, / New Teacher of the Town I mean not to make . . .'[55] Jonson first gives sustained attention to the news trade in his masque *News from the New World*, produced in 1620; in that year corantos (single news-sheets in folio) reporting events on the Continent began to appear in London with some regularity, and a rash of pamphlets was published there dealing with current European politics.[56] These developments owed much to the onset of the Thirty Years War, which had intensified in 1619 with the action of the Elector-Palatine, James I's son-in-law Frederick, in accepting the crown of Bohemia, and so created an immediate demand in England for news of the conflict. The war gave a stimulus to the already well-established news trade on the Continent, sending a flood of reports along the European trade-routes to centres like Amsterdam, where in 1620 small folio news-sheets in English were printed and exported across the Channel. This particular expedient, like the use of fictitious imprints like 'At the Hage' on early London news publications, was designed to get round the strict controls on the printing of political news in England; but in the following year (1621) a licence was issued to one N. B. (probably Nathaniel Butter) to print in London news 'honestly translated out of the Dutch'.[57] By October 1622 a syndicate of several booksellers had been formed, and serial publication of news – with the single-sheet coranto replaced by a quarto newsbook of 16–24 pages – became a reality. The news printed at this time was exclusively foreign (a Star Chamber ban on domestic reporting remained in force until 1641), and in practice mainly confined to accounts of the war extracted from Dutch news-sheets, modified or augmented by other printed sources and 'relations' (newsletters) from private correspondents on the Continent.

A glance at the big Staple scene (III.ii) in Jonson's play, with its endless trickle of military rumour, confirms the topicality of his satire on the news trade;[58] and it is necessary at the start to consider some of the ways in which these developments might have engaged Jonson's attention. The issue of the Palatinate was a contentious one in England: James I was very unwilling to get involved, whilst committed Protestants were anxious to lend support to the fight against the Catholic alliance in Europe. The great likelihood is that Jonson was on the king's side in this; and Sara Pearl has shown how in a number of works written in the 1620s he echoes James's hostility to public debate of the Palatinate question and seems to be formulating a repressive argument against political commentary and satire in general.[59] The editor of some of the early newsbooks, Captain Thomas Gainsford, had earlier written propaganda for the Protestant cause, and Jonson may have seen these newsbooks as whipping up public support for the war through the careful manipulation of report. But it would be wrong to restrict Jonson's satire on news to immediate national controversy. His political sympathies are rarely in doubt, but it is unlikely that he would have paid much attention to the predictable bias and distortions of the newsbooks (generally the product of routinely anti-Spanish feeling) if he had not first seen in them a more basic threat to civilised communication. Accordingly, it is to the larger implications of the new Jacobean journalism that we must now turn.

    News from the New World provides a convenient diagram of Jonson's concerns. It brings together a 'Printer of Newes' who will 'give any thing for a good Copie now, be't true or false', a chronologer who pads out his book with political gossip 'to give light to posteritie in the truth of things', and a 'Factor of newes' who makes a living out of newsletters sent to the provinces. Jonson parades before us three figures who seek to carve up the literary market and turn writing into a commodity. His indictment has points of contact with the distaste felt by many contemporaries for the hack writers who turn out ephemera – almanacs and broadsheets – and disastrously undermine the effort of genuine poets to educate the public, who (as Nashe put it) 'no sooner spy a new Ballad, and his name to it that compilde it: but they put him in for one of the learned men of our time'.[60] But for Jonson the problem was compounded in that he was prepared neither to confound the scribblers as Nashe and Dekker did by producing superior journalism in pamphlet form, nor to eschew the medium of print as beneath the dignity of a man of letters. Jonson's self-appointed mission to educate his public not only via the stage but also through publication of his works committed him to elevating the tone of literary endeavour, and also to raising standards in the book trade, and he identifies as his natural antagonists the poetasters and hacks who exploit the popular audience, and the booksellers who stand to profit from their labours.

    A great deal of the material coming from the press in Jonson's lifetime falls into the broad category of news. It has been calculated that nearly one-quarter of titles entered in the Stationers' Register for the years 1591–4 are concerned with current news, and that some 450 news publications appeared in England between 1590 and 1610.[61]

These generally take the form of prose pamphlets or ballads; G. B. Harrison notes that it 'was common for news pamphlets to be rendered into verse',[62] and this was one way in which literary drudges were employed to make incoming accounts of battles, marvels or natural disasters more accessible to the buying public (many of whom were illiterate). Such writers were adept at supplying instant broadsides in response to a sensational murder or notable execution, and to their sententious moralising and graphic detail the publisher would almost invariably add a crude but arresting illustration. They might also be asked to translate foreign news, or paid to cast verbal reports or rumours in the form of first-hand descriptions which would carry greater credence with readers. Many of these journalistic efforts are the true ancestors of today's tabloid press, and they formed the basis of a stable trade in popular 'news' which remained largely untouched by political or national events.

Nor were they in any sense regular 'serial' publications, but simply occasional products of the book trade. It was not until 1589 that the first tentative moves were made towards a periodical press, when the printer and bookseller John Wolfe created for his newsbooks a distinctive title-page consisting only of the short title, house block and imprint; he dated his news, and made tentative promises to the reader to publish further instalments of a story as they came in. He also set an example to the trade in the art of newsgathering, culling his material from foreign printed corantos, private letters from contacts, official news (obtained through his contacts in government), and letters bought from agents.[63] Wolfe's enterprise was relatively short-lived, and had no immediate successor; but it makes plain the challenge that improved communications and the spread of education presented to the book trade. Broadside ballads had long been a profitable way of exploiting public curiosity about current sensations; but the growth of literacy and awareness of the world at large, especially as England became more involved in Continental politics, created the conditions for a new kind of journalism, one that might demand a more sustained effort from the reader and mediate responsibly between news and its recipients.[64] Moreover, whereas earlier printers had tended to work the ballad market in response to the monopoly on profitable book-titles by a few wealthy stationers, by the 1590s a man like Wolfe had several presses set up in Stationers' Hall, conveniently near to London's principal centres of trade and gossip. The newsmongers were beginning to come into their own, laying the foundations for the careers of men like Nathaniel Butter, Nicholas Bourne and Thomas Archer, all of whom during the reign of James I acquired extensive experience in news publishing before they came together in the syndicate of 1622.

Yet it cannot really be said that journalism decisively altered its character in this period. Part of the reason lies with Elizabethan censorship, which effectively stifled political debate at a time when people were ready to learn the language of that debate. Wolfe's foreign newsbooks are basically official propaganda (some of them bear the legend 'Published by Authority') and domestic news – such as it is – generally continues to avoid the hazards of solid fact for marvels, eclipses and monstrous births. The mental habit of moralising an unlikely story, extracting omens and hidden significance from the incredible, was one that died hard, and it proved difficult to reconcile with unprejudiced analysis of news. Furthermore, while foreign wars may have been a stimulus to journalistic activity, in the short term the reporting of them encouraged rather than allayed the bigotry and partisan hysteria which disfigured so much public debate of the time. These are perennial weaknesses of the news trade, of course, and we can easily find examples in the journalism of our own time.

In Jonson's day, however, the absence of tried journalistic method made the news trade particularly susceptible to the censure of contemporaries. Anthony Smith, writing about the conditions necessary for a periodical press, comments that 'Journalism does not become professionalised ... until it requires the essential tool of double-checking; until then it remains a mere appendage of printing or, in its grander forms, a sub-branch of diplomacy'.[65] We have seen already that Wolfe got his news from more than one source (though whether he was able to corroborate a story by this means we do not know), and there are signs in the 1620s newsbooks of an attempt to sort out the muddle of conflicting report and give the public a reliable account. But it is abundantly clear that news publishers had only limited control over the flow of information, few ways of checking its accuracy when it arrived, and lacked the editorial skills to guide their readers in its reception. They were also faced with the problem of adjusting to the public role of the newspaper, with everything this implies about the kinds of information presented, the audience addressed, the ends sought. When Jonson attacks newsmongering as a profiteering activity, he is suggesting on one level that there is a fundamental absurdity about information being for sale, that the rules governing social communication are somehow transgressed. The Countrywoman who asks for a 'groatsworth of any news – I care not what' (I.iv.11) is doing what people have always done and picks up whatever news is going; but when she proceeds to pay for it she displays not only her naiveté but also her vulnerability in a new set of social and economic assumptions. Yet the newsmen were also in a difficult position. Much of the foreign news they printed really was what Smith calls 'a sub-branch of diplomacy': treaties, proclamations, the doings in foreign courts. Such news was only very gradually becoming public property, in that traditionally it flowed along channels reserved for exclusive and specialist purposes, and became available to publishers in a form which usually took little account of the public right to know.

The point can be made by citing Sir Henry Wotton's terse comment, writing in his capacity as Ambassador at Venice to his counterpart in Spain in 1621: 'frequent couriers are sent hither, with lies in their mouths and truth in their packets, as the fashion is; whereof the last has filled all this town with a voice of an encounter ... But a fresh letter doth correct this vain noise.'[66] One wonders how, and how much, the contents of this letter were publicised. The patrician attitude to information revealed here prevailed throughout the sixteenth century, and the means of communicating news were only slowly and reluctantly made available to the unprivileged public. Those means, almost exclusively, were the posts, which began as a royal service but were gradually extended under the Tudors to nobility and the merchants (who had their own postmaster).[67] Burghley and Walsingham used the system to develop their own news network, with agents acting as correspondents in the capitals of Europe. Control over dispatches was firmly maintained by a 'Master of the Posts and Courriers', and in James's reign, with the appointment of a naturalised Dutchman, Matthew de Quester, and his son as special postmasters 'for Forraine Parts', we begin to get a fuller picture of how these important and lucrative appointments functioned in an age of developing communications. During the 1620s there was a lengthy dispute over control of the foreign posts between de Quester, Charles Stanhope, official Master of the Posts, and the merchants, who fiercely defended their right to 'a post of their own election'. Jonson appears to allude to de Quester, and to this particular dispute, in The Staple of News;[68] and a contemporary audience might have detected in the play's central notion of a news monopoly a further gloss on this drawn-out squabble over special preserves. It is interesting in this regard to compare the organisation of the Staple office, with its desks and files and systems of registration (I.v.2–7), with the postal service arrangements as described by Howard Robinson: 'De Quester had a public office near the Exchange where two clerks kept a list of all letters sent and received. A table of schedules was hung up for the benefit of the public . . . The office had writing desks for public use, as well as a table on which the outgoing letters were accumulated.'[69] Jonson probably had less confidence than Wotton in the truth in couriers' packets, and the emphasis on written news in *The Staple* is in part his satire on the letter-writers who transcribed the latest gossip in Paul's and the Exchange and mailed it to friends and contacts. In *Neptune's Triumph* Jonson clarifies the process in the relationship between 'Grave Mr. *Ambler*, Newes-master of *Poules*' and the Dutchman Buz who acts as his emissary;[70] it seems likely that he saw de Quester's shop as a clearing-house for worthless information, a place where gossip is turned into commerce.

But there were other, and for Jonson more significant, ways in which written news served the growing trade. In I.v he deploys considerable resources of irony to suggest that Cymbal's new enterprise has abolished at a stroke the old way of doing things: instead of trading gossip in taverns and barber-shops, and patching up antiquated pamphlets, newsletters are collected at a central point and their contents retailed. The Staple emissaries assigned to the nerve-centres of social and commercial life, together with the 'special friends' and 'men of correspondence i' the country' (I.v.17–18), postulate a news-gathering and distribution system on a national scale, something that could scarcely be contemplated by the news trade in reality until English law permitted the printing of home news. Yet Jonson's picture, wherein laboriously attested accounts of incredible events are replaced by a streamlined news agency purveying up-to-date information, is a legitimate extrapolation from contemporary trends, and it shows us where his own principal concerns lie: not so much with the crude and easily satirised pamphlets of popular fancy, as with the organised exploitation of contemporary reality by men able to take advantage of a ready flow of information and an increasingly volatile political atmosphere. In this respect, the trade in hand-written reports that could not be printed was almost as significant in the 1620s as the newsbooks coming off the press; for future developments, including the journalism of the Civil Wars, it was probably more so.[71]

The commercial potential of hand-written news had in effect been demonstrated by its organised circulation amongst the upper classes in England over several decades. Stanley Morison describes examples of commissioned newsletters from the 1560s, both the personal kind where an 'intelligencer' or journalist writes by arrangement to a particular nobleman, and the more general digest of news which could be sent out in multiple copies.[72] In reading the correspondence of Jacobean times we can see how the one type of letter often shades into the other: as the contract between newsmonger and recipient became clearly defined, the dispatches frequently dispense with florid courtesies and preambles and take on an efficient, businesslike air, adopting the sub-divisions of news items by place and date that were customary in foreign newsletters and corantos.[73] This process reflects the fact that from early on stationers were employing agents to gather and reproduce reports which could be dispatched to clients on a subscription basis. In 1625 Sir Simonds d'Ewes concludes a letter of news to Sir Martin Stuteville by saying: 'I would onlie entreate you to let a copie of these articles bee written by anye of youre servants & at your next best opportunitie ... to bee sent to Dr Gibson';[74] but this early advocacy of the chain letter is evidence of a demand that could be satisfied more efficiently (and profitably) in other ways. This can be seen above all in the case of parliamentary reports.

In their pioneering introduction to the *Commons Debates for 1629*, Notestein and Relf stress the importance of the semi-official trade in manuscripts of parliamentary proceedings to the formation of organised political dissent and the growth of a domestic news industry.[75] The practice of preparing and circulating Commons speeches increased with the growth of Puritan opposition in Parliament, since members became sufficiently interested in giving their views a wider airing to attempt evasion of the traditional rules of secrecy that bound their proceedings. As we might expect, the scriveners and stationers were not slow to exploit the situation, and by the time *The Staple of News* appeared it was common practice for them to make and sell multiple copies of parliamentary speeches.[76] The play's 'emissary Westminster' presumably has his type in the scriveners and booksellers' agents who hung around Parliament in search of employment or information; and when neither was readily forthcoming, it seems that they were not above forging speeches on a recent topic of interest and attributing them to a particular member.[77] MPs struck deals with the stationers to distribute their pronouncements, or supplied them with notes of proceedings from which newsletters could be constructed. (The latter took the form of daily or weekly digests of Parliament, and were a prime means of keeping the provinces in touch with developments.) Because so few examples have been preserved from James's reign, it is impossible to know how regular or organised the service in newsletters then was; but it seems likely that Jonson's Factor in *News from the New World*, who in 1620 dispatches his week-ly bulletins throughout the shires, is based to some extent on observ-able practice; and Notestein and Relf find evidence for circulating 'remembrances' of parliamentary proceedings in 1626.[78] It was of course traditional practice to read and exchange unprinted writings in manuscript copies, especially in the case of verse: many of Jonson's own poems must have circulated thus amongst friends and patrons, and he was no doubt familiar with the dissemination of court news by this means. But never before had written news threatened to become the adjunct of a book trade prepared to use its know-how in matters of selling and distribution to exploit what it could not print.

The real point at issue here is the growing power of the stationer, who, as George Wither complained in 1625, had come to dominate the craftsmen of his profession – the printers, binders and clasp-makers – and thus fragmented a 'mystery' which once consisted of 'divers Trades incorporated together'.[79] Increasingly, the imprints on seven-teenth-century title-pages reveal that the printer and bookseller are separate individuals, the one often producing job-work for the other; and it is easy to see how ambitious stationers might decide to extend their enterprise into areas where, as yet, they could have no use for the printer at all. This kind of initiative patently subordinated trade principles to profit, and in the case of parliamentary newsletters, of-fered the alarming prospect (to a conservative mind like Jonson's) of political debate escaping its proper arena and, lacking even the con-trols entailed by printing regulations, losing its function in a wilder-ness of supposition and rumour.

Yet in the way he sets up his staple of written news, Jonson is look-ing beyond the immediate problem of irresponsible scriveners and unlicensed manuscripts. He sees clearly that such trends will not only ensure an organised trade in newsletters (such as actually came about after the Restoration),[80] but also, and more important, must even-tually remove the barriers standing in the way of domestic printed journalism. This inevitable prospect is imaged in the structure of Cymbal's enterprise, which relies on a network of correspondents and stores its news in rolls, yet consistently apes the rituals of London publishing in general and newsbook production by Butter & co. in particular. As McKenzie observes, the 'examining and registering of news' by Staple officials in Act I 'is an exact parallel to that of licensing and entering the copy for a book';[81] while at least two of the men actively involved in the production of newsbooks in 1623 are caricatured in the play. Jonson's strategy is not to distinguish one element of the news trade from another, but to link them in a single indictment: witness how in III.ii he builds on the earlier description (I.v) of a home industry in written news with examples redolent of the printed newsbooks reporting foreign wars.

This conflation seems all the more plausible when we examine the circumstances in which printed news was retailed. Our modern experience of print is that it establishes an impersonal relationship between producer and consumer; while it mediates between them, it also severs the possibility of direct contact. This was true only in a limited sense in the book trade of Jonson's time, and in early serial journalism, before the days of newspaper mass production, an informal relationship between the purveyor and recipient of news seems to have been quite common. Jonson touches on this when he calls news 'a weekly cheat to *draw* money' (my emphasis: a 'trick of alluring money to the Office and there cozening the people'). A preface to one of Butter's newsbooks understandably sees the transaction in rather different terms, but agrees that it can be an intimate one: '*Gentle Reader*, Custome is so predominant in every thing, that both the Reader and the Printer of these Pamphlets, agree in their expectation of weekely Newes, so that if the Printer have not wherewithall to afford satisfaction, yet will the Reader come and aske every day for new Newes; not out of curiosity or wantonness, but pretending a necessity, either to please themselves, or satisfie their Customers.'[82] Jonson turns this informality to his own purposes, suggesting that all the newsbooks do is to usurp the time-honoured trade in gossip and hearsay: Tattle complains that she has heard better news at the bakehouse and conduits in the street (III.Int.19–20), and refuses to be impressed by the Staple's claim to superior methods and sources. This sense of the book trade as an agency of rumour is vividly caught in a remark of Sir Henry Wotton's, in a letter of 1626 in which he announces his intention to publish a book in Oxford: he speaks of 'a little ambitious vanity stirring in me, to Print a thing of my Composition there, which would else in *London* run through too much noise before hand, by reason of the Licences that must be gotten, and an eternal trick in those *City-Stationers*, to rumour what they have under Press'.[83] Where the news trade is concerned, its critics probably regarded the product offered for sale as indistinguishable from the process by which it was advertised: the grapevine retailing itself to a credulous public. Jonson finds in this relatively informal transaction not a comfortable familiarity but a simple confidence trick: the evils of commercial newsmongering writ small and clear in ordinary human transactions.

To journalism's detractors Thomas Gainsford, who for a time was responsible for editing Butter's newsbooks, offered this counterblast:

> But why should you thus carelesse be? when all
> The earth for newes a scrutinie doth call:
> Besides, who ever mastred nature so,
> But he was well content since to bestow
> Upon fair rumour of the worlds designes,
> Which either men, or their prepar'd assignes
> Hunt after with full greedinesse, till they
> Doe understand what other men can say;
> And so doe rectifie their ignorance,
> And either custome, or some fairer chance
> The Common-wealths rich curtaines draw aside,
> That they may see, what therein doth abide . . . [84]

Gainsford's rather conventional eloquence lacks the spirit of some of his prose expostulations in the newsbooks, where he expertly projects himself as the overworked editor dedicated to serving an ungrateful public. But the lines do at least attempt to define the purpose and value of the news trade in terms which can be debated. Jonson, of course, with his own firm ideas about knowledge and education, would find the suggestion that journalism is leading men out of uncertainty and error into truth impossible to take seriously; and he brings to his critique in *The Staple* a powerful awareness of cultural issues and incipient change of which Gainsford has no inkling. Yet at the same time, the idea that a responsible journalism can communicate to ordinary people and 'rectifie their ignorance' has profound implications in the early seventeenth century; it directly and usefully challenges Jonson's central assumptions about the function of the writer in society, and it needs to be borne in mind when we come to attempt an evaluation of his art and thought in this play.

5. THE PLAY

When Canter concludes his tirade in Act IV and takes Pecunia home with him, the effect is to declare redundant the play's various settings, real and imagined, in favour of a solid and virtuous context:

> I will take home the lady to my charge,
> And these her servants . . . A seat

> Is built already, furnished too, worth twenty
> Of your imagined structures, Canters' College.   (IV.iv.121–5)

He points his son to the beggar's cloak he has thrown off, ironically conflating his special use of 'cant' with its usual application to vagrant language:

> Tomorrow you may put on that grave robe
> And enter your great work of Canters' College,
> Your work, and worthy of a chronicle.   (177–9)

The last line reminds us that Pennyboy Junior's ambitious designs on Pecunia, announced at the end of Act I, have ended in ignominious failure, and with them have evaporated the educational scheme on which he planned to prostitute his wealth, the news office that would have chronicled his deeds, and above all the great festive occasion in Apollo planned and executed by Lickfinger. Only one setting remains to be purged, and this is the house of Pennyboy Senior, where Pecunia was previously confined and which in the last Act becomes a crazy parody of a law-court, before the usurer's wits are restored and he hands over to his nephew 'my house, goods, lands, all but my vices, / And those I go to cleanse' (V.vi.55–6). We are not told that he will go and preach the end of the world in a turnip cart, like Mammon in *The Alchemist*, perhaps because this would be out of keeping in a play which preaches the golden mean and whose concluding affirmations are so resolutely abstract. Similarly the feast at home, if there is to be one, will not be a tolerant extension of the play's action like the supper at Justice Overdo's, but a withdrawal from contexts which have seen the perversion of living ideals. In this sense at least the ending restores an image of moral security which is tarnished by the accommodations of *The Alchemist* and *Bartholomew Fair*; although arguably it is achieved at some cost in a play whose settings are designed as theatrical counterfeits, challenges to the working context of the dramatic poet. As the Staple to which Cymbal acts as midwife, the saturnalian masque of Act IV and the college conceived by Pennyboy Junior are thrust aside, we may feel that the 'hard labour' of the play itself prophesied by the Prologue (Induction, 61) has been essentially a work of denial and exclusion, in which Jonson shuts up his circle against some of the most pressing concerns of his audience.[85]

Much remains to be said, however, about the ways in which the play engages our attention through the course of five acts, and in general criticism has not done justice to the complexity of its dramatic method. Partly this is so because *The Staple* is on the face of it a play where Jonson tells us what to think, rejecting what Douglas Duncan calls 'the oblique method of teaching'[86] he had used in *Bartholomew Fair* and a number of earlier comedies, and so eschewing the dense ironies and conflicting perspectives which that strategy tends to provoke. It is certainly true that the use of overt allegory and of a commentator-figure in Pennyboy Canter, together with the underdeveloped characterisation of most of the satiric butts, can give the impression that Jonson is ramming home his message at the expense of profitable ambiguity; moreover, the progress of his moral fable is at times stiffly predictable since Pennyboy Junior lacks the capacity of a Bartholomew Cokes to enliven his own story and carry us with him wherever he goes. Yet within the obligatory episodes of the prodigal plot the play is intricately organised to yield a rich thematic vein, linking and juxtaposing its various concerns in ways that complicate our response and on occasion – as with Pecunia and the masque in Act IV – deliberately unsettle us and compel a suspension of judgement.

Jonson is unusually attentive to details of setting in the first half of the play in establishing the dimensions of his plot and suggesting something of its thematic structure. In Act I he initially encourages a sense of unity of place by introducing the Staple as 'here i' the house, almost on the same floor' (I.iii.64) as Pennyboy Junior's lodgings, and the feckless 'town' atmosphere of the opening *levée* scene influences our early impression of the Staple as a fashionable, fly-by-night venture which strives to give itself an air of solidity:

> Master Cymbal
> Is Master of the Office: he projected it.
> He lies here i'the house, and the great rooms
> He has taken for the Office, and set up
> His desks and classes, tables, and his shelves.   (I.ii.41–5)

These proximate venues become ironically complementary: whereas the prodigal is a magnet for tradesmen who come to prey on his new-found wealth with an over-priced outfit, the news office lures credulous customers to itself in order to capitalise upon their greedy curiosity. In each case the emphasis is not so much on financial cupidity as on the vanity of consumer demand. It is of course part of Jonson's purpose to suggest that the Staple is simply another 'tailor of the times' serving the needs of a giddy society, a point sardonically reinforced when Pennyboy Junior goes to the office in I.v. and is enraptured by its devices of fabrication. But the spurious air of efficiency projected by Cymbal and his cronies also tends to suggest that organised enterprise, however empty, has a shaping effect of its own, and the last scenes of Act I vividly show the disparity between Penny-boy's absurd gestures of patronage: 'Keep me fair, sir, / Still i'your Staple. I am here your friend, / On the same floor' (I.v.145–7) and the stealthy way in which the Staple has made him effectively their creature.

This emphasis upon the misuse of wealth is echoed in Act II, where we are introduced to Pennyboy Senior, the miser who monopolises Pecunia in his own house and is shown to be as enslaved to her as his nephew is to the latest fashions. The introduction of Pecunia brings out the classic opposition between avarice and prodigality, as Jonson buttresses his plot with discreet echoes of two familiar story-lines: the usurer's daughter running off with spendthrift young man (the *Merchant of Venice* situation), and the rivalry of grasping old age and virile youth for the hand of an heiress.[87] But the diagram of the play is meanwhile complicated by other ideas. Pecunia has already been announced at the end of Act I, where Picklock explains to the prodigal how he must compete with journalism for her favours:

> Now, sir, Cymbal thinks –
> The master here and governor o'the Staple –
> By his fine arts and pomp of his great place
> To draw her. He concludes, she is a woman,
> And that so soon as sh'hears of the new Office
> She'll come to visit it, as they all have longings
> After new sights and motions. But your bounty,
> Person and bravery must achieve her.   (I.vi.55–62)

The skilful infusion of the allegory of Lady Money into a realistic plot perceptibly quickens the dramatic pulse, for we see clearly for the first time that Pennyboy's bounty is not something to be spent or merely protected – as at I.iii.31 – but something to be *achieved* (the word 'bounty' is later used of Pecunia herself); in the elaborately ironical encomium offered by Picklock and Canter, wealth is put through her paces as a high-class whore ('All sorts of men and all professions') and emerges as a test of virtue and discrimination:

> P. *Canter*. And you to bear her from all these, it will be –
> *Picklock*. A work of fame –
> P. *Canter*.   Of honour –
> *Picklock*.   Celebration –
> P. *Canter*. Worthy your name.   (85–7)

The comedy of this climax derives less from any incongruity in the praise of money than from Pennyboy Junior's manifest inadequacy to grasp what is being offered to him, for behind the disclosure that Cymbal is the prodigal's main rival for Pecunia's attention lies the more significant truth that Pecunia is a rival to the Staple for his own. She becomes a dramatic centre in her own right, as Act II makes clear, and a moral challenge to Pennyboy's self-importance:

> I'll undertake it ... for since I came
> Of mature age, I have had a certain itch
> In my right eye – this corner here, do you see? –
> To do some work, and worthy of a chronicle. (89–93)

Jonson's personification of money in this play, as I have already suggested in discussing the tradition behind Lady Pecunia, seems designed to free the idea of wealth from fixed definitions and recover from it an image of value. The undertaking is finally inseparable from Jonson's work in masque, for it is there that he transforms the allegorical materials of morality drama into a new expression of working ideals and exemplary modes of conduct; and in so doing he pushes beyond the satirical treatment of wealth and its pursuit in his earlier plays. The depraved fantasies of Volpone and Mammon, in which the myth of a Golden Age is distorted into immediate sensual gratification, reappear in *The Staple* in contexts which not only expose these transgressions but also seek to give expression to the vision of life they betray. Jonson is not altogether successful in this, partly because in seeking to transcend the powerful obsessions of his earlier debauchées and realise another kind of imaginative potential, he loses touch with some of the raw vitality of his own art. But the endeavour is an ambitious and interesting one, and will repay close attention to its key moments in the play.

In the course of Act II Pecunia is gradually defined in relation to the world which seeks to exploit her. In the first scene, Pennyboy Senior's grovelling worship is calmly questioned in a way that establishes her dignity and moderating role ('Cannot my grace be gotten, and held too, / Without your self-tormentings . . . ?'), and the predatory visit of the jeerers in II.iv reminds us of the bankrupt milieu that awaits her outside. Jonson is careful to avoid the conventional imagery of money-bags and chests at this early stage of characterisation; instead, he uses the vicious flyting between the jeerers and Pecunia's guardian to hint at the quality of her confinement:

I have heard you ha' offered, sir, to lock up smoke
And caulk your windows, spar up all your doors,
Thinking to keep it a close prisoner wi' you,
And wept when it went out, sir, at your chimney.   (II.iv.168–71)

The usurer's arid routines are effectively evoked in Almanac's male-
volent taunt that he

               Sweeps down no cobwebs here
But sells 'em for cut fingers; and the spiders,
As creatures reared of dust and cost him nothing,
To fat old ladies' monkeys.   (175–8)

And the trivialising of Lady Money by her context is further under-
lined in Statute's advice to Pecunia not to 'make your grace too cheap'
(II.i.59) in the eyes of her suitors, echoing Nathaniel's cynical counsel
that Staple customers should be made to 'attend in name of policy'
(I.iv.20), and thus reducing Pecunia, like news, to a mere commodity.
Her monopoly by the usurer denies her the independent life that dramatic personification entitles her to:

Band.   I fear your grace
      Hath ta'en too much of the sharp air.
Pecunia.   O no!
      I could endure to take a great deal more
      (And with my constitution) were it left
      Unto my choice.   (II.i.45–9)

This is altogether more robust than Argurion's 'wandring and giddy
disposition' in *Cynthia's Revels*, and lends Pecunia a sophisticated
poise which tactfully supports a prevalent theory of monetary circulation, releasing wealth from the torpid grip of the usurer.[88] As
the gossips later remind us, Pecunia is not costumed after the manner of the emblem books (as she might be in a city pageant), but
'pranked up like a prime lady' (II.Int.19);[89] and the effect is literally
and figuratively to enrich the allegory, making it capable of bearing
the weight of modern problems. The consequences of this emphasis
are fully felt in II.v, where the three Pennyboys and Picklock are
audience to an impressive spectacle: *The study is opened where she sits
in state* (II.v.43.1), and Pecunia is introduced to the prodigal in an
elaborate ceremony of kissing and mutual declaration. The encounter
itself is verbally disappointing, being rather too obviously a patchwork of classical references, but its main effect is clearly visual and
choreographic, a kind of mating game ('Ay, he does kiss her. I like
him') which anticipates the curious rituals of Act IV. Pecunia's

fashionable elegance is an essential part of the scene, matching Pennyboy Junior's 'bravery' with a display calculated to express the range of
Jonson's feelings about conspicuous wealth, forcing us to respond to a
spectacle of munificence and civilised splendour but also to sense the
prodigal's vulnerability to empty ostentation. The scene is Jonson at
his most Jacobean, cultivating the grandeur of state as he had learnt
to do at court and exploiting all he knew of its inner conflicts and
pressures. An important element in his own response surfaces later
when Pecunia is prostituted to the Staple, and Canter comments:

> Why, that's the end of wealth! Thrust riches outward
> And remain beggars within; contemplate nothing
> But the vile sordid things of time, place, money ...   (III.ii.241-3)

But in the present scene the conventional attitude to sumptuous display is ironically centred in Pennyboy Senior, who offers Pecunia to
his nephew as a temptation to extravagance and ruin ('I shall have all
at last, my hopes do tell me', II.iv.203); and we sense a finer challenge
implicit in the occasion, to marry magnificence to an inner virtue and
sense of decorum.

This may be an over-confident statement of Jonson's design; certainly his handling of Pecunia's adventures in the next two acts is
morally complex and teasing, and the dramatic sequence which cul-
minates in her adoration in Apollo rarely permits a straightforward
response. Its next major landmark is Cymbal's attempt to seduce
Pecunia to the news office:

> If it will please your grace to sojourn here
> And take my roof for covert, you shall know
> The rites belonging to your blood and birth,
> Which few can apprehend .... I would have
> You waited on by ladies, and your train
> Borne up by persons of quality and honour.
> Your meat should be served in with curious dances,
> And set upon the board with virgin hands
> Tuned to their voices, not a dish removed
> But to the music, nor a drop of wine
> Mixed with his water without harmony.   (III.ii.222-34)

The banquet of sense is offered to Pecunia as the traditional temptation to power and influence:

> Come forth, state and wonder
> Of these our times, dazzle the vulgar eyes
> And strike the people blind with admiration.   (238-40)

In joining forces with the news trade, she will become the siren figure who lures others to 'taste the *cornucopiae* of her rumours' (119). But the identification also increases Pecunia's own vulnerability. If news is 'the diet of the times', something that Lickfinger gathers to 'strew out the long meal withal' (183), Pecunia, by being the occasion of a banquet, also becomes its object. In the later revels in Apollo, Pennyboy Junior's tactless apostrophe makes clear what is involved in Cymbal's persuasions:

> O, how my princess draws me with her looks
> And hales me in, as eddies draw in boats
> Or strong Charybdis ships that sail too near
> The shelves of love! The tides of your two eyes,
> Wind of your breath, are such as suck in all
> That do approach you.
>
> *Pecunia.*   Who hath changed my servant?
> *P. Junior.* Yourself, who drink my blood up with your beams
> As doth the sun, the sea! Pecunia shines
> More in the world than he, and makes it spring
> Where'er she favours. Please her but to show
> Her melting wrists or bare her ivory hands,
> She catches still! Her smiles, they are love's fetters!
> Her breasts his apples! Her teats strawberries!
> Where Cupid, were he present now, would cry,
> Farewell my mother's milk, here's sweeter
>   nectar!   (IV.ii.42–56)

The Siren-figure crudely meshes with the idea of a radiant, fertilising centre to turn Pecunia into something to be tasted and enjoyed. The curiously repellent quality of Pennyboy's language may be traceable to the way the speech inverts a common (and often vulgar) convention, that of describing female beauty in terms of material wealth. The imagery of treasure-trove pervades the love poetry of the sixteenth century, with uncountable references to teeth like pearls, lips like rubies, hair (even) like gold wire; but beyond a reference to 'ivory hands', and a fleeting comparison in line 70, Pecunia is not described in these terms. Instead, reversing the tendency to turn the loved one into a precious inanimate object, wealth, Lady Money, is translated back into images of perishable nature, which quickly reveal her as an object to be consumed. The images of breasts like apples, and so forth, are of course conventional enough in themselves, and provide an apt vehicle for Pennyboy's banalities; but their unpleasantly tangible quality here seems deliberately contrived to make a further point.

What Jonson is doing resembles the process of 'unmetaphoring' that Rosalie Colie has discovered in Marvell's poetry:[90] he takes the trope of Money as a lady and shows how indiscriminate worship destroys the analogy's mystique by turning a figurative meaning (the 'consumption' of money) into a quasi-literal one. It comes across as an *abuse* of allegory, a point that is emphasised by the momentary reference to the positive, creative associations of Pecunia's bounty (she 'makes it spring / Where'er she favours'), contaminated in the lines that follow by a purely appetitive sense of her value.

We cannot fully grasp what Jonson is doing here, however, without looking at his overall strategy in Act IV and its implications for his art in the play as a whole. The establishing context for Pecunia's praises is the great testimonial to the powers of the cook delivered just prior to this by Lickfinger, in answer to Madrigal's claim that poetry is allied to the 'quick cellar':

> Seducèd poet, I do say to thee,
> A boiler, range and dresser were the fountains
> Of all the knowledge in the universe.
> And they're the kitchens, where the master cook
> (Thou dost not know the man, nor canst thou know him,
> Till thou hast served some years in that deep school
> That's both the nurse and mother of the arts,
> And hearst him read, interpret and demonstrate!) –
> A master cook! Why, he's the man o' men
> For a professor. He designs, he draws,
> He paints, he carves, he builds, he fortifies,
> Makes citadels of curious fowl and fish;
> Some he dry-ditches, some moats round with broths.

Lickfinger concludes by insisting on the cook as universal man:

> He is an architect, an engineer,
> A soldier, a physician, a philosopher,
> A general mathematician.   (IV.ii.11–23, 35–7)

And Madrigal's acknowledgement of gastronomic wisdom ('It is granted') leads into the apostrophe just discussed, followed by the mock-encomium of Pecunia by the jeerers.

Lickfinger's speech is a complex double allusion to the classics, drawing on the fragments of Greek comedy that make up Athenaeus's banquet-symposium *Deipnosophistae*, and at the same time echoing the maxims of Vitruvius in the opening chapter of his *De Architectura*, where he insists upon the versatility of the architect, his acquisition

of a wide range of skills to equip him for a uniquely demanding voca-
tion.[91] This clearly links the speech to Jonson's running dispute with
Inigo Jones about the relative status of poet and designer in the making
of court entertainments (which was later to produce Jonson's bitter
remark that 'Painting and carpentry are the soul of masque');[92] and
the cooking analogy neatly catches the slightly facile opportunism of
architecture's claim to blend all disciplines in the comprehensive art
of building. It is no accident that this testament to the cook's powers
also has a solid context in the well-wrought feasts of the time, and
Jonson was presumably not slow to catch the irony that the scenic
wonders of the masque were staged in Jones's neo-classic Banqueting Hall. But we need to tread carefully here. Although there is an
obvious vein of parody in this strenuous assertion, its overall dramatic
purpose and effect are not easily classified as satire, partly because
Jonson was himself deeply committed to the masque ethos and often
drew on the metaphor of cooking to express his own vision of theatrical synthesis. Our primary (or initial) response to Lickfinger must be
to see him as an embodiment of festivity, a character whose energy is
slightly suspect but who nonetheless is a vital presence in the play.
We cannot help noticing that his skills as well as his appearance re-
semble those of a figure evoked right at the start, in Mirth's vivid
description:

> Yonder he is within (I was i'the tiring-house awhile to see the actors
> dressed) rolling himself up and down like a tun i'the midst of 'em, and
> spurges. Never did vessel of wort or wine work so! His sweating put me in
> mind of a good Shroving-dish (and I believe would be taken up for a service
> of state somewhere, an't were known) – a stewed poet! He doth sit like an
> unbraced drum with one of his heads beaten out. For that you must note, a
> poet hath two heads as a drum has, one for making, the other repeating; and
> his repeating head is all to pieces. They may gather it up i'the tiring-house,
> for he hath torn the book in a poetical fury, and put himself to silence in
> dead sack; which, were there no other vexation, were sufficient to make him
> the most miserable emblem of patience.   (Induction, 62–75)

This early association of poet and cook is the basis for the more complex linking of ideas to follow. Mirth, always the most perceptive
of the gossips, is allowed to glimpse the element of vulnerability in
Jonson's flamboyant grossness: the poet who has been serving up
court entertainments for the past nine years (a regular 'service of
state') is now trying once again to write for the public theatre, a
medium in which he could never be certain of success. But beyond
the defensive posture, which is perhaps Jonson's admission that, like

Face, he seeks new guests, lies a cunning use of persona. Critics tend to use words like 'charming' or 'genial' to describe this comic portrait,[93] noting that some of the sting has gone out of Jonson's satire generally and made way for good-humoured self-mockery. Yet it may be less whimsical than it seems. By promising from the start to haunt his play in the likeness of an old fat man, Jonson allies his creative function to the 'spirit of Shrovetide' embodied and announced by Mirth but at the same time undertakes to use the drama of occasion to a larger purpose than simple revelry. The picture of the silent, impotent poet seemingly contradicts the festive occasion, but in reality it is designed to interrogate it, setting up a tension between the holiday chatter of the gossips and the hard-won eloquence of the play which contains them. In a similar way, Jonson's own art is neither to be identified with Lickfinger's or completely dissociated from it, for it includes it, in a work which draws on both the traditional energies of festivity and the language of masque to achieve its resolution.

The point can be developed by looking more fully at the context of Lickfinger's speech. It has the air of a set-piece, which indeed it is, being lifted directly and almost verbatim from the unperformed masque *Neptune's Triumph*. In the masque the Cook who delivers it has an antagonist altogether more impressive than Madrigal, in the Poet who comes on at the start 'to disperse the Argument' (7). He is interrupted by the Cook (shades of the Prologue and gossips in *The Staple*), who browbeats him about his qualifications for the job, and then offers his own claim to mastery. After the big speech, however, we actually hear the Poet's Argument, an exalted summary of the masque's theme, Albion's return to the Court of Neptune, and the action unfolds accordingly, punctuated by an entertaining anti-masque of newsmongers emerging from an *olla podrida*. The effect is to balance the claims of poet and cook, in what Angus Fletcher calls 'a parody of transcendence',[94] and to accept by implication the partnership of poetry and spectacle in the hybrid creation of masque. The former holds its own against the 'vulgars chime' (162), the Cook's desire to please every palate, but the Poet's unJonsonian refusal to provide an antimasque is successfully overruled by the other. The episode is revealing about the accommodations Jonson made as a writer of court masques, as well as about the ways his own dramatic language is stretched by the medium. But what we notice is that in *The Staple* Lickfinger's praise of cooking has no creative complement or significant counter-argument except in the total context of the play itself.

In many respects the scenes set in Apollo which comprise Act IV form a kind of multiplying antimasque, variants upon a saturnalian theme which is curtailed only by Canter's self-revelation at the end, which itself may be said to imitate the triumphant disclosure of truth that normally climaxes a Jonsonian masque. The ugly jeering of the first scene precipitates an undertaking on his part to show that 'the whole world are canters' (IV.i.56), but before he does so we witness Lickfinger's big moment, the praise of Pecunia with Madrigal's insipid verses, the antic dance which follows it, the intervention and expulsion of Pennyboy Senior, and the proclamation of Pecunia's pedigree at the start of IV.iv. It is a sequence with its own momentum, like the 'dancing engines' savagely observed by Canter (IV.ii.138), and Jonson seems to be fascinated by its profane logic, its shadow-relationship to the workings of genuine art. The perversely compelling quality of this bacchanale is at its strongest perhaps in IV.iii, where Pennyboy Senior breaks in upon the proceedings to rescue Pecunia and is ritually baited before being thrown out. As representative of the anti-festive principle ('Thou and thy cups, too, perish!'), he is exposed to the full hostility of the revellers, and Jonson touches a primitive nerve in his audience with the spectacle of the miser's humiliation:

> Madrigal.   You have now no money –
> Shunfield. But are a rascal.
> P. Senior.   I am cheated, robbed,
>   Jeered by confederacy.
> Fitton.   No, you are kicked
>   And used kindly, as you should be.
> Shunfield.   Spurned
>   From all commerce of men, who are a cur.   (IV.iii.71–5)

Even Pecunia's attendants move into a strange mechanical limbo as they refashion their own dramatic constituents into a weapon of mockery:

> Band. H'has left my fellow Wax out, i'the cold –
> Statute. Till she was stiff as any frost, and crumbled
>   Away to dust and almost lost her form.
> Wax. Much ado to recover me.
> P. Senior.   Woman jeerers!
>   Have you learned too the subtle faculty?   (47–51)

Their rebellion is a seizing of licence which has our uneasy assent but which comes across as artificially stimulated by the hectic atmosphere of Apollo; the servants are like puppets in a carnival parade whose vitality derives essentially from the contrast with their quotidian obscurity. In this respect they are a grotesque minor epitome of the play's teaching on the danger of extremes, as they move from being lifeless 'concentrics' revolving around Pecunia (II.ii.56) to the frenzied revels of Act IV.

What we have in this scene is a negative image of the play's larger pattern of conflict and resolution. The traditional battle between Carnival and Lent is allegorised (and humanised) into the disruptive revels of prodigality versus life-denying avarice; but what is largely missing in Apollo, as long as Pecunia is besieged by the jeerers and Canter remains a bystander, is the reconciling middle term, the arbitration of the golden mean. Pennyboy Senior is cast in the role of Shrove puppet or scapegoat, the Jack-a-Lent (see V.v.35) whose ritual destruction purges and renews the community; but in practice the atavistic note ('A snarling rascal. Hence!') does not induce order and harmony, which must wait upon the very different humbling of the miser in Act V. Like most of his contemporaries Jonson probably accepted the derivation of carnival from the Roman Saturnalia, but he also seems to follow the common interpretation of Shrovetide as a meeting-point 'of holy day and holiday, Lent and Carnival, feasting and fasting',[95] a festival in which the wisdom of temperance is clearly signalled. Elsewhere in his work he touches upon the necessity of decorum in celebration, honouring occasion in the proper way; and in *The Staple* the point is made partly through contrast, showing how the festive arts of Lickfinger (who in an important sense is the miser's true opposite) lack this kind of civilised balance and tumble into a licentious parody of the holiday spirit. The fact that so much powerful criticism of excess is put into Pennyboy Senior's mouth in this play has to do, I think, with Jonson's basic distrust of carnival, its unfrugal disruption of normal order, at the same time that he recognised its energies as a profoundly important side of human creativity, one that needed to be harnessed and used just as he always sought to make something of his own Dionysian side – the heavy drinking, for example, and the rebellious 'fantasy, which ... ever mastered his reason'.[96] There is a certain appropriateness in Mirth's description at the start of a poet who is both a drunken lord of misrule and a dramatist trying to keep recalcitrant actors under control, for his play explores and seeks to order the lubberlands of false festivity which are ambiguously related to genuine occasion, the sort that is marked, ideally, by the performance of a Ben Jonson play.

When we call *The Staple of News* a 'festive drama', then, we should not allow the label to simplify our understanding of the play's design. Jonson finds little to celebrate in his society, and there is practically nothing of the solidarity with his audience, precarious but real, that he established in *Bartholomew Fair*. *The Staple* is a much more self-protective work, assimilating the threat to the poet's authority by giving it fictional status within the dramatic structure and effectively precluding a free assessment of its implications. As D. F. McKenzie suggests (in a fine analysis of this aspect of the play) it is a 'forbiddingly intellectual effort of containment',[97] one which may leave us more aware of Jonson's ingenuity in constructing his critique than of its efficacy as an indictment of contemporary trends. But if *The Staple* runs the risk of solipsism – of being caught in its own fictional web, and turning social satire into a game with structures – this is testimony also to the play's formidable engagement with the problem of how truth and reality can be mediated through human systems of communication. Here we need to consider for a moment Jonson's extensive concern in *The Staple* with the question of language.

For Jonson, '*Speech* ... is the Instrument of *Society*',[98] a prime index of a community's moral health, and it hardly needs to be said that throughout his work he laments the decay of language and civilised discourse in his own time. Jonson's sense of decorum of speech and writing is clearly set forth in *Discoveries* and in dramatic episodes like the one from *Poetaster* where Crispinus is made to vomit up some of John Marston's more bizarre linguistic innovations. Nearly all his work implies the view that the socially responsible poet is more than a mere custodian of expression, and that an important part of keeping a tradition alive is to assess the new and exert influence upon contemporary progress: '*Custome* is the most certaine Mistresse of Language, as the publicke stampe makes the current money. But wee must not be too frequent with the mint, every day coyning.'[99] In *The Staple*, however, Jonson seems to contemplate the prospect of 'custom' losing its power of arbitration, its capacity through the agency of the poet to shape a developing culture: as stable centres of communication like the theatre or pulpit are challenged by other contexts, he implies, agreed usage in language gives way to competing modes of expression which both reflect and help to accelerate the breakdown of civilised consensus. This concern is visible in the way Jonson establishes a quasi-rhetorical contrast between the news office, with its smooth devices of persuasion (punning repeatedly on 'butter' to reinforce the idea of a bland and enervating enterprise) and the noisy aggression of the jeerers, whose violation of language reflects both their bankrupt imaginations and their poverty of manners:

> *Almanac.*   Let's upon him,
> And if we cannot jeer him down in wit –
> *Madrigal.* Let's do't in noise.   (V.v.21–3)

But Jonson goes further than this in investigating how language becomes disengaged from stable meanings and the expression of truth. The curious episode towards the end of Act IV, where Canter anatomises the jargon of the assembled jeerers, is revealing less for what it tells us about the insensitive opportunism of these characters than as an attack on developments in language itself and its social and professional uses. For instance, the exposition of medical cant (IV.iv.37–47) primarily suggests – as in much of what Subtle says in *The Alchemist* – the obscuring power of technical language: on this view, such terminology serves no other purpose than to safeguard the prestige of its user, and so is hostile to the traditional uses of words. It is a simple enough point, and Jonson's concern with jargon in all its forms as a corruption of language and a divisive factor in social relations is familiar to us from several of his plays; the immediately relevant comparison is with Volpone's mountebank speech, with its use of learned terms to inflate and deceive. But there is an important difference in dramatic situation. Jonson's normal method is to show the misuse of language in action, as something that reveals the character of the user and guides our assessment of him; and elsewhere in *The Staple* he does just this, not only in exposing the news office and the jeerers but also in satirising the affectations of the prodigal. But when it comes to the analysis of professional jargon, we are offered in this scene a kind of ritual condemnation, a parade of terminology which in most cases illuminates none of the vices of these characters as we have perceived them earlier in the play. The effect is to disengage the critique of language and profession from the interrogation of the individuals concerned. Furthermore, despite Canter's later insistence in condemning Almanac: 'Do I despise a learn'd physician, / In calling him a quacksalver?' (IV.iv.164–5), we could be forgiven for thinking that the distinction between the charlatan and the true doctor has actually been obscured by the attack on medical jargon at IV.iv.37–47. Given Jonson's evident hostility to the more arcane side of doctoring – judicial astrology and the like – we can see how easily he might have shown the way in which jargon tends to conflate medicine and pseudo-science, physiology and star-gazing, by making both sound equally impressive (and meaningless) to lay ears, and thus perpetuates a spurious and disabling association between the two. But he conspicuously neglects the opportunity to do this. The real effect of Canter's speech is to run the two practices together and parade their vocabularies as joint evidence of professional vanity and, beyond that, of how the modern rage for definition progressively hardens the arteries of normal communication. Furthermore, because the speech avoids the obvious distinction between the quack and the genuine practitioner, we are unlikely to gather from it that Jonson is simply attacking the misuse of terminology by the former. We are much more likely to draw the conclusion that clinical science just as much as astrology stands condemned by its reliance on a technical vocabulary, the 'darke, and obscure tearmes' in which (Jonson claims in one of his masques) 'the monster ignorance stil covets, to enwrap it self'.[100]

Canter's initiative is essentially rhetorical in nature: its tactical, even playful quality is apparent, for instance, in the way Picklock plays the accomplice at lines 103–8 and offers a specimen of legal jargon when asked to do so. What it does is to create a symbolic arena in which the voice of the poet-critic can impose its authority, in a relentlessly impartial way, on a world which seems disinclined to listen. It reveals Jonson's awareness of the growing fragmentation of the learned and professional world, a situation in which, to use Lawrence Stone's terms, a 'status hierarchy' was gradually giving way to 'competitive status agglomerations',[101] and men's occupations are measured by the values of the market-place. Jonson clearly regarded this situation as a kind of Babel, where the idiom of the poet has to compete with a variety of dialects to be heard, and language is emptied of moral significance. He may also have sensed something of the radical shift in linguistic thought during the Renaissance which was to change the conceptual relationship between *word* and *thing*: from the belief in language as a real description of the world, something settled and God-given, in which words have an organic relationship to things, to a theory of language as an arbitrary set of signs, in which meanings and definitions must be fixed precisely because there is no 'natural' relationship between an object and its descriptive term.[102] Jonson's sense of a world that is literally 'encoded', its disparate activities each defined by the idiom it employs, might be said to anticipate a good deal of modern linguistic theory; but he differs from the new grammarians (and from progressive thinkers in his own day) in his insistence that this state of affairs is a betrayal of essential human interests, and represents a short-sighted surrender to pluralism. We cannot know how clearly or in exactly what terms Jonson saw

this issue, but he understood very well that literature cannot claim
the moral and educative function he himself insisted upon unless the
reality it seeks to imitate is acknowledged as something larger than
individual vested interests and ways of seeing.

The climactic folly of *The Staple of News* is Pennyboy Junior's
'noble whimsy' of a Canters' College (IV.iv.80): staffed by the jeerers,
this monstrous conception brings out into the open Jonson's anxiety
about education in a society crudely obsessed with fact and rumour. It
has been suggested that Canters' College is Jonson's response to new
educational initiatives in England at this time, and the insistent satire
in the play on technological innovation and enquiry may partly reflect a distaste for the emphasis on practical training at institutions
like Gresham College in London.[103] This is an important subject,
which cannot be dealt with adequately in the space available here; but
it must be said that by implicitly linking Canters' College with the
Staple via the jeerers (who support both institutions) and Pecunia
(who is nominally invested in both) and through unlikely news stories
about the latest scientific inventions,[104] Jonson comes perilously near
to inventing a conspiracy theory about the assault on genuine learning
by upstart purveyors and seekers of information. At the same time
though (as the repeated 'midwife' metaphor implies: see Induction,
60, and I.v.77) he saw how news, like the theatre, is able to create its
own image of reality – 'things (like truths) well fain'd' – and how the
jargon of urban cliques is capable of becoming the recognised language of power and status, usurping the public voice which Jonson,
particularly in his poetry, articulated so effectively.

In the last Act of *The Staple* the triumph of Jonson's art is on
one level complete, as the news office blows up, Picklock's plot is
thwarted by a superior stratagem, and the jeerers are scattered by the
arrival of Canter 'with his forces':

> *Fitton.* He's a flame.
> *Shunfield.*   A furnace.
> *Almanac.*   A consumption,
>   Kills where he goes.   (*They all run away.*)   (V.v.55–6)

Canter seems to be armed, quite simply and irresistibly, with the
cleansing power of truth; and his moral fury, unlike the 'short madness' of his miserly brother, is lucid and purposeful, sowing confusion
in the minds of his opponents to bring about a new understanding:

> You see by this amazement and distraction
> What your companions were, a poor, affrighted

And guilty race of men that dare to stand
No breath of truth, but conscious to themselves
Of their no-wit or honesty, ran routed
At every panic terror themselves bred.   (V.vi.1–6)

The father's device to educate his son is complete, and the moral
driven home; but in Jonson's scheme this speech gains much of its
force and assurance from the momentum built up in Act V, as he uses
a lively intrigue and the hilarious farce of the dog-trial in scene iv to
create fresh interest in his plot and win the audience's assent to the
achievements of comic art. Picklock's 'fresh cheat' is a distillation of
the knavery which in various forms has operated throughout the play,
and his defeat is an opportunity to affirm some basic moral impera-
tives: Pennyboy Junior promises to stop the lawyer's mouth with
'truth' (V.ii.56), and wins his father's trust, in more than one sense,
by successfully capturing the deed held for Picklock by Lickfinger:

> *Picklock.*   I am lost. A plot! I scent it.
> *Lickfinger.* Why, and I sent it by the man you sent,
>   Whom else I had not trusted.
> *Picklock.*   Plague o'your trust.
>   I am trussed up among you.   (V.iii.12–15)

The word-play is nimble but emphatic, highlighting Picklock's de-
viousness and effectively neutralising it. In a comparable way Pennyboy Senior is also to be the victim of his own ingenuity, when in the
next scene his demand for honest testimony from his dogs ('The truth
now!', V.iv.40) merely emphasises the extent of his delusion, and
leads to the humbling which must precede his return to sanity.

We may well decide, however, that the pace and energy of Act V do
not quite sustain the moralising of the closing scene, and the pristine
declarations of the few characters who survive Canter's scourging tend
to indicate that the main concerns of the play have not been resolved
so much as simply left behind. It perhaps matters little that Pennyboy
Senior's reformation is unconvincing, for the events of the last scene
are purely exemplary, and dedicated to the working out of a pattern;
but the tenuous relationship of the play's final teaching to many of its
earlier themes is more of a problem. The iteration throughout Act V
of words like *truth, liberty, uses, trust,* and so on, is clearly intended by
Jonson as a stay against moral and linguistic incoherence; but it does
not mend the vices of canting and jeering, whose practitioners are
refused the comic dispensation to be wise hereafter and simply disappear from sight. A similar point must be made about the treatment

of journalism. Jonson is ultimately unable to convince us that news has anything to do with the theme of prodigality and the teaching on the golden mean, partly because the Staple never quite comes alive as a creature of Hydra-like excess, a creature painted full of tongues and ears whose proliferation threatens the health of the body politic. As a consequence, by the time we reach Act V the news trade has been assimilated into the ignorant and uncouth elements in Jonson's society without any clear demonstration of its 'buffon licence' or of how it violates the decorum of serious knowledge and ideas. Canter's flame-like descent upon the 'guilty race of men' is an arresting moment in the play's allegory, and coming soon after his denunciations in Act IV it adequately represents the power of *eloquentia* to silence mindless chatter and verbal distortion. But although (as I shall suggest shortly) this abrupt suppression of folly has its warrant in the techniques of Jonson's masques, it also reveals the tendency of his art in *The Staple* to subdue rather than fully interpret a difficult reality.

6. THE PLAY ON THE STAGE

When Jonson came to prepare *The Staple* for publication he can have had few illusions about its chances of surviving in the theatre, although he may have hoped that by giving it a permanent literary form the play would appeal to the stable judgement of later times and thereby regain the stage. As far as I know there is no record of this ever happening. We can speak with certainty of only a single production by the King's Men, who gave the play in February 1626 at Blackfriars and again at court, the latter performance almost certainly taking place at Shrovetide, which in that year fell on 19–21 February.[105] As we have seen, there is much in the play to connect it with carnival festivity and renunciation, from Mirth's announcement of herself as 'the daughter of Christmas and spirit of Shrovetide' (Induction, 11–12) to the anticipations of Lent in the Second Inter-mean, 63, and III.ii.84–5. There may have been further performances during that season, for in other ways as well the play was a topical one, and registered sufficiently in certain circles to give currency to the 'sinister' interpretation of its meaning which Jonson tried to quell in a note attached to the published version (see 'To the Readers' following Act II). 'Such complaints do not accompany successful plays', as Bentley points out;[106] yet *The Staple* was apparently thought of well enough to be imitated on at least two occasions, and one of these – Thomas Randolph's *The Drinking Academy* –

was written in the 1620s before Jonson sent his play to the press, and so perhaps reflects a response to its virtues in performance.[107]

The play seems to have been neglected for the remainder of the seventeenth century: Dryden probably administered the *coup de grace* with his classification of the late works as 'dotages'. In any case, the number of Jonson's plays considered stageworthy (or stageable) in the Restoration and eighteenth century was always small, and it has increased only slightly in recent years. The sole attempt that I know of to test our play's theatrical qualities came in 1973, on the occasion of Jonson's quatercentenary, when D. F. McKenzie organised a production under the auspices of the English Department at Victoria University of Wellington, New Zealand.[108]

The main obstacle to modern performance of *The Staple*, I suspect, is the dense topicality of much of its satire. The critical problems we have noted of underwritten characters and thematic disjunctions might prove unimportant in a well-paced and judiciously pointed production, but the scenes upon which Herford and Simpson thought the play's reputation rests – those set in the news office – would probably present serious difficulties in staging. This is at any rate true of III.ii, with its now excessively remote burlesque of contemporary news reports. Yet the scene is a fine one, and well worth salvaging via the kind of modest reworking that Peter Barnes brought to his production of *The Devil is an Ass* a few years ago, modifying and updating parts of the Jacobean frame of reference.[109]

In other respects the play might gain considerably from the challenge of performance. In particular the allegorical portrayal of Pecunia, which has generally found disfavour with critics on the grounds of its supposed stiffness and inconsistency, could be realised in the visual terms that are clearly central to Jonson's conception. As already suggested, Pecunia is not so much a creature out of a morality play as one out of a masque; and the ambivalent allure of wealth is potent in episodes of ironic high ceremonial like her disclosure at II.v.45 or the mock-encomium in Apollo in IV.ii. At moments of this kind Jonson seems to be extending and complicating the dramatic effects he engineered in Volpone's hymn to gold or in the presentation of the Queen in *Cynthia's Revels*, seeking the reality of Pecunia not in conventional character terms but in her operation as a radiant centre, as a symbol of ambiguous potentialities. The moral diagram of the play comes to life in a series of stage images in which she is the constant factor but which prompt in each case a subtly different way of looking at her: Pecunia worshipped by a thin, unwholesome, kneeling miser,

Pecunia clumsily wooed by the frills and feathers of the prodigal, Pecunia in stark contrast to the rags of the liberal Canter who will deliver her from abuse. Her circulation also brings her into contact with the calculating prosperity of Cymbal and the more fleshly extravagance of Lickfinger, who in variously elaborating the theme of ironic festivity initiated by the prodigal's riot (in the diversions of the Staple, and the Act IV banquet) help to create new contexts for Pecunia's splendour and at the same time define the need for her to act as a moderating, refining presence, the attractive catalyst of Canter's designs. What I am suggesting is that this part of Jonson's design above all requires the context of performance, and it is possible that the play might thereby reveal a dynamic which is not always evident to literary-critical inspection.

The play seems generally well adapted to the layout and resources of the Blackfriars stage (as far as we understand them). Two 'discoveries' are required, as are two eavesdroppings, and in addition there is the question of how the Staple was 'opened' in Acts I and III. Eugene Waith has suggested that booths were used to represent the Staple and a room in the house of Pennyboy Senior, placed against, respectively, the stage right and left-hand doors in the tiring-house façade.[110] This would facilitate the provision of a permanent Staple 'set' (until its dismantlement after Act IV) which could be closed by drawing a curtain, while the other booth would enhance the discovery of Pecunia 'in state' at II.v.43. But my own instinct is for a simpler arrangement, with the side-doors used for exits and entrances, and the central doorway curtained and reserved for eavesdroppings and discoveries,[111] and the storage of furniture and props which could be carried on stage when needed. Without wishing to resurrect notions of an 'inner stage', it is conceivable that parts of the news office were represented behind the curtain line (perhaps bookshelves and desks), with certain pieces brought forward in the actual Staple scenes. So, for example, at the start of I.iv the clerks enter through one of the side doors, draw the curtain and put a carpet on the table which is already on stage (see headnote), while the countrywoman enters at the other door and waits to be served. The curtain would be closed up until V.iv for scenes other than those in the news office, except to reveal Pecunia in II.v; it is also used to conceal Pennyboy Senior in II.ii and Tom 'behind the hangings' in V.i–ii.

The only difficulty with this arrangement concerns the second 'discovery' in V.iv, where Pennyboy Senior 'is seen' at his table preparing to interrogate his dogs. This splendid scene can hardly have been played entirely within a discovery-space, and yet it would spoil the mock-formality of the proceedings to have the miser leave his seat and move downstage. Waith suggests that a booth is 'almost essential' for this scene,[112] and certainly such a device would heighten the effect of confined lunacy. But perhaps there would be no great difficulty in the table being carried out from behind the curtain with Pennyboy Senior quickly taking up his place to begin the scene.

A greater problem emerges when we consider the play's staging needs in relation to its dramatic structure. As Eugene Waith points out, the decisive event in *The Staple* is Canter's self-revelation at the end of Act IV; while there is more intrigue to come, this is the real moment of enlightenment and restoration, so that the last Act 'has somewhat the quality of a coda'.[113] There is a clear analogy here with Jonson's masques, which make the rout of error and falsehood into a structural climax, to be succeeded by expansive affirmation. This climax generally reveals its meaning through a visual transformation, a graphic altering of the scene in which Jonson's moral design is realised by the staging devices of Inigo Jones. Jonson came to distrust this reliance upon the visual (witness the cautionary remarks in both prologues to *The Staple*), but arguably here his overall conception requires it. The immediate and inevitable consequence of Canter's recovering Pecunia is the destruction of the news office ('Shivered, as in an earthquake! Heard you not / The crack and ruins?' – V.i.40–1); but the play's critics have never been content with this report, feeling with Gossip Expectation that Jonson has let the Staple 'fall most abruptly', and insisting that a final news office scene is required to balance the play's structure. It may be that what is needed rather is a convincing demonstration of the Staple's demise, in the eloquent theatrical vocabulary of masque.[114] Of course, there is a case for saying that the Staple's disintegration, like that of Subtle's laboratory, must be an offstage event because what is dispersed is already a kind of fiction: to show it being blown up is to credit it retrospectively with solidity and significance. But whereas *The Alchemist* offsets the chimera of alchemy with the human reality of Face's survival, in *The Staple* the explosion is prelude to a more comprehensive renewal: it cleanses the commonwealth, and a new world stands revealed. (Like Prospero, Canter delivers the characters – or some of them – from 'amazement and distraction' into fresh existence.) This is not to say of the news office, as of Shakespeare's Antony, that the 'breaking of so great a thing should make / A greater crack', but that the radical purge of illusion and misty error demands its precise theatrical expression.

Blackfriars apparently did not provide this, not so much because its technology was limited (it was certainly capable of staging complex spectacles like the masques in *The Tempest* and *The Maid's Tragedy*), but more because Jonson's conception is uneasily poised in this respect between masque and conventional theatre. All this should however encourage the modern stage to attempt a revival of what D. F. McKenzie aptly calls 'a play of shows',[115] as intricate a piece of writing as any of Jonson's plays, and one that exploits a wider theatrical vocabulary than most.

NOTES

1 Edward Arber, ed., *A Transcript of the Registers of the Company of Stationers of London, 1554–1640*, IV.156.

2 *Ibid.*, IV.260.

3 The title-page of *B.F.* was printed on A2R, leaving the first leaf blank, presumably for a general title when the volume was completed. It subsequently bore the 1640 title-page.

4 *H.&S.* I.211.

5 W. W. Greg, *A Bibliography of the English Printed Drama to the Restoration*, III.1075. One such volume appears to be copy 5 under the shelfmark Ah/J738/+B641 in the Humanities Research Center at Austin, Texas. It consists of the three plays ordered chronologically in a binding whose boards are detached but whose spine appears to be original. Copy 15 under the same number is a stitched, unbound copy of *D.A.* (1631), which may have been one of those privately distributed.

6 *H.&S.* IX.101.

7 W. P. Williams, 'Chetwin, Crooke, and the Jonson Folios', *S.B.*, XXX (1977), 75–95.

8 In the same year Jonson arranged the separate publication of *N.I.* in octavo by Thomas Alchorne. See Arber, IV.251.

9 Letter to the Earl of Newcastle, undated (*H.&S.* I.211).

10 Arber, IV.388. Crooke and Legatt did not enter their copies until 1 July 1637, following action by the Stationers' Court. See Williams, p. 77.

11 Williams, pp. 79f.

12 F. Marcham, 'Thomas Walkley and the Ben Jonson "Works" of 1640', *The Library*, 4th Ser., XI (1930–1), 226.

13 Greg calls the 1631–40 issues of the three plays alone 'Volume 2', and the 'Walkley' material published in 1641, Volume 3 (*Bibliography*, III.1076–9).

14 I have ignored for the purposes of this discussion the additional complications surrounding *D.A.*, of which the stock ran out sooner than that of the other two 1631 plays. See Williams, pp. 92–4.

15 Distinctive periods used in running titles are simply transferred from one

play to the next; the persistence (and deterioration) of broken rules in skeleton A (see top right-hand corner) can be detected on, for instance, *B.F.*, p. 71, *D.A.*, p. 165, *Staple*, p. 13.

16 *H.&S.* I.211.

17 Skeleton A has a chipped S in STAPLE (running title, recto), and the letter A was damaged during the printing of p. 33; on the verso there is a deformed N in NEWES. Skeleton B has a broken T in *The* (recto) and a defective *f* in *of* (verso). Skeleton C has none of these features and differs slightly in layout; it was used to set the outer formes of sheets 1, 4, 13, 16, 17, and the inner forme of sheet 19.

18 This indirectly provides the most substantial evidence for setting by formes. In sig. G there is a heavy run on W which eventually requires the compositor to use four double-V in completing the outer forme of the gathering (pp. 49 and 56). Immediately prior to this, on the same sheet, he has been forced to use two almost identically deformed letter W, one on each page, which have already appeared on pp. 50 and 55 respectively (i.e., on the inner forme of the sheet). Both damaged pieces recur on p. 69. The other incontestable example of type recurrence within the early pages of a gathering is the appearance of a damaged double-s on p. 33 (line 37) and p. 36 (line 11).

19 An example is the letter Y in the first word of III.ii on p. 38, which was damaged during printing (it is intact in some copies) and recurs on pp. 44, 52 and 56.

20 Most recently by G. R. Hibbard in his New Mermaid edition of *Bartholomew Fair* (London 1977), pp. xxxiii–iv. It is worth noting that a particular aberration in this volume is always found in skeleton A: that of page misnumbering through a failure to strip the chase properly after imposition, so that a new sheet is set with the previous page numbers still in place. This happens with *Staple* pp. 19 and 22 (sheet 6, outer forme) which are numbered 9 and 16. We may be seeing here the persistent errors of an individual compositor in Beale's team looking after A; although *Staple* at least reveals no evidence of distinctive habits and practices, such as spelling preferences, which might enable us to distinguish two or more compositors at work. The volume is consistent in layout and method.

21 Hibbard, p. xxxiv.

22 *H.&S.* VI.276.

23 The two Bodleian copies (Gibson 518 and 519) were formerly owned by W. W. Greg and not seen by Simpson. The two newly discovered variants, neither of which affects the text, are the alteration of 'idle' to 'idle,' at III.ii.118, and the correction of 'deriver' to 'derive' at I.vi.79.

24 *H.&S.* I.84.

25 *Ibid.*, p. 85.

26 Paul R. Sellin, 'The Performances of Jonson's *Newes from the New World Discover'd in the Moone*', *E.S.*, 61 (1980), 495.

27 G. B. Johnston, 'Notes on Jonson's Execration upon Vulcan', *M.L.N.*, 46 (1931), 150–3.

28 Richard James, 'To Mr. Benj: Johnson on his Staple of News first presented', in *The Jonson Allusion Book*, ed. J. F. Bradley & J. Q. Adams (New Haven, 1922). p. 137.

29 *The Magnetic Lady*, Induction, 104–5 (*H.&S.* VI.511).

30 *The London Prodigal* was unconvincingly claimed by the Yale editor in 1905 as a source for *The Staple*, on the basis of minor resemblances in language and plot situation, the most substantial being the fact that in both a disguised father brings the news of his own death. Jonson had no need either to imitate or parody such a play in 1625.

31 These are discussed by Alan Young, *The English Prodigal Son Plays* (Salzburg, 1979), pp. 274–8.

32 *Ibid.*, p. 166.

33 *H.&S.* comment that the collapse of the Staple 'is told . . . in terms which might describe the sudden annihilation of some wizard's den' (II.177–8).

34 Two important discussions which advance understanding of the play in these terms are Richard Levin, 'The Staple of News, The Society of Jeerers, and Canters' College', *P.Q.*, 44 (1965), 445–53, and D. F. McKenzie, '*The Staple of News* and the Late Plays', in *A Celebration of Ben Jonson*, ed. William Blissett *et al.*, pp. 83–128.

35 *The Nicomachean Ethics*, transl. J. A. K. Thomson (Harmondsworth, 1976), p. 109.

36 *Ibid.*

37 *Ibid.* See also Young, *Prodigal Plays*, pp. 148–50.

38 See *H.&S.*'s introduction to the play, and A. B. Stonex, 'The Sources of Jonson's *The Staple of News*', *P.M.L.A.* 30 (1915), 821–30. But it is doubtful whether either work is really a more formative influence than Plautus' *Aulularia*, which Jonson uses selectively to fill out the portrait of the miserly Pennyboy Senior (II.iv.168f), or the scene in Aristophanes' *Wasps* (891–1008) which inspired the dog trial in V.iv.

39 *Selected Satires of Lucian*, ed. L. Casson (Chicago, 1962), pp. 245, 250.

40 Cf. K. W. Salter, 'Of the Right Use of Riches'. *E.&S.* 16 (1963), 101–4.

41 Horace, *Epistles*, I.vi.1, 5–6: 'Marvel at nothing . . . what think you of the gifts of earth, or what of the sea's, which makes rich far distant Arabs and Indians' (Loeb ed., p. 287).

42 *The Poems of Horace*, ed. A. Brome (1666; rpt. New York, 1978), p. 315.

43 *Epistles*, I.vi.24–5 (Loeb ed., p. 289).

44 Jonson quoted the lines approvingly in *Discoveries*; see note to III.iv.45–68.

45 The resemblance was first pointed out by A. B. Stonex (see note 38). It should be noted however that in discussing this *H.&S.* (X 259) inadvertently present lines from *Staple* as belonging to the earlier play.

46 Dodsley 8.337.

47 Dodsley 8.382.

48 Dodsley 3.299. Irena Janicka in *Kwartalnik Neofilologiczny*, 15 (1968), 301–7, makes a case for *The Trial* as a source for *Staple*, but there is little in the earlier play that is of direct use to Jonson, and we have no reason to believe he knew it.
49 Dodsley 3.293.
50 *Cynthia's Revels*, II.iii.164–5.
51 Richard Barnfield, *The Encomion of Lady Pecunia* (1598), p. 91.
52 Raymond Southall, *Literature and the Rise of Capitalism* (London, 1973), p. 20.
53 Dodsley 6.406.
54 Grosart IV.165.
55 John Cleveland, 'How the Commencement growes new', in *Poems* 1653 (rpt. Scolar Press 1971), p. 66.
56 See *S.T.C.* 10808–16. On the first corantos in English, see Dahl, pp. 31–54, and L. Hanson, 'English Newsbooks 1620–41', *The Library*, 4th Ser. XVIII (1937–8), 355–65.
57 Letter from Joseph Mead to Sir Martin Stuteville, 22 September 1621 (*Harl.* MS 389), quoted by Hanson, p. 363.
58 Joseph Frank, *Beginnings of the English Newspaper* (1971), offers an illuminating and well-illustrated account of the early news trade; Hanson, 'English Newsbooks', and M. A. Shaaber, 'The History of the First English Newspaper', *S.P.*, 29 (1932), 551–87, have detailed discussions of the period in question; apart from his valuable *Bibliography*, Folke Dahl has written about the Continental background in 'Amsterdam– Cradle of English Newspapers', *The Library*, 5th Ser. IV (1949), 166–78.
59 Sara Pearl, 'Sounding to present occasions: Jonson's masques of 1620–5', in David Lindley (ed.), *The Court Masque* (1984), 60–77.
60 Thomas Nashe, *Pierce Penilesse* (1592): McKerrow I.194.
61 G. B. Harrison, 'Books and Readers 1591–4', *The Library*, 4th Ser. VIII (1927), 285; P. M. Handover, *Printing in London* (London 1960), p. 102.
62 G. B. Harrison, 'Books and Readers 1599–1603', *The Library*, 4th Ser. XIV (1933–4), 10. For the myriad forms of popular news in the sixteenth century, see M. A. Shaaber, *Some Forerunners of the Newspaper in England, 1476–1622* (London 1966).
63 See Handover, pp. 104–9.
64 Recent research has suggested a figure of seventy percent illiteracy 'among men in the rural England of 1642–4, with the home counties and metropolitan areas somewhat better' (David Cressy, 'Literacy in seventeenth-century England', *J.I.H.*, 8 (1977), 144). But historians are agreed that the Elizabethan educational movement had a considerable impact on reading habits and capacity, especially in areas where Puritan influence was strong. See also Peter Clark's discussion of book ownership in *Schooling and Society*, ed. L. Stone (1976), pp. 95–111.
65 Anthony Smith, 'The long road to objectivity', in *Newspaper History from the seventeenth century to the present day*, ed. George Boyce et al. (1978), p. 155.

66 Letter to Sir Walter Aston, 18 June 1621. L. P. Smith, *The Life and Letters of Sir Henry Wotton* (Oxford, 1907), II.213.

67 On the posts at this time, see Howard Robinson, *The British Post Office* (Princeton, 1949), pp. 5–36, and *Carrying British Mails Overseas* (New York, 1964), pp. 15–21.

68 See I.ii.68–73 and notes.

69 *Carrying British Mails Overseas*, p. 20.

70 *N.T.*, 295–7. In 1908 J. B. Williams, in his *History of British Journalism*, pp. 20–2, suggested that the 'fine-paced gentleman' Ambler, emissary Paul's (I.ii.68–9) is intended as a caricature of John Chamberlain, the prolific letter-writer who became special correspondent to Dudley Carleton, Ambassador to the Hague. This proposal has not found favour since, perhaps because Williams is often wrong in his attributions; but we should not assume that Chamberlain lay outside the orbit of Jonson's satire. He was a highly visible gossip, a self-styled 'Paul's walker', and Jonson might have singled him out as representative of a class of dilettantes who lent respectability to the news trade. Chamberlain's letters to the Hague were presumably carried by de Quester.

71 When the Star Chamber was abolished in 1641, taking with it the licensing system, much material relating to Parliamentary affairs became available to the press for the first time, an important factor in the emergence of the first English newspapers. See Williams, *History*, pp. 32–4.

72 Stanley Morison, 'The Origins of the Newspaper', in *Selected Essays on the History of Letter-Forms in Manuscript and Print* (Cambridge, 1980), p. 329. See also W. S. Powell, *John Pory* (1977), pp. 51–9.

73 See the letters to Joseph Mead in *Harl.* MS 383; and Morison, *Origins*, p. 329.

74 *Harl.* MS 383: 32.

75 W. Notestein & F. H. Relf, *Commons Debates for 1629* (Minneapolis, 1921), pp. xxii, liv.

76 *Ibid.*, p. xxxv. Notestein and Relf record that William Stansby, who published the 1616 Jonson Folio, had been collecting parliamentary manuscripts 'as early as 1626'.

77 *Ibid.*, citing Sir Simonds d'Ewes on 'beggarly scholars who did in alehouses invent speeches and make speeches of members of the house'.

78 *Ibid.*, pp. xlii–iii.

79 George Wither, *The Schollers Purgatory* (London, 1625), p. 9.

80 E.g. the newsletter service of Joseph Muddiman. The following satire 'On Intelligencers or News-Mongers', from a pamphlet by L. Meriton published in 1696, describes a situation very close to Jonson's vision of an organised news system:

> The News-Mongers themselves Insinuate
> Into their favour, who can tell the state
> And Face of Things, how they are mannag'd here,
> And how transacted and design'd elsewhere;

To their Amanuenses they Indite,
Who take the Heads, and several Letters write
Of News at large, then to the Country send 'em,
And to th'Imployers there, do recommend 'em:
Thus Post by Post, they let them understand
Th'Intreagues a foot aswel by Sea as Land,
Money for this, they quarterly receive
From their Imployers, thus they bravely Live:
Then to th'Imployers Houses Men repair,
And Money spend, to read News-Letters there;
Thus both News-mongers, and Imployers gain
Money on this account, or it is plain,
No News at home, from Foraign States, or *France*,
We should receive, but rest in Ignorance.

(*Pecuniæ Obediunt Omnia*, pp. 96–7; Wing 1821A.)

81 D. F. McKenzie, *The London Book Trade in the Later Seventeenth Century*.
Sandars Lectures, Cambridge 1976 (unpublished), p. 5.
82 *Newes from Europe*, 19 March 1624, p. 1.
83 *Reliquae Wottonianae* (London 1672), p. 321.
84 Thomas Gainsford, *An Answer to Wither's Motto* (London 1625), sig. E4.
85 A similar point is made by D. F. McKenzie in '*The Staple of News* and
the Late Plays', *loc. cit.* (note 34), p. 107. My debt to this searching essay
is considerable.
86 Douglas Duncan, *Ben Jonson and the Lucianic Tradition* (1979), p. 226.
87 See Glenn H. Blayney, 'Wardship in English Drama, 1600–50', *S.P.*,
53 (1956), 482.
88 See S. Todd Lowry, 'The Archaeology of the Circulation Concept in
Economic Theory', *J.H.I.*, 35 (1974), 429f.
89 Compare the illustrations (see p. 15) to the ballad 'The World's Sweetheart' in *The Roxburghe Ballads*, III.81–3, which show Pecunia as an
aristocratic and sumptuously attired lady. The allegorical tradition is
represented by Ripa's *Iconologia* (1603), p. 384.
90 Rosalie Colie, '*My Ecchoing Song*': *Andrew Marvell's Poetry of Criticism*
(1970), p. 79.
91 'The architect should be equipped with knowledge of many branches of
study and varied kinds of learning, for it is by his judgement that all work
done by the other arts is put to the test' (*The Ten Books on Architecture*,
transl. M. M. Morgan (1914), p. 5).
92 'An Expostulation with Inigo Jones', 50.
93 L. A. Beaurline calls it 'a charming piece of comic dissimulation' (*Jonson
and Elizabethan Comedy: Essays in Dramatic Rhetoric* (1978), p. 31).
94 Angus Fletcher, *The Transcendental Masque* (1971), p. 26.
95 R. Chris Hassel, *Renaissance Drama and the English Church Year* (1979),
p. 116.

96 *Conv. Drum.*, 692.
97 McKenzie, p. 86; and see pp. 90–103.
98 *Disc.*, 1881–3.
99 *Ibid.*, 1926–8.
100 *Love Freed from Ignorance and Folly*, 98 (marginal note).
101 Lawrence Stone, 'Social Mobility in England, 1500–1700', *P.&P.*, 33 (1966), 17.
102 On this, see Martin Elsky, 'Bacon's Hieroglyphs and the Separation of Words and Things', *P.Q.*, 63 (1984), 449–60.
103 See McKenzie, pp. 120–1. Canters' College has some literary and colloquial precedent in popular writing, e.g. Joseph Hall's *Mundus Alter et Idem* (*c.* 1605), whose third book describes the land of Fooliana, which boasts a university town with two colleges. Cf. Rabelais, *Pantagruel*, V.31, where Hearsay keeps a 'school of vouching', with its 'forty cartloads of modern historians ...' (II.330–2). On the kind of education provided at Gresham College, see I. R. Adamson, 'The Administration of Gresham College', *History of Education*, 9 (1980), 13–23.
104 See, for instance, III.ii.41–107. F. R. Johnson has shown that there was 'a close association, in scientific investigations, of the Gresham College professors and the sea captains, the shipbuilders, and the administrative officials of the English navy' ('Gresham College: Precursor of the Royal Society', *J.H.I.*, 1 (1940), 429). It was at Gresham, also, that Kenelm Digby and others carried out chemical and astronomical experiments, and the mathematician Henry Briggs edited John Napier's work on logarithms, which Jonson was wittily to make part of the usurer's exploitative system in *M.L.*, I.vi.31–40. Endowments to provide practical lectures in the vernacular for the benefit of artisans were fairly common at this time, and in 1608 Francis Bacon was making notes on the possibility of the 'Foundac. of a college for Inventors' (quoted by Rosalie Colie, 'Two Jacobean Models for Salomon's House', *H.L.Q.*, 18 (1954–5), 246).
105 Bentley, IV.630.
106 *Ibid*, p. 632.
107 The other was Davenant's *News from Plymouth*. Gifford thought he detected Jonson's influence in the 'military dinner' in II.i of Cartwright's *The Ordinary*, and in the master-cook of Fletcher's *Rollo, Duke of Normandy* (see note to IV.ii.24). The play was clearly admired amongst Jonson's own circle, as the quotation on p. 11 attests.
108 In a letter to the present editor, McKenzie describes this as 'a well-rehearsed costumed reading, with full stage movements in a 300-seat lecture room. The acting area was broad and deep, but not raised. There was minimal lighting, and there were sound effects. The actors were a mixed crew of students and staff, but with some professionals'. The reading was directed by Jim Spalding.
109 Such adaptation is however controversial: see Dennis Marks, 'Hands off the classics – asses and devilry', *The Listener*, 99 (1978), 17–19.

110 Eugene M. Waith, 'Things as They Are and the World of Absolutes', *The Elizabethan Theatre* IV, ed. George Hibbard, pp. 113–14.

111 Richard Hosley (whose reconstruction of Blackfriars I am largely following) claims that the so-called discovery space was rarely used as such, but rather as a place where characters could be concealed or stage items stored. (See *Revels History of Drama in English*, III.233–4) It is very unlikely that whole scenes or episodes were ever acted within such a space: a 'discovered' character would immediately step forward if required to take part in the ensuing action.

112 Waith, *loc. cit.*, p. 114.

113 *Ibid.*, p. 116. Nonetheless the formal impact in stage terms of Picklock's 'fresh cheat' should not be underestimated.

114 This surely casts doubt on the idea that the Staple was represented by a booth: the prosaic dismantling of such a structure after Act IV in full of the audience would further weaken the latter's imaginative grasp of the momentous 'crack and ruins' when the news office falls. But perhaps Jonson would have relished the ironic discrepancy between humble representation and inflated idea.

115 McKenzie, *loc. cit.*, p. 104.

The Persons of the Play

PENNYBOY [JUNIOR], *the son, the heir and suitor.*
PENNYBOY [CANTER], *the father, the canter.*
PENNYBOY [SENIOR], *the uncle, the usurer.*
CYMBAL, *Master of the Staple and prime jeerer.*
FITTON, *Emissary Court and jeerer.*   5
ALMANAC, *doctor in physic and jeerer.*
SHUNFIELD, *sea captain and jeerer.*
MADRIGAL, *poetaster and jeerer.*
PICKLOCK, *man o'law and Emissary Westminster.*
PIEDMANTLE, *pursuivant at arms and heraldet.*   10

1–3. *PENNYBOY*] a family name which hints at the play's concern with wealth but which, unlike the remainder of the cast list, does not define the moral character or occupation of the individuals involved. With it Jonson can. contrive to recall familiar appellations like 'truepenny' (a trusty fellow, as in *Ham.*, I.v.158, and clearly suited to the Canter here) and 'pennyfather', the traditional name for a skinflint, but at the same time avoid their fixed and unalterable definitions of character.

2. *CANTER*] beggar; the word could also describe gypsies and other vagrant bands who used their own language or 'canting' dialect (see Dekker, *Non-Dramatic Works*, ed. Grosart, III.82f, 187–204), but Jonson does not exploit their vocabulary in the play.

4. *CYMBAL*] like 'sounding brass or a tinkling cymbal' (Corinthians, xiii.1) since he deals in empty rumour. The phrase 'sounding brass' conventionally described the headquarters of Fame (see Golding's translation of Ovid's *Metamorphoses*, xii.50), but Jonson prefers the more belittling epithet. See also note to III.ii.115.

5. *FITTON*] *O.E.D. fitten* (v. & sb.), to feign, lie. Cf. *C.R.*, I.iv.22–3: 'He doth feed you with fittons, figments, and leasings.'

Emissary ... jeerer] See notes to I.ii.47 & 65.

8. *MADRIGAL*] a verse form Jonson seems to have associated with would-be poets. Cf. Daw's 'madrigal of Modesty' in *S.W.*, II.iii.24–42.

9. *PICKLOCK*] Cf. *B.F.*, III.v.280 (Revels): 'some crafty fellow, some picklock o'the law!' The word could refer simply to the skill of lawyers in dealing with the intricacies of law, but often expressed a popular prejudice about their capacity for exploitation and guile.

Westminster] Westminster Hall, where the Courts of Common Law were held.

10. pursuivant at arms] junior 'follower' or attendant in the College of Arms; one of the four members of the third and lowest grade of heralds. The

Register, *of the Staple or Office.*
NATHANIEL, *first clerk of the Office.*
THOMAS BARBER, *second clerk of the Office.*
PECUNIA, *Infanta of the Mines.*
MORTGAGE, *her nurse.*   15
STATUTE, [*her*] *first woman.*
BAND, [*her*] *second woman.*
WAX, [*her*] *chambermaid.*
BROKER, *secretary and gentleman-usher to her Grace.*
LICKFINGER, *a master-cook and parcel-poet.*   20
Fashioner, *the tailor of the times.*
Linener.
Haberdasher.
[LEATHERLEG, *a*] *Shoemaker.*
Spurrier.   25
Customers, *male and female.*
Porter.
Dogs, *two.*
[Prologue.
Gossip MIRTH.   30

---

pursuivants are Rouge Dragon, Blue Mantle (which Jonson burlesques in Piedmantle's name), Portcullis and Rouge Croix.
  heraldet] petty herald.
  14. *PECUNIA*] Lady Money; *Pecuniæ obediunt omnia* is proverbial at this date. See Erasmus, *Adagia*, I.iii.87 (*Works,* transl. M. M. Phillips, vol. 31, p. 306); and cf. Tilley M1052, 1060.
  Infanta] the title given to a daughter of the Spanish Royal Family; but it came to be used more loosely, and often ironically, to describe a great lady. Cf. *D.A.*, IV.ii.71, where the disguised Wittipol is 'the very *Infanta* of the *Giants!*'
  17. *BAND*] bond, security.
  19. secretary] one entrusted with the secrets of another (Kifer). In the popular demonology of the time, a broker acted as pander between Money and the usurer.
  20. *LICKFINGER*] 'He is an ill cook that cannot lick his own fingers' (Tilley C636).
  parcel-poet] part-poet.
  21. *Fashioner*] tailor.
  22. *Linener*] dealer in linen goods; more specifically, a shirt-maker.
  23. *Haberdasher*] dealer in small wares, such as thread, tape and ribbons. But he could also be exclusively a hatter in Jonson's day (see *O.E.D.*) and is so described at I.iii.11.
  29. *Prologue*] actor who speaks the play's prologue (and also, presumably, the epilogue); often a boy player in Jonson's theatre.
  30. *Gossip*] See note to Induction, line 19.

Gossip TATTLE.
Gossip EXPECTATION.
Gossip CENSURE.
Musicians.
NICHOLAS, *a boy singer*.]   35

THE SCENE
LONDON.

The Induction

The PROLOGUE *enters. After him,* Gossip MIRTH, Gossip TATTLE, Gossip EXPECTATION, *and* Gossip CENSURE, *four gentlewomen lady-like attired.*

Prologue. For your own sake, not ours –
Mirth. Come, gossip, be not ashamed. The play is *The Staple of News*, and you are the mistress and lady of Tattle; let's ha' your opinion of it. Do you hear, gentleman? What are you, gentleman-usher to the play? Pray you, help us to some   5 stools here.
Prologue. Where? O'the stage, ladies?
Mirth. Yes, o'the stage. We are persons of quality, I assure you, and women of fashion, and come to see and to be

---

1–76.] *Italic in F.*

0.1. The ... enters] In Jonson's theatre, usually following a concert of vocal and instrumental music (for which Blackfriars was noted) and probably heralded by a fanfare.

2. Come ... ashamed] In Beaumont's *The Knight of the Burning Pestle* (1607), Induction, 45, the Wife is similarly bashful at first: 'shall I come up, husband?'. Seats on the stage were reserved for men, and usually taken by gallants; the practice is deplored in the Prologue to *D.A.* and Induction to *C.R.* Like Beaumont's Wife, the ladies are presumably planted in the audience and ascend the stage from the front, generally following Dekker's recommendation in *The Guls Horn-booke,* Ch. 6: 'Present not your selfe on the Stage (especially at a new play) untill the quaking prologue hath (by rubbing) got culor into his cheekes, and is ready to give the trumpets their Cue, that hees upon point to enter' (Grosart II.250).

5. gentleman-usher] not a theatrical employee in the modern sense of 'usher' but personal servant to a lady of standing. Mirth is putting on airs. However, Bentley records an 'usher of the revels' at Court performances (VI.284), and probably there was some shepherding of the audience at the private theatres. See next note. Richard Brathwaite records that one of the gentleman-usher's duties was 'to be versed in the perusall of *Play-bils*, which he presents to his Lady with great *devotion*; and recommends some especiall one to her view' (*A Boulster Lecture* (1640), p. 163).

5–6. help ... stools] Cf. *B.F.*, V.iii.60–1 (Revels): 'Ha' you none of your pretty impudent boys, now, to bring stools, fill tobacco, fetch ale, and beg money ...?'

seen: my gossip Tattle here, and gossip Expectation, and   10
my gossip Censure; and I am Mirth, the daughter of
Christmas and spirit of Shrovetide. They say 'It's merry
when gossips meet'. I hope your play will be a merry one.
Prologue. Or you will make it such, ladies. Bring a form here.
[*A bench is brought. They sit.*] But what will the noble-   15
men think, or the grave wits here, to see you seated on the
bench thus?
Mirth. Why, what should they think, but that they had
mothers, as we had, and those mothers had gossips (if their
children were christened) as we are, and such as had a   20
longing to see plays and sit upon them, as we do, and
arraign both them and their poets?
Prologue. O, is that your purpose? Why, Mistress Mirth, and
Madame Tattle, enjoy your delights freely.
Tattle. Look your news be new and fresh, Master Prologue,   25
and untainted. I shall find them else, if they be stale or

15. S.D.] *Gifford.*

8–10. *We . . . seen*] Mirth rallies her companions with a declaration of social
intent like Fitzdottrel's in *D.A.*, I.vi.31–8. The dangers of such behaviour
in women are constantly stressed by male commentators and moralists; cf.
Jonson's satire on the lady collegiates in *S.W.*, IV.i. The diaries of the
Venetian embassy at Court for 1617–18 record the 'theatres are frequented
by a number of respectable and handsome ladies, who come freely and seat
themselves among the men without the slightest hesitation!' (*Quarterly Review*,
102 (1857), 416; see also Bentley VI.151).

9–10. *to see . . . seen*] translated from Ovid's *Ars Amatoria*, 99: 'Spectatum
veniunt, veniunt spectentur ut ipsae' (*H.&S.*).

11. *Mirth*] associated with festival and holiday, similarly personified as
'heart-easing Mirth' in Milton's *L'Allegro*, 13.

11–12. *the . . . Shrovetide*] Shrovetide marks the end of the season of
festivity commencing at Christmas; the latter's offspring (not including Mirth)
are brought on in Jonson's *Christmas, His Masque*, presented at Court in 1616.

12–13. *'It's . . . meet'*] proverbial (Tilley G382), as Jonson acknowledges
when he begins a song in *An Entertainment at the Blackfriars* (1620): 'They say
it is merrye when Gossips doe meete'. It is also the title of a 1602 verse pamphlet by Samuel Rowlands; on the vogue for 'gossip' literature during this
period, see Linda Woodbridge, *Women and the English Renaissance* (1984),
Ch. 9.

19. *gossips*] godmothers; a corruption of O.E. *godsibb*, meaning godparent.
Elsewhere in *Staple* the word is used either as a term of greeting or endearment
between women, or in its modern sense of idle chatterers.

21. *sit upon*] sit in judgement upon.

26. *find*] find out, expose; cf. Cotgrave, '*trouver* . . . light on, take in the
manner'.

fly-blown, quickly.

Prologue. We ask no favour from you; only we would entreat of
Madame Expectation –

Expectation. What, Master Prologue?   30

Prologue. That your ladyship would expect no more than you
understand.

Expectation. Sir, I can expect enough.

Prologue. I fear, too much, lady, and teach others to do the
like.   35

Expectation. I can do that too if I have cause.

Prologue. Cry you mercy, you never did wrong, but with just
cause. What's this lady?

Mirth. Curiosity, my lady Censure.

Prologue. O, Curiosity! You come to see who wears the new   40
suit today, whose clothes are best penned (whatever the
part be), which actor has the best leg and foot, what king
plays without cuffs and his queen without gloves, who
rides post in stockings and dances in boots?

Censure. Yes, and which amorous prince makes love in drink,   45
or does overact prodigiously in beaten satin and, having

---

35. like.] *like?* F.

stale] perhaps with the extra implication of 'stolen' (it is an obsolete form
of the past participle), as in *C.A.*, I.ii.48–9, where the poetaster Balladino
assures Onion that 'I do use as much stale stuff ... as any man'.

27. *fly-blown*] i.e. decayed, stale news.

31–2. *expect ... understand*] Jonson criticises his audience in these terms
at III.ii.301–2, and in *N.T.*, 54–61.

37–8. *you ... cause*] Cf. *Disc.*, 661–6, where Jonson admonishes Shakespeare for writing 'Caesar did never wrong, but with just cause', in *Caes.*,
III.i.47–8. In the First Folio (1623) the text reads differently, yet Jonson
clearly expected his audience to recognise the echo. *Caes.* was frequently
revived, and if Jonson's version indeed represents Shakespeare's first thoughts,
it may have survived as such in the prompt-book. See J. Dover Wilson in
Shakespeare Survey, 2 (1949), 38–43.

41. *are ... penned*] have the most feathers (*H.&S.*) – but with a pun on
'described'.

42–4. *what ... boots?*] This may be a topical reference (cf. next note); but
more likely it is a gibe at misplaced attention to detail among a section of the
audience.

45. *amorous prince*] perhaps Pharamond in Beaumont and Fletcher's *Phil-
aster*, which appeared in three quarto editions in the 1620s and was clearly
prominent in the repertory of the King's Men.

got the trick on't, will be monstrous still, in despite of
counsel.

Bookholder. [*Within.*] Mend your lights, gentlemen. Master
Prologue, begin.   *The Tiremen enter to mend the lights.*   50

Tattle. Ay me!

Expectation. Who's that?

Prologue. Nay start not, ladies. These carry no fireworks to
fright you, but a torch i'their hands to give light to the
business. The truth is, there are a set of gamesters within   55
in travail of a thing called a play, and would fain be delivered of it; and they have entreated me to be their man-
midwife, the Prologue, for they are like to have a hard
labour on't.

Tattle. Then the poet has abused himself, like an ass, as he is.   60

Mirth. No, his actors will abuse him enough, or I am deceived.

---

49. *Within.*] *Gifford.*   50. S.D.] *Printed in F margin.*

---

46. *beaten*] embroidered (Kifer).

49. Bookholder] prompter.

Mend ... *lights*] Kifer suggests that lights are used here not simply to provide indoor illumination but also to suggest an early morning scene to follow.
There is little evidence for this view, although lighting effects probably assisted the illusion of darkness in instances where a sense of mystery or obscurity was important. Here the point is simply that the gossips are holding up
the performance of a play. *Mend* = trim.

50. Tiremen] stage-hands.

53. *fireworks*] used in the outdoor theatres for a variety of effects, but rather
less so in houses like Blackfriars, where they were both malodorous and excessively noisy, and might also be a fire hazard. See R. B. Graves, 'Elizabethan
Lighting Effects', *Renaissance Drama* XII (1981), 62–7. The Prologue's
insinuation is that the gossips expect the vulgar practices of the popular stage.

55. *gamesters*] rarely used of actors; the word usually describes gamblers and
wastrels, though Nano uses it to describe himself and his fellow-grotesques
when they perform in *Volp.*, I. ii.1 (Revels). In the present context the word
seems to reflect something of Jonson's hardening attitude to the popular stage
and its practitioners in his later years.

57–8. *man-midwife*] This conceit appears to have been recalled by Richard
Brome in *The Antipodes* (1637), I.iii.6–7: 'Play the man-midwife and deliver
him / Of his huge timpany of news – of monsters, / Pigmies, and giants, apes,
and elephants' (Regents ed.).

60. *Then* ... *ass*] Kifer points out the allusion to the proverb 'He is an ass
that hurts himself' (Tilley A377); but her suggestion of sexual innuendo is
barely supported by O.E.D. or the context. Tattle's comment is more likely a
jibe at the Prologue's youthfulness and the poet's stupidity in choosing such a
midwife.

Yonder he is within (I was i'the tiring-house awhile to see
the actors dressed) rolling himself up and down like a tun
i'the midst of 'em, and spurges. Never did vessel of wort
or wine work so! His sweating put me in mind of a good   65
Shroving-dish (and I believe would be taken up for a service of state somewhere, an't were known) – a stewed poet!
He doth sit like an unbraced drum with one of his heads
beaten out. For that you must note, a poet hath two heads
as a drum has, one for making, the other repeating; and his   70
repeating head is all to pieces. They may gather it up i'the
tiring-house, for he hath torn the book in a poetical fury,
and put himself to silence in dead sack; which, were there
no other vexation, were sufficient to make him the most

62–6. *Yonder* . . . *Shroving-dish*] satirising his own corpulence, as in *Und.*
9 and elsewhere in his work. More generally, Jonson adapts to his own purposes the familiar figure of Carnival, who 'usually took the form of a fat man,
pot-bellied, ruddy . . . seated on a barrel' (P. Burke, *Popular Culture in Early
Modern Europe*, p. 185). Cf. the vigorous description in *Vox Graculi* (1622),
H3: 'give room I say: for here must enter that wadling, stradling, bursten-
gutted *Carnifax* of all Christendome; vulgarly enstiled *Shrove-Tuesday*, but
more pertinently, sole-monarch of the Mouth, high Steward to the Stomack,
chiefe Ganimede to the Guts, prime Peere of the Pullets, first favorite to the
Frying-pans'.
64. *spurges*] froths, foams. Mirth's next sentence also suggests the more
specialised and still-current sense of 'emit or throw off impure matter by
fermentation' (*O.E.D.*).
64. *wort*] unfermented beer.
65–7. *sweating* . . . *poet*] anticipating the identification of poet and cook in
IV.ii. Cf. John Taylor, *Jacke-a-Lent*, on 'Cookes in Great mens Kitchins [who]
sweat in their owne grease, that if ever a Cooke be worth the eating it is when
Shrove Tuesday is in towne, for he is so stued and larded' (*Workes* 1630,
p. 114).
66–7. *service of state*] i.e. a sumptuous banquet.
68. *unbraced*] with the tension taken off.
69. *heads*] membranes; with a pun on the sense (looking back at 63–4) of
the flat end of a barrel.
70. *making* . . . *repeating*] creating . . . reciting.
72. *poetical fury*] ironic self-deprecation by Jonson, recalling old battles.
The satirical vein of Asper in *E.M.O.* is called 'right Furor Poeticus' (Induction, 147), but in *Poet.*, IV.iii.108 Jonson has Tucca call Demetrius (Dekker)
'my poore poeticall Furie'; a similar phrase describes Crispinus (Marston) in
Satiromastix, IV.iii.70 (Bowers I.361). Its use here suggests a genuine poetic
strength driven to desperate expedients.
73. *dead*] flavourless, stale.

miserable emblem of patience.   75
Censure. The Prologue, peace.

THE PROLOGUE FOR THE STAGE

For your own sakes, not his, he bade me say,
Would you were come to hear, not see, a play.
Though we his actors must provide for those
Who are our guests here in the way of shows,
The maker hath not so. He'd have you wise   5
Much rather by your ears than by your eyes,
And prays you'll not prejudge his play for ill
Because you mark it not and sit not still,
But have a longing to salute or talk
With such a female, and from her to walk   10
With your discourse, to what is done, and where,
How, and by whom, in all the town but here.
Alas, what is it to his scene to know
How many coaches in Hyde Park did show

---

75. *emblem of patience*] A common motif; cf. the figure of *Patienza* which
appears on p. 381 of Cesare Ripa's *Iconologia* (1603), a book which Jonson used
extensively in preparing masques at court.

1–30.] Designed for the Blackfriars playhouse; for the play's premiere, see
Introduction, p. 49.
    1. *not his*] Cf. the interrupted opening of the Induction, 1 (*not ours*). The
preliminary skirmish with the gossips brings out Jonson's combative in-
dividualism.
    2. *hear, not see*] the dogmatic insistence of the later Jonson; in the second
prologue to *S.W.*, 5–6, he is more open to the range of theatrical stimulus:
'this play, which we present tonight, / . . . make the object of your eare, and
sight'. Nonetheless *Staple* is not without its appeal to our visual sense.
    5. *maker*] Jonson's preferred term for the poet, as in *Disc.*, 2346–51.
    13. *scene*] dramatic design. The word was commonly used for performance,
but Jonson was probably more aware than most of its origin in the classical
scena or stage set.
    14. *coaches . . . Park*] Cf. *N.N.W.*, 247–9, on the moon-dwellers: 'Ha' they
any places of meeting with their Coaches, and takeing the fresh open aire . . .
as in our Hide-Parke, or so?'. Coaches had been introduced into England in
the mid sixteenth century, and became very popular with the citizenry. John
Taylor the Water-Poet complained that 'The World runnes on Wheeles', in
'upstart, fantasticall, and Time-troubling *Coaches*' (*Workes* 1630, p. 235);
Jonson frequently satirises the trend. Cf. III.iv.37–8.

Last spring, what fare today at Medley's was,   15
If Dunstan or the Phoenix best wine has?
They are things – But yet the stage might stand as well
If it did neither hear these things nor tell.
Great noble wits, be good unto yourselves
And make a difference 'twixt poetic elves   20
And poets: all that dabble in the ink
And defile quills are not those few can think,
Conceive, express, and steer the souls of men,
As with a rudder, round thus, with their pen.
He must be one that can instruct your youth   25
And keep your acme in the state of truth,
Must enterprise this work. Mark but his ways,
What flight he makes, how new. And then he says,
If that not like you that he sends tonight,
'Tis you have left to judge, not he to write.   [*Exit.*]   30

---

15. *Medley's*] a fashionable ordinary (tavern which also served meals) situated in Milford Lane, running south from the Strand.

16. *Dunstan*] the Devil Tavern in Fleet St, whose inn-sign showed St Dunstan tweaking the Devil's nose. It was probably more often known as *Dunstan* after 1608, when the landlord Simon Wadlow 'was required to reforme his signe of St. Dunstan and the Divell and to put the Divell Cleane out of yt and to leave St. Dunstan aloane' (quoted in F. C. Chalfant, *Ben Jonson's London*, p. 66). The tavern was much frequented by Jonson, and since he sets Act IV in its Apollo Room and rehearses the argument between cellar and kitchen there, the quality of Dunstan's wine is of more significance to the play than the Prologue suggests.

Phoenix] another tavern, of uncertain location. Gifford places it near the Phoenix theatre in Drury Lane, and edd. have followed him, but there is no evidence to confirm this. See Chalfant, p. 142.

20. *poetic elves*] i.e. small-time poets, rhymers of negligible ability.

24. *round thus*] The Prologue presumably suits the action to the word, perhaps with a quill he is holding.

25–6.] H.&S. compare the Epistle to *Volp.*, 22–5 (Revels) on the poet's ability to 'inform young men to all good disciplines, inflame grown men to all great virtues, keep old men in their best and supreme state or, as they decline to childhood, recover them to their first strength'. On the classical and Renaissance sources for this exalted view, see R. B. Parker's note on 22–8 (*loc. cit.*).

26. *acme*] maturity, adult life. The first appearance of the word in English; Jonson uses the Greek form in *Disc.*, 923 (H.&S.).

27. *enterprise*] undertake.

29. *like you*] meet with your approval.

30.] i.e. it's your judgement that has deteriorated (since Jonson last wrote for the public stage) and not his art.

THE PROLOGUE FOR THE COURT

A work not smelling of the lamp, tonight,
But fitted for your Majesty's disport,
And writ to the meridian of your court,
We bring, and hope it may produce delight:
The rather being offered as a rite   5
To scholars, that can judge and fair report
The sense they hear, above the vulgar sort
Of nutcrackers, that only come for sight.
Wherein, although our title, sir, be News,
We yet adventure here to tell you none,   10
But show you common follies, and so known,
That though they are not truths, th'innocent Muse
Hath made so like, as fant'sy could them state
Or poetry, without scandal, imitate.   [*Exit.*]

1–14.] *Italic in F.*   9. title ... News] *both words roman in F.*

This was designed for the performance at court which probably took place during Shrovetide, 19–21 February 1626. Unlike the Blackfriars prologue, this one has no organic link with the Induction, and obviously belongs to a different kind of occasion; it is most likely that the scenes involving the gossips were omitted in this performance. Edd. record Jonson's apparent dislike of the sonnet-form (*Conv. Drum.* 60–3), but it is conceived as a worthy vehicle in a play where the chosen forms of poetasters (like the madrigal in IV.ii) are readily vulgarised.

    8. *nutcrackers*] *H.&S.* compare Beaumont and Fletcher's *The Scornful Lady*, IV.ii.66–7, on fellows that 'goe hungry to a play, and crack / More nuts than would suffice a dozen Squirrels' (*B.&F.* II.523–4).

    12–14. *though ... imitate*] Cf. *S.W.*, 2nd Prologue, 9–14, and the Horatian precept which follows 'To the Readers' (between Acts II & III of this play).

THE STAPLE OF NEWS

Aut prodesse volunt, aut delectare poetae:
Aut simul & jucunda, & idonea dicere vitae.

Horace, in *Ars Poetica*

Aut ... Poetica] epigraph from the title-page in *F*, taken from Horace's *Art of Poetry*, 333–4, which Jonson translates as 'Poets would either profit, or delight, / Or mixing sweet, and fit, teach life the right' (see *H.&S.* VIII 327).

Act I

[*Enter*] PENNYBOY JUNIOR [*and*] LEATHERLEG. *His shoemaker has pulled on a new pair of boots, and he walks in his gown, waistcoat and trouses, expecting his tailor.*

[*P. Junior.*] Gramercy, Leatherleg. Get me the spurrier,
    An' thou hast fitted me.
Leatherleg.   I'll do't presently.   [*Exit.*]
P. Junior. Look to me, wit, and look to my wit, land:
    That is, look on me, and with all thine eyes,
    Male, female, yea, hermaphroditic eyes,   5
    And those bring all your helps and perspicils

0.1–3. *His . . . tailor*] Printed in F margin; succeeding examples of this practice will be recorded only when not incorporated into text.   2. *An'*] Whalley; And F.

I.i.o.3. trouses] close-fitting underhose of ankle length (Linthicum, p. 210).
    2. *presently*] immediately.
    3. parodying Donne's 'Elegie on Prince Henry' (1612), opening line: 'Looke to mee faith, and look to my faith, God' (F. A. Pottle in *M.L.N.*, 40 (1925), 223–4). Jonson told Drummond that Donne claimed to have written the poem 'to match Sir Ed: Herbert in obscurenesse' (*Conv. Drum.*, 127), and perhaps this made it a suitable object of parody in his eyes.
    land] (*a*) inheritance (*b*) fellow-countrymen (in the audience).
    5. *hermaphroditic*] echoing a widespread diagnosis of contemporary fashion; cf. Prynne, *Histriomastix* (1633) on 'our English Man-women monsters' (pp. 188, 201). In 1620 there was a pamphlet war on the subject, starting with *Hic Mulier: or, The Man-Woman*, and in the same year James I ordered the clergy to preach against the 'insolencie of our women, and theyre wearing of brode brim'd hats, pointed doublets, theyre haire cut short or shorne, and some of them stilettoes or poinards' (see *Letters of John Chamberlain*, ed. N. E. McClure, II.286–7).
    6. *perspicils*] optic glasses, telescopes. In satirising the prodigal's attention-seeking, Jonson discourages the narrow perspective of the idle spectator in favour of the comprehensive viewpoint his play demands. Cf. *N.I.*, Dedication, 5–6 (Revels), deploring those 'impertinents' who 'never made piece of their prospect the right way.' The analogy was a popular one at a time of much

74

To see me at best advantage, and augment
My form as I come forth, for I do feel
I will be one worth looking after shortly.
Now, by and by, that's shortly.
He draws forth his watch and sets it on the table.
             'T strikes! One, two,   10
Three, four, five, six. Enough, enough, dear watch,
Thy pulse hath beat enough. Now sleep and rest;
Would thou couldst make the time to do so too.
I'll wind thee up no more. The hour is come
So long expected! There, there, drop my wardship,   15
        He throws off his gown.
My pupil age and vassalage together.
And Liberty, come throw thyself about me,
In a rich suit, cloak, hat and band, for now
I'll sue out no man's livery but mine own.
I stand on my own feet, so much a year,   20

---

experimentation with lenses and the newly invented telescope; P. Junior's vanity also initiates Jonson's satire in the play upon this practical vogue.

12. *pulse ... enough*] Striking watches had been in existence since the fifteenth century, but were still a relative novelty in England, where the watch and clock trade was slow to establish itself. The highly ornamented pendant timepieces of the 1620s were worn as conspicuous jewellery as much as for practical purposes.

14. *The hour is come*] i.e. the start of the 'civil' day, bounded by the rising and setting of the sun. It was more usual to count the start of the legal day from midnight, as in modern practice; but Jonson makes the attainment of majority coincide with the traditional *levée* scene at the start of the play.

15–17. *There ... me*] P. Junior's gown is presumably a nightgown, which could be worn during the day in public, but being less elaborate than most attire was rarely worn by young men as an outer garment (Linthicum, pp. 182–3). The theatrical device of costume-shift to signify change in station and moral worth, here and at the start of Act V, is part of the native tradition which Jonson recalls in this play.

17–18. *Liberty ... band*] Criticism of extravagant dress is a constant in the period, from Stubbes, *Anatomie of Abuses* (1583), 'this contagious infection, of Pride in Apparell' (B7*v*), to Brathwaite in *The English Gentleman* (1630), 'Delight not then in your *shame*, but in a decent and seemely manner affect ... that attire which gives best grace to modesty, and hath neerest correspondence with Gentilitie' (p. 25).

18. *band*] linen collar worn about the neck of a shirt or bodice; in Jacobean times it was increasingly ornamented and often coloured.

19. *sue ... livery*] 'institute a suit as heir to obtain possession of lands which are in the hands of the court of wards' (*O.E.D.*). But there is a pun on *livery* meaning 'servant's attire' – the dependent status which is now thrown off.

Right, round and sound, the lord of mine own ground,
And (to rhyme to it) threescore thousand pound!
He goes to the door and looks.
Not come? Not yet? Tailor, thou art a vermin,
Worse than the same thou prosecut'st and prickst
In subtle seam – (Go to, I say no more),   25
Thus to retard my longings, on the day
I do write man, to beat thee. One and twenty
Since the clock struck, complete! And thou wilt feel it,
Thou foolish animal! I could pity him
(An' I were not heartily angry with him now)   30
For this one piece of folly he bears about him,
To dare to tempt the fury of an heir
T'above two thousand a year, yet hope his custom!
Well, Master Fashioner, there's some must break –
A head, for this your breaking.

[*Enter* Fashioner.]

Are you come, sir?   35

ACT I   SCENE ii

[*Fashioner.*] God give your worship joy.
P. *Junior.*   What, of your staying?

28. struck] *F3;* strooke *F.*

23–5. *Tailor ... seam*] combining disparagement of the tailor as a 'prick-louse' with a familiar innuendo: tailor's needle = penis, as in *Temp.*, II.ii.54, 'Yet a tailor might scratch her where'er she did itch' (see Hilda Hulme's note in *J.E.G.P.*, 57 (722–4). Tailors were traditionally lecherous: cf. *E.H.*, I.ii.60–9 (Revels).

25. *subtle*] narrow – with the suggestion of 'ingeniously contrived', which assists the bawdy pun.

27. *write man*] reach manhood. A common expression: cf. *E.M.O.*, III.iv.52–3.

33. *hope*] hope for.

35. S.D.] The Blackfriars stage is generally thought to have had three doorways in the tiring-house façade; the centre one was probably curtained and used more as a discovery-space or place of concealment than for routine entries and exits. See Introduction, p. 51. A plausible staging might have P. Junior first entering at the door stage right, as if from an inner chamber; whilst the opposite door (used by the Fashioner and subsequent entrants in this Act) leads to the street and also to the Staple office elsewhere in the building.

And leaving me to stalk here in my trouses
Like a tame hernshaw for you?
Fashioner.   I but waited
  Below, till the clock struck.
P. Junior.   Why, if you had come
  Before a quarter, would it so have hurt you   5
  In reputation to have waited here?
Fashioner. No, but your worship might have pleaded nonage
  If you had got 'em on ere I could make
  Just affidavit of the time.
P. Junior.   That jest
  Has gained thy pardon. Thou hadst lived condemned   10
  To thine own hell else, never to have wrought
  Stitch more for me or any Pennyboy.
  I could have hindered thee, but now thou art mine.
  For one and twenty years, or for three lives –
  Choose which thou wilt – I'll make thee a copyholder,   15
  And thy first bill unquestioned. Help me on.
          He 'says his suit.
Fashioner. Presently, sir. I am bound unto your worship.

I.ii] ACT. II. SCENE. II. / FASHIONER. PENIBOY. THOMAS / BARBER.
HABERDASHER. *F.*   3. hernshaw] *Her'n-sew F;* heronsew *Wilkes.*   4.
struck] strooke *F.*   13–14. mine. / For ... lives –] mine. / For ... lives,
F; mine/For ... lives. *1716.*   16.1 'says] *Whalley; sayes F.*

I.ii.3. *hernshaw*] heron. The image of a long-legged bird is a natural one
for the gallant; cf. Bartholomew Cokes with 'his Sir Cranion legs' in *B.F.*,
I.v.96–7 (Revels). The combination with *tame* may imply a bird with its wings
clipped and able only to strut; the phrase also suggests exploitation, as in
O.E.D.'s gloss on 'tame-goose' (which Jonson uses in *C.A.*), 'a person who is
made a convenience by his friends'. Herons were a favourite prey in hawking,
and the image also creates a context for the tradesmen's designs upon the
prodigal. See note to line 139.
  7. *pleaded nonage*] claimed you were not responsible for your debt to me
(because you were still under-age).
  11. *hell*] place under a tailor's shop-board for shreds and trimmings
(*O.E.D.*).
  14. *three lives*] a lease which remains in force during the lifetime of the
longest lived of three specified persons (*O.E.D.*).
  15. *copyholder*] one who holds lands belonging to a manor; 'who at the first
held but at the free will of the Lord; yet now by usage and continuall granting
time out of minde, they have gotten an estate after the Custome, that doing
their Services and behaving themselves well, they cannot by Law or Reason be

P. Junior. Thou shalt be when I have sealed thee a lease of my
custom.
Fashioner. Your worship's barber is without.
P. Junior.   Who? Tom?
Come in, Tom.

[*Enter* THOMAS BARBER.]

                    Set thy things upon the board   20
And spread thy cloths. Lay all forth *in procinctu*,
And tell's what news.
Thomas.   O sir, a staple of news!
Or the new staple, which you please.
P. Junior.   What's that?
Fashioner. An office, sir, a brave young office set up.
I had forgot to tell your worship.
P. Junior.   For what?   25
Thomas. To enter all the news, sir, o'the time –
Fashioner. And vent it as occasion serves. A place
Of huge commerce it will be!
P. Junior.   Pray thee, peace:
I cannot abide a talking tailor. Let Tom
(He's a barber) by his place relate it.   30

20. S.D.] *Gifford.*   21. cloths] *Whalley;* clothes *F.*

put from them' (G. Calthorpe, *Coppy-hold* (1635), p. 7). Presumably specific
terms like P. Junior's were often proposed in order to prevent lands being
claimed in perpetuity: Calthorpe stresses that when tenure is longer than 'the
memory of man' it is a 'good Coppy-hold' (pp. 18–19).
   16.1. 'says] essays, tries on.
   21. in procinctu] in readiness; 'since barbers doubled as surgeons, they
were expected to know some Latin' (Kifer). Their shops were also prime
centres for the dissemination of gossip.
   23. *staple*] originally, a town appointed to be the exclusive market for a
particular class of goods. Protectionist systems of this kind were an important
means of regulating trade in Renaissance Europe. By Jonson's time the word
was often used loosely to mean a business centre, but the idea of monopoly is
alive in his use of it here.
   24. *brave*] fine.
   27. *vent*] a) publish, give out b) sell (punning on 'vend').
   30. *He's a barber*] and therefore a qualified newsmonger. Cf. *S.W.*, III.v.23–
5: 'Why, did you ever hope, sir, committing the secrecie of it to a barber, that
lesse then the whole towne should know it?'.

What is't, an office, Tom?
Thomas.   Newly erected
Here in the house, almost on the same floor,
Where all the news of all sorts shall be brought,
And there be examined, and then registered,
And so be issued under the seal of the Office,   35
As Staple News, no other news be current.
P. Junior. 'Fore me, thou speakst of a brave business, Tom.
Fashioner. Nay, if you knew the brain that hatched it, sir –
P. Junior. I know thee well enough. Give him a loaf, Tom;
Quiet his mouth; that oven will be venting else.   40
Proceed.
Thomas.   He tells you true, sir. Master Cymbal
Is Master of the Office: he projected it.
He lies here i'the house, and the great rooms
He has taken for the Office, and set up
His desks and classes, tables, and his shelves.   45
Fashioner. He's my customer, and a wit, sir, too.
But h'has brave wits under him –
Thomas.   Yes, four emissaries.
P. Junior. Emissaries? Stay, there's a fine new word, Tom!
Pray God it signify anything. What are emissaries?

---

36. *current*] Jonson's controlled placing of the word allows its several meanings to emerge, underlining the fatuity of Tom's claim. The Staple will decide
not only what people read and hear, but also what constitutes authentic news.
For the latter, now obsolete sense of *current*, compare *1H4*, II.i.118–20:
'unpay the villainy you have done ... with current repentance'.

39. *loaf*] Tailors' fondness for bread was proverbial. Cf. *B.F.*, V.iii.75–8
(Revels).

40. *venting*] discharging or pouring out (smoke) – with the implication that,
like the Staple news, everything the tailor utters will be hot air.

42. *projected*] contrived, set up.

43. *lies*] lodges.

45. *classes*] plural of *classis*, originally equivalent to 'stall', a case of bookshelves standing out at right angles to the wall (*O.E.D.*).

47. *emissaries*] persons sent on a mission to get information, implying something odious in the object of the mission, or underhand in its manner (*O.E.D.*).
This is the earliest entry in *O.E.D.* in this sense, but Jonson had already used
it thus in *D.A.*, V.v.47, and in *Und.*, 2.viii.17 he has 'your emissary eye',
deriving the phrase from Plautus, *Aulularia*, 41: 'Circumspectatrix cum oculis
emissiciis' (*H.&S.*). Jonson's sense of the politics of information is clearest in
Disc., 1191–3: 'the merciful *Prince* ... needs no Emissaries, Spies, Intelligencers, to intrap true Subjects. Hee feares no Libels, no Treasons.'

Thomas. Men employed outward, that are sent abroad   50
  To fetch in the commodity.
Fashioner.   From all regions
  Where the best news are made –
Thomas.   Or vented forth –
Fashioner. By way of exchange or trade.
P. Junior.   Nay, thou wilt speak –
Fashioner. My share, sir. There's enough for both.
P. Junior. (*He gives the tailor leave to talk.*) Go on then.
  Speak all thou canst. Methinks the ordinaries   55
  Should help them much.
Fashioner.   Sir, they have ordinaries
  And extraordinaries, as many changes
  And variations as there are points i'the compass.
Thomas. But the four cardinal quarters –
P. Junior.   Ay those, Tom –
Thomas. The Court, sir, Paul's, Exchange, and Westminster
  Hall.   60
P. Junior. Who is the chief? Which hath precedency?
Thomas. The governor o'the Staple, Master Cymbal.
  He is the chief, and after him the emissaries.
  First, emissary Court, one Master Fitton.
  He's a jeerer too.
P. Junior.   What's that?

---

55. *canst*] knowest.
  ordinaries] eating places. Dekker (*Guls Horn-booke*, Ch. 5) says that at the
ordinary a gallant 'shall ... receive all the newes ere the post can deliver his
packet' (Grosart II.245).
  56–8. *they ... compass*] The tailor takes *ordinaries* to mean 'couriers' or
'postal services': *O.E.D.* sb.6, first example from 1667; but Florio (1611) has
'*Ordinario* ... a carier of Letters, or an ordinarie messenger.' The post ordinary was distinguished from post haste, which is perhaps what the tailor means
by *extraordinaries*.
  60. *Paul's ... Hall*] Samuel Rowlands, *The Knave of Harts* (1612), A3v,
singles out these three as principal locations where 'Knaves does ... daily
meete'; Westminster Hall was the home of the Courts of Common Law and
Chancery, and almost as notorious a centre of gossip as St Paul's and the Royal
Exchange. John Earle, *Microcosmographie* (1630), L9r, calls Paul's centre aisle
'the generall Mint of al famous lies'; see also Barnabe Rich, *My Ladies Looking
Glasse* (1606), p. 52: 'The News-monger ... about ten of the clocke in the
fore-noone, you may hitte upon him in the middle walke in *Pauls*: but from
aleaven to twelve, hee will not misse the Exchange' (*H.&S.*).

Fashioner.   A wit.   65
Thomas. Or half a wit. Some of them are half-wits:
   Two to a wit, there are a set of 'em.
   Then Master Ambler, emissary Paul's,
   A fine-paced gentleman as you shall see walk
   The middle aisle. And then my froy Hans Buz,   70
   A Dutchman; he's emissary Exchange.
Fashioner. I had thought Master Burst the merchant had had
   it.
Thomas. No,
   He has a rupture; he has sprung a leak.
   Emissary Westminster's undisposed of yet.
   Then, the Examiner, Register, and two clerks.   75
   They manage all at home, and sort and file
   And seal the news, and issue them.
P. Junior.   Tom, dear Tom,
   What may my means do for thee? Ask, and have it:

65.] Early in the play Jonson establishes a link between newsmongering and
the social abuse of language: in both, as with the vapours game in *B.F.*, IV.iii
(which the jeering in this play recalls), honest communication is shown to be
subverted by fashionable modes of exchange.
   68–70. *Ambler ... Buz*] These figures (who do not appear in the play) are
conceived in *N.T.*, 295–7: 'Grave Mr. *Ambler*, Newes-master of *Poules*, /
Supplies your Capon; and growne Captaine *Buz* (His Emissary) underwrites
for Turky'. On the possible identity of Ambler, see Introduction, p. 57, note
70. Buz has plausibly been identified with Matthew de Quester, a naturalised
Dutchman who controlled the foreign posts from early in James' reign, and
in 1619 was promoted together with his son to be official 'Postmasters for
Forraine Parts' (J. B. Williams, *A History of British Journalism*, p. 22).
   70. *froy*] handsome, dapper (Dutch *fraay*) (Kifer).
   71–3.] This seems to refer to a dispute in 1625 over management of the
foreign posts, in which de Quester sought to extend his authority over the
Merchant Adventurers, who had long enjoyed their own mail service, but
whose postmaster had recently died. The merchants managed to obtain the
appointment of one Henry Billingsley as his successor, and thereafter both he
and de Quester had offices in the Exchange area where they received letters
for transmission. (See Howard Robinson, *Carrying British Mails Overseas*,
pp. 19–20.) A proclamation of 14 January 1626, however, forbade Billingsley
to 'carry foreign letters to and fro London' until the dispute with de Quester
was settled (R. Steele, *A Bibliography of Royal Proclamations*, I.172).
   73. *sprung a leak*] gone bust – like his namesake in *N.I.*, IV.ii.11 who
'breaks out bankrupt' (Revels). The phrase was also current slang for catching
venereal disease.

I'd fain be doing some good. It is my birthday,
And I'd do it betimes. I feel a grudging   80
Of bounty, and I would not long lie fallow.
I pray thee think, and speak or wish for something.
Thomas. I would I had but one o'the clerks' places
   I'this News Office.
P. Junior.   Thou shalt have it, Tom,
If silver or gold will fetch it. What's the rate?   85
At what is't set i'the market?
Thomas.   Fifty pound, sir.
P. Junior. An't were a hundred, Tom, thou shalt not want it.
Fashioner. O noble master!
         The tailor leaps and embraceth him.
P. Junior.   How now, Aesop's ass!
Because I play with Tom, must I needs run
Into your rude embraces? Stand you still, sir.   90
Clowns' fawnings are a horse's salutations.
How dost thou like my suit, Tom?
Thomas.   Master Fashioner
Has hit your measures, sir. H'has moulded you
And made you, as they say.
Fashioner.   No, no, not I –
I am an ass, old Aesop's ass.
P. Junior.   Nay, Fashioner,   95
I can do thee a good turn too. Be not musty,
Though thou hast moulded me, as little Tom says.
         He draws out his pockets.
I think thou hast put me in mouldy pockets.
Fashioner.   As good
Right Spanish perfume, the lady Estifania's;

---

80. *grudging*] secret longing. *H.&S.* compare the French *avoir envie*; cf.
Cotgrave, '*envie* . . . a desire, or lust unto, a longing after'. Not in *O.E.D.* in
this sense.
   88. *Aesop's ass*] the ass who acted like a dog; J. Brindley, *Esops Fables*
(1617): 'his master returning home, hee about to try the matter, runs forth to
meet him, leapes upon him beates him with his hooves . . . the foolish asse,
which thought himselfe civill, is beaten with a club.'
   96. *musty*] peevish, with a play on 'mouldy' (Kifer).
   98–9. *pockets . . . perfume*] Spanish leather was prized for its suppleness,
and was sometimes perfumed. Cf. *Alch.*, IV.iv.13–14 (Revels).
   99. *Estifania's*] apparently a perfume dealer: Jonson mentions her in *D.A.*,

They cost twelve pound a pair.
P. Junior.   Thy bill will say so.   100
  I pray thee tell me, Fashioner, what authors
  Thou readst to help thy invention. Italian prints?
  Or arras hangings? They are tailors' libraries.
Fashioner. I scorn such helps.
P. Junior.   O, though thou art a silkworm
  And dealst in satins and velvets and rich plushes,   105
  Thou canst not spin all forms out of thyself:
  They are quite other things. I think this suit
  Has made me wittier than I was.
Fashioner.   Believe it, sir,
  That clothes do much upon the wit as weather
  Does on the brain, and thence comes your proverb: 110
  'The tailor makes the man'. I speak by experience
  Of my own customers. I have had gallants,
  Both court and country, would ha' fooled you up
  In a new suit with the best wits in being,
  And kept their speed as long as their clothes lasted   115
  Han'some and neat; but then as they grew out
  At the elbows again, or had a stain or spot,
  They have sunk most wretchedly.
P. Junior.   What thou reportst

---

110. thence comes] *F;* thence [sir] comes] *conj. Gifford.*

IV.iv.40. He seems to have been knowledgeable about cosmetics generally; see
this passage and *Cat.*, II.i and *Sej.*, II.i.
  100. *Thy* ... *so*] This dry response simultaneously anticipates P. Canter's
counsel at I.iii.25–31, and demonstrates the frivolous vanity which blinds his
son to such counsel.
  101–2. *authors* ... *prints*] H.&S. suggest two such sources in their note to
C.R., II.iv.70 (IX 504).
  103. *arras hangings*] rich tapestry fabrics hung on wooden frames set out
from the wall, and frequently depicting legends or historical episodes. Those
imported from abroad probably gave many Englishmen their clearest idea of
foreign styles of dress.
  106–8. *Thou* ... *was*] Cf. Littlewit in *B.F.*, I.i.1–3 (Revels); as E. A.
Horsman notes, this was 'clearly taken by Jonson as a feeble witticism'.
  111. *The* ... *man*] proverbial (Tilley T17). For Jonson, fine clothes are
sanctioned by nobility of character; cf. *N.I.*, V.ii.3–4 (Revels): 'Rich gar-
ments only fit / The parties they are made for; they shame others.'
  112–18. *I* ... *wretchedly*] H.&S. compare *Disc.*, 1502–8.
  113. *fooled* ... *up*] fooled you completely.

Is but the common calamity, and seen daily;
And therefore you've another answering proverb: 120
'A broken sleeve keeps the arm back'.
Fashioner.   'Tis true, sir.
And thence we say that such a one plays at peep-arm.
P. Junior. Do you so? It is wittily said. I wonder gentlemen
And men of means will not maintain themselves
Fresher in wit – I mean in clothes – to the highest.   125
For he that's out o'clothes is out o'fashion,
And out of fashion is out of countenance,
And out o'countenance is out o'wit.
Is not rogue Haberdasher come?

[*Enter* Haberdasher, Linener *and* LEATHERLEG.]

Haberdasher.   Yes, here, sir.
I ha' been without this half hour.
P. Junior. (*They are all about him, busy.*) Give me my hat.   130
Put on my girdle. Rascal, sits my ruff well?
Linener. In print.
P. Junior.   Slave –
Linener. [*Showing him a mirror.*] See yourself.
P. Junior. [*Scrutinising his attire.*]   Is this same hat
O'the block passant? Do not answer me:
I cannot stay for an answer. I do feel
The powers of one and twenty like a tide   135
Flow in upon me, and perceive an heir
Can conjure up all spirits in all circles.

120. you've] you'have *F.*   131. sits] *F*; fits *Gifford.*   132. S.D.s] *This
ed.*

---

121. *A . . . back*] proverbial (Tilley S53); *broken* = torn.
122. *peep-arm*] *O.E.D.*, citing only this example, glosses 'to let the arm be
seen as briefly as possible'. Perhaps the reference is to provocative female
fashions.
131. *girdle*] sword belt, elaborately decorated.
132. *In print*] perfectly. The term was proverbial (Tilley M239); See *E.M.O.*,
II.v.19, 'you are a gallant in print'. But there may be an allusion to the 'small
printed ruffs' favoured by Puritans (see *B.F.*, III.ii.112, Revels), and perhaps P. Junior interprets the Linener's comment as a risky jest on his neat
appearance.
133. *O'the . . . passant*] in the current fashion. The block was the wooden
model on which the hat was moulded.

Rogue; rascal; slave; give tradesmen their true names
And they appear to 'em presently.
Linener. [*Aside*].   For profit.
P. Junior. Come, cast my cloak about me. I'll go see   140
This Office, Tom, and be trimmed afterwards.
I'll put thee in possession, my prime work!

His Spurrier *comes in.*

Godso, my spurrier! Put 'em on, boy, quickly.
I'd like to ha' lost my spurs with too much speed.

ACT I   SCENE iii

[*Enter*] PENNYBOY CANTER *to them, singing,* [*in a patched and
ragged cloak*].

[*P. Canter.*] Good morning to my joy, my jolly Pennyboy,
     The lord and the prince of plenty!
I come to see what riches thou bearest in thy breeches,
     The first of thy one and twenty.
What, do thy pockets jingle? Or shall we need to mingle   5
     Our strength both of foot and horses?
These fellows look so eager, as if they would beleaguer
     An heir in the midst of his forces!

---

139. S.D.] *Kifer.*   144. I'd] I'had *F.*   I.iii.0.1–2. *in . . . cloak*] *Gifford.*
1–12.] *Italic in F.*

138.] Cf. *N.I.*, I.iii.116–17 (Revels): 'Rogue, bawd, and cheater, call you
by the surnames / And known *synonyma* of your profession.'
     139. *appear . . . 'em*] i.e. materialise (continuing the conjuring metaphor).
As the tradesmen cluster round the intoxicated Pennyboy, Jonson may intend
a stylised image of the gull inviting organised attack, anticipating the reference
to birds of prey at II.iv.42–8.
     142. *in possession*] i.e. of the clerk's place (see line 83).
     143. *Godso*] apparently a nonce form in fashionable use (like 'Godsokers'
later in the century), though it may be a pious corruption of an oath derived
from It. *cazzo* = penis (cf. 'Gadso').
     I.iii.0.1–2. *in . . . cloak*] Gifford's S.D. is supported by Dekker, *The
Belman of London*, on 'a *Clapperdugeon*: his upper garment is an olde cloake
made of as many pieces patch'd together, as there be villanies in him' (Grosart
III.99).

I hope they be no sergeants that hang upon thy margents:
This rogue has the jowl of a jailor.   10

The young Pennyboy answers in tune.

P. Junior. O Founder, no such matter: my spurrier and my
    hatter;
My linen-man and my tailor.
[*Breaks off the song.*] Thou shouldst have been brought in
    too, shoemaker,
If the time had been longer, and Tom Barber.
How dost thou like my company, old Canter?   15
Do I not muster a brave troupe? All bill-men!
[*To them.*] Present your arms before my Founder here.
This is my Founder, this same learned Canter.
He brought me the first news of my father's death,
I thank him, and ever since I call him Founder.   20
Worship him, boys. [*He takes their bills.*] I'll read only the
    sums

---

13. S.D.] *This ed.*   14. time] *F;* tune *conj. Theobald, recorded Whalley.*
22. S.H. Leatherleg] *H.&S.;* SHO. *F.* S.H. *Other tradesmen*] *This ed.;* REST.
F.

---

9. *sergeants*] Empowered to arrest for debt, these officers are depicted in
contemporary satire as the natural enemy of improvident gallants; see W.
Fennor, *The Compters Commonwealth* (1617), 'I hold them very religious men,
for they will continually watch and pray, watch a whole day together to catch
young Gentlemen, and after they have clutcht them pray upon them' (p. 40).
    margents] flanks.
    10. *jowl . . . jailor*] Cf. Mynshul, *Essays and Characters* (1638): 'Your Keepers
most commonly are insinuating knaves, and mercinary rascals . . . in full proportion they look like the picture of envy, with their hands continually diving
into poore prisoners pockets' (p. 28). Canter is probably commenting on the
spurrier (fastening the spur like a leg-iron?) as he looks up to observe the new
arrival.
    16. *bill-men*] For the quibble, cf. *Tim.*, III.iv.88–9, where besieged by his
creditors ('All our bills') Timon exclaims 'Knock me down with 'em: cleave me
to the girdle'. The weapons carried by watchmen and infantry soldiers were
called halberds or bills.
    17. *Founder*] one who institutes or sets up (*O.E.D.*). But since Canter is
'bred i'the mines' (line 56), there may be a suggestion of *founder* meaning 'the
Point at which a Vein of Ore shall be first found' (*O.E.D.* sb.5.3, first example
from 1653). The prodigal must learn to value his founder-father above the
spurious vein of wealth opened up to him at the start of the play.
    22. *Now . . . him*] presumably a traditional toast; cf. the proverb 'Bless-

And pass 'em straight.
Leatherleg. [*Proposing a toast.*] Now ale –
Other tradesmen.   And strong ale bless him.
P. Junior. Godso, some ale and sugar for my Founder!
     Good bills, sufficient bills; these bills may pass.
                              [*Puts them in his pockets.*]
P. Canter. I do not like those paper-squibs, good master.   25
     They may undo your store – I mean of credit –
     And fire your arsenal, if case you do not
     In time make good those outerworks, your pockets,
     And take a garrison in of some two hundred
     To beat these pioners off, that carry a mine   30
     Would blow you up at last. Secure your casemates.
     [*Producing a money-bag.*] Here Master Picklock, sir, your
          man o'law
     And learn'd attorney, has sent you a bag of munition.
P. Junior. What is't? [*Takes the bag.*]
P. Canter.   Three hundred pieces.
P. Junior.   I'll dispatch 'em.

24.1.] *This ed.; He takes the bils, and puts them vp in his pockets. in F margin next
to lines 20–3.*   30. pioners] F (*Pyoners*); *Pioneers F3.*

---

ing of your heart, you brew good ale' (Tilley B450), and *The Masque of Augurs*,
181–3.
     23. *sugar*] used to sweeten wine and ale.
     24. *sufficient*] properly drawn up.
     27. *if case*] perchance.
     30. *pioners*] It seems inadvisable to modernise to 'pioneers'; as in *Ham.*,
I.v.171, the word is used in its unfamiliar (now obsolete?) sense of 'under-
miners' – usually, in Jonson's day, soldiers who dig tunnels under city walls to
weaken them or blow them up. Cf. Dekker, *Worke for Armorours* (1609),
describing a siege: 'Pioners had digd at least a quarter of a mile under the
earth, and the mine [sic] with gun powder to blow up one quarter of the Cittie'
(Grosart IV.154).
     31. *casemates*] Florio (1611), p. 87: 'Casamatta, a Casamat, a Canonrie or
slaughter-house so called of enginers, which is a place built low under the wall
or bulwarke not arriving unto the height of the ditch, and serves to annoy or
hinder the enemie when he entreth the ditch to scale the wall.'
     34. *dispatch*] Canter in his reply (see next line) understands this word in its
rare sense of 'stow away' (*O.E.D.* v.6.c) and on the surface P. Junior would
appear to be assuring him that he will pocket the money rather than spend it all
immediately. The more usual meaning of *dispatch* threatens, however, and is
confirmed at line 37.

P. Canter. Do: I would have your strengths lined and   35
        perfumed
    With gold as well as amber.
P. Junior.   God-a-mercy,
    Come, *ad solvendum*, boys! (*He pays all.*) There, there, and
        there, &c.
    I look on nothing but *totalis.*
P. Canter [*Aside.*]   See
    The difference 'twixt the covetous and the prodigal!
    'The covetous man never has money, and   40
    The prodigal will have none shortly'.
P. Junior.   Ha,
    What says my Founder? [*Tradesmen bow and start to leave.*]
    – I thank you, I thank you, sirs.
Tradesmen. God bless your worship, and your worship's
        chanter.
    [*Exeunt* LEATHERLEG, Fashioner, Linener *and* Haberdasher.]
P. Canter. I say 'tis nobly done to cherish shopkeepers
    And pay their bills without examining, thus.   45
P. Junior. Alas, they have had a pitiful hard time on't,
    A long vacation from their cozening.

---

35. *strengths*] fortifications, continuing the metaphor at line 28. Cf. *Disc.*,
335–8: 'the rashnesse of talking should ... be fenced in, and defended by
certaine strengths placed in the mouth it selfe, and within the lips'.

36. *amber*] ambergris, used in making perfumes. Cf. the description of a
gallant in Dekker's *1 Honest Whore*, III.ii.27–8: 'he smells all of Muske and
Amber greece, his pocket full of Crownes' (Bowers II.66). See also *C.R.*,
II.i.60–2.

God-a-mercy,] i.e. God reward you (*a* = have). The comma marks P. Junior's
smooth, inevitable movement from getting to spending.

37. *Come ... solvendum*] settling up time.

38. *totalis*] Jonson may be glancing at Dekker's advice to gallants in a
tavern, in *The Guls Horn-booke*, Ch. 7: when faced with 'the terrible Reckoning ... cast your eie onely upon the *Totalis*, and no further; for to traverse the
bill would betray you to be acquainted with the rates of the market' (Grosart
II.259–60). But the expression was probably a commonplace in fashionable
London (*H.&S.*).

40–1.] from Seneca, *De Remediis Fortuitorum*, x.3, *Multum habet* ('He has
much'): 'whether the rich man be a miser or a spendthrift, if the former, he has
nothing; if the latter, he will have nothing' (*H.&S.*).

43. *chanter*] singer. The pun on Canter's name is motivated by his entry
('singing') at the start of the scene.

47. *long vacation*] De Winter suggests an allusion to the catastrophic plague

Poor rascals, I do do it out of charity.
I would advance their trade again, and have them
Haste to be rich, swear and forswear wealthily.   50
[*To the Spurrier.*] What do you stay for, sirrah?
Spurrier.   To my box, sir.
P. Junior. Your box? (*He gives the* Spurrier *to his box.*)
                    Why, there's an angel. If my spurs
Be not right Ripon –
Spurrier.   Give me never a penny
If I strike not through your bounty with the rowels.
                                                [*Exit.*]
P. Junior. Dost thou want any money, Founder?
P. Canter.   Who, sir, I?   55
Did I not tell you I was bred i'the mines
Under Sir Bevis Bullion?
P. Junior.   That is true,
I quite forgot: you mine men want no money;
Your streets are paved with't. There the molten silver
Runs out like cream on cakes of gold.

---

from which London was still recovering in early 1626; this is given support by
John Taylor, *The Fearefull Summer* (1625): 'The Mercers, Grocers, Silk-men,
Goldsmiths, Drapers, / Are out of Season, like noone burning Tapers, / All
functions faile almost, through want of buyers' (*Workes* 1630, p. 60). But
complaints about slack trading during the long summer vacation in the Inns of
Court were habitual: cf. *D.A.*, III.ii.12, and Westminster's complaint in
Dekker, *The Dead Tearme* (Grosart IV.22).
    50. *swear ... wealthily*] a common expression for dishonesty and sharp
practice; cf. Dekker, *The Seven Deadly Sinnes of London*: 'What fooles then are
thy *Buyers* and *Sellers* to be abused by such hell-hounds? *Swearing* and *For-
swearing* put into their hands perhaps the gaines of a little Silver, but like those
pieces which *Judas* received, they are their destruction' (Grosart II.35). In his
last letter to his wife, Robert Greene lamented that 'for my swearing and for-
swearing, no man will beleeve me' (*A Groatsworth of Wit* (1592), F3*v*).
    51. *To my box*] i.e. soliciting a tip. P. Junior's contribution (an angel was
worth ten shillings) is suitably excessive.
    53. *right Ripon*] proverbial: 'As true steel as Ripon rowels' (Tilley S841).
H.&S. cite Nares: 'Rippon ... is a Town famous for the best *spurs* of *England*,
whose *rowels* may be enforced to strike through a shilling'.
    57. *Sir ... Bullion*] 'A neat pseudonym for Sir Bevis Bulmer, a famous
mining engineer and speculator knighted in 1604' (*H.&S.*). He amassed a
considerable fortune from various projects, including a silver mine in Devon,
but over-extended himself and died in debt in 1615.
    59–61. *Your ... strawberries*] This whimsical day-dream, which has some
of the satiric extravagance of Mammon's fantasies in *Alch.*, II.i, is initially

P. Canter.   And rubies   60
    Do grow like strawberrries.
P. Junior.   'Twere brave being there.
    Come, Tom, we'll go to the Office now.
P. Canter.   What office?
P. Junior. News Office; the new staple. Thou shalt go too.
    'Tis here i'the house, on the same floor, Tom says.
    Come, Founder, let us trade in ale and nutmegs.   65
                                                    [*Exeunt.*]

ACT I SCENE iv

[Enter] Register, [NATHANIEL *the*] *Clerk* [*at one door, and at
another door enter*] *a* Countrywoman [*who*] *waits there.*

[*Register.*] What, are those desks fit now? Set forth the table,
    The carpet, and the chair. Where are the news

I.iv.0.1–2.] *This ed.*; REGISTER. CLERKE. VVOMAN. F, *which has in margin
next to lines 11–12 'A countrey-woman waites there'.*

prompted by the contemporary image of New World riches, such as 'the great
and Golden Citie of . . . El *Dorado*' (from the title of Raleigh's *Discoverie of
Guiana* (1596)). In that putative mine country, says Raleigh, 'all the rocks,
mountains, all stones in the plaines . . . are in effect thorow shining, and
appeare marveylous rich, which . . . are the trew signes of rich mineralles' (*To
the Reader*). But it is characteristic of Jonson's art in this play that his topical
comment should be mediated through literary allusion which shapes our
response to it; and his opulent description evokes a tradition which includes
Raleigh's sardonic vision in 'The Pilgrimage' of the 'blessed paths' to Heaven,
'Strowed with rubies thick as gravel' (31–2), and Mammon's temptation of
Guyon in *The Faerie Queene* with 'fruits, whose kinds mote not be redd' since
they are poisoned by materialism (Bk. II.vii.51, line 5). In Chaucer's House of
Fame the walls, floors and ceilings are set thick with 'the fynest stones faire, /
. . . As grasses growen in a mede' (*Works*, ed. F. N. Robinson, p. 295). Again,
it was a Renaissance commonplace that Solomon 'made silver to be in Jerusalem
as stones' (I Kings, x.27). The ambivalent allure of wealth is evoked by Jonson
preparatory to the introduction of Pecunia in Act II.
    65. *trade in*] occupy ourselves with, indulge in; cf. *Ant.*, II.v.1–2: 'music,
moody food / Of us that trade in love.'
    nutmegs] used to flavour ale.
    I.iv.1–2. *desks . . . chair*] It seems likely that the Staple scenes were quite
elaborately furnished on Jonson's stage. The table is already there from the
opening scene (see I.i.10); and the other items are either carried in or dis-
closed by drawing a curtain (possibly one at the front of some kind of booth).
See Introduction, p. 51.
    2. *carpet*] Edd. gloss this as 'tablecloth', but carpets (especially oriental

That were examined last? Ha' you filed them up?
Nathaniel. Not yet, I had no time.
Register.   Are those news registered
That emissary Buz sent in last night   5
Of Spinola and his eggs?
Nathaniel.   Yes sir, and filed.
Register. What are you now upon?
Nathaniel.   That our new emissary
Westminster gave us of the Golden Heir.
Register. Dispatch. That's news indeed, and of importance.
[Countrywoman *approaches*.] What would you have, good
      woman?
Countrywoman. I would have, sir,   10
A groatsworth of any news – I care not what –
To carry down this Saturday to our vicar.
Register. O, you are a butterwoman! Ask Nathaniel

---

4. S.H. *Nathaniel.*] *Gifford (Nath.), so passim;* CLE. *F.*   10. S.D.] This ed.
13. you are] *F;* you're *Whalley.*

ones) were extensively used as table coverings, and provided an air of established opulence which would suit the Staple's purposes.
    3. *filed ... up*] The obvious meaning is dominant here, but the idea of
'polished, improved' may also be present.
    6. *Spinola*] Ambrogio di Spinola, an Italian general who served Spain in
the Thirty Years War and whose campaigns were frequently reported in the
English newsbooks; he overran the Palatinate in 1620, ousting James I's son-
in-law Frederick, and captured the city of Breda in 1625. See notes to III.ii.26
and, for *his eggs,* III.ii.46.
    8. *Golden Heir*] i.e. Pennyboy, whose change of fortune has been noted in
legal circles. But the grandiloquent phrase may have helped to provoke the
charge that Jonson's play depicted existing people and institutions (see 'To the
Readers' following Act II). This 'sinister interpretation', as D. F. McKenzie
says, must 'have found parallels ... between the prodigal Pennyboy Junior
and Charles I, who assumed his full patrimony with his coronation robes on
2 February 1626, only a week or two before the play was performed' (*A Celebration of B.J.*, ed. Blissett, p. 124). Not long before, the nation had anxiously
awaited the outcome of Charles's protracted marriage negotiations abroad.
    10.] The Countrywoman, who has been visible from the start of the scene,
now approaches the stage area defined by furniture and props (and pͬ ᴀaps a
booth) as the Staple office.
    11. *groatsworth*] A groat was worth fourpence.
    13. *you ... Nathaniel*] The first of several allusions to the publisher and
bookseller Nathaniel Butter, who in 1622 issued the first ɾegular newsbooks.
See Introduction, p. 22. Butter is frequently satirised in writings of the period,
e.g. *The Fair Maid of the Inn*, IV.ii.74–80: 'a spirit to informe you ... it shall

The clerk there.

Nathaniel.   Sir, I tell her she must stay
Till emissary Exchange or Paul's send in,   15
And then I'll fit her.
Register.   Do, good woman, have patience.
It is not now as when the Captain lived.
                                                  [*Exit* Countrywoman.]
Nathaniel. You'll blast the reputation of the Office
(Now i'the bud) if you dispatch these groats
So soon. Let them attend in name of policy.   20

ACT I SCENE V

[*Enter to them*] CYMBAL [*and*] FITTON [, *introducing*] PENNYBOY
[JUNIOR]; THO [MAS] BARBER [*and* PENNYBOY] CANTER [*enter
after them and stand apart*].

18–19. Office / . . . bud)] Office, / . . . Bud, *F.*

---

be the ghost of some lying Stationer, a spirit shall looke as if butter would
not melt in his mouth, A new Mercurius Gallobelgicus' (Lucas IV.204). Cf.
Brathwaite's portrait of 'a Corranto-Coiner': 'the vulgar doe admire him, holding his Novels oracular. And these are usually sent for Tokens or intermissive
Curtsies betwixt City and Countrey' (*Whimzies* (1631), p. 15).
    14. *stay*] wait.
    16. *fit her*] fix her up, provide her with what she wants. The complete half-
line recalls the cadence of Hieronymo's promise in *The Spanish Tragedy*,
IV.i.70 (Revels): 'Why then I'll fit you', and this seems to prompt the more
explicit quotation from Kyd's play in the next line.
    17. *It . . . lived*] Cf. *The Spanish Tragedy*, III.xiv.111: 'It is not now as when
Andrea liv'd'. The quotation from an old and much satirised play frames an
allusion to Thomas Gainsford, a soldier and traveller who turned to journalism
and was involved in editing Butter's newsbooks for a period in the early 1620s.
Jonson elsewhere disparages 'Captain Pamphlet's horse and foot, that sally /
Upon the Exchange, still, out of Pope's Head Alley' ('An Execration upon
Vulcan', 79–80); and here he ironically contrasts the rough and informal
methods of Gainsford and Butter with the Staple's more organised exploitation
of public curiosity. Gainsford died of the plague in August 1624.
    19. *groats*] punning on the sense of 'hulled oats' (Kifer). As the Country-
woman exits and the mask drops, Nathaniel's words recall Mosca and Face in
the resourceful, calculated use of insubstantial lures.
    20. *Let . . . policy*] i.e. it's politic to keep them waiting.

    I.v.o.2–3. enter . . . apart] Tom and Canter are evidently on hand to be
called into the 'office' later (see lines 84–92), and perhaps should be visible
from the start, to one side (and downstage?) from the main acting area. Canter
is often in the play a silent attender on the prodigal's vanity.

[*P. Junior.*] In troth, they are dainty rooms. What place is this?
Cymbal. This is the outer room, where my clerks sit
    And keep their sides; the Register i'the midst;
    The Examiner, he sits private there within;
    And here I have my several rolls and files   5
    Of news by the alphabet, and all put up
    Under their heads.
P. Junior.   But those too, subdivided?
Cymbal. Into authentical, and apocryphal;
Fitton. Or news of doubtful credit, as barbers' news –
Cymbal. And tailors' news, porters' and watermen's news.   10
Fitton. Whereto, beside the *coranti* and *gazetti* –
Cymbal. I have the news of the season –
Fitton.   As vacation news,
    Term news, and Christmas news.

I.v.0.1–2. *Enter* ... JUNIOR] *Gifford subst.*   0.2–3. THOMAS ... *apart*]
This ed.; PENIBOY. CYMBAL. FITTON. THO: / BARBER. CANTER. *F.*

---

3. *keep* ... *sides*] look after their own sections. The division of responsibility is explained at III.ii.62–9.
4. *Examiner*] presumably an editor. There is limited evidence of systematic editing in the early newsbooks; see M. A. Shaaber, 'The History of the First English Newspaper', *S.P.*, 29 (1932), 551–87, and Appendix B. Jonson may have been thinking of (and 'improving') Thomas Gainsford's role in Butter's venture; the comic conception of the Staple thrives on the suggestion of a detailed hierarchy.
    private ... *within*] Cymbal probably indicates one of the side doors in the façade, or possibly an area within the discovery space; see also III.i.41 note.
9–10. *barber's* ... *watermen's*] John Taylor (the Water-Poet) declares in *Taylor's Travels* that 'at Barbar-shops, / There tidings vented are, as thicke as hops' (9–10; *Workes* 1630, Hhh5). But his own credibility as a reporter is queried in Overbury's *Characters* (1615), where *A Water-man* 'is evermore telling strange newes; most commonly lyes' (Lucas IV.37).
11. *coranti* ... *gazetti*] Corantos or 'currants' (from the French 'courante') were the single-sheet digests of news from various parts of Europe which immediately preceded the first regular newsbooks and in the 1620s supplied the latter with much of their information. They were also known as 'Gazetts': cf. Florio, '*Gazzette*, running reports, daily newes, idle intelligences, or flim flam tales ... daily written from Italie'.
12–13. *vacation* ... *news*] town gossip, of the kind which became institutionalised in Restoration newspapers; cf. Chamberlain's letters to Carleton and others. The notion of *vacation news* is almost oxymoronic in this context (see note to I.iii.47); but cf. *S.W.*, II.v.105–10, where Morose tells Cutbeard: 'Your knighthood ... shall cheat at the twelve-penny ordinary ... for it's diet all the terme time, and tell tales for it in the vacation, to the hostesse'.

Cymbal.   And news o'the faction –
Fitton. As the Reformèd news, Protestant news –
Cymbal. And Pontifical news; of all which several   15
    The day-books, characters, precedents are kept,
    Together with the names of special friends –
Fitton. And men of correspondence i'the country –
Cymbal. Yes, of all ranks and all religions –
Fitton. Factors and agents –
Cymbal.   Liegers, that lie out   20
    Through all the shires o'the kingdom.
P. Junior.   This is fine
    And bears a brave relation! But what says
    Mercurius Britannicus to this?
Cymbal. O sir, he gains by't half in half.
Fitton.   Nay, more:
    I'll stand to't. For, where he was wont to get   25
    In hungry captains, obscure statesmen –

14–21. *As . . . kingdom*] adapted from *N.N.W.*, 33–43.
15. *of . . . several*] whereof in each case.
16. *day-books*] in which the occurrences or transactions of the day are
entered (*O.E.D.*).
    characters] ciphers. *precedents*] originals.
20. *Factors*] agents.
    Liegers] obsolete form of 'ledger'. a resident agent or representative.
20–1. *Liegers . . . kingdom*] probably adapting to a domestic context Sir
Henry Wotton's famous definition of an ambassador: '*Legatus est vir bonus,
peregre missus ad mentiendum Reipub[licae] causa*. In English, being only this
Jest; An Ambassador is an honest man sent to lye abroad for the Commonwealth' (*Reliquae Wottonianae* (1672), e8v). Jonson was fond of the pun: cf.
Disc., 288–90, where he comments on the decline of learning and letters: 'The
Writer must lye, and the gentle Reader rests happy, to heare the worthiest
workes misinterpreted; the clearest actions obscured'.
22. *bears . . . relation*] makes impressive hearing.
23. *Mercurius Britannicus*] The third numbered series of newsbooks to
appear in England bore the legend 'printed for *Mercurius Britannicus*', and
came to an end in January 1626. They were produced by Butter and Nicholas
Bourne. Once again Cymbal's brave new enterprise is improving on a recent
venture.
24. *gains . . . half*] makes 100% profit; or perhaps, has doubled his profits.
O.E.D. (*half in half*) glosses 'by half the total amount, cent per cent'; cf.
· Massinger, *The Guardian*, II.iv.100: 'cheating Vintners not contented / With
half in half in their reckonings' (*E.&G.* IV.145). Both here and in Jonson the
phrase seems to imply improved takings by dubious means.
26. *hungry captains*] Soldiers' news were considered especially unreliable.

Cymbal.   Fellows
   To drink with him in a dark room in a tavern
   And eat a sausage –
Fitton.   We ha' seen't.
Cymbal.   As fain
   To keep so many politic pens
   Going to feed the press –
Fitton.   And dish out news,   30
   Were't true or false –
Cymbal.   Now all that charge is saved.
   The public chronicler –
Fitton.   How do you call him there?
Cymbal. And gentle reader –
Fitton.   He that has the maidenhead
   Of all the books.

28–9. seen't. As fain / . . . pens] *F (subst.);* seen it / As fain . . . pens *Gifford.*
29. politic] *F (politique);* politician *conj. H.&S.*   32. How] How, *F,*
H.&S.

Cf. *Ep.* 107, 'To Captain Hungry', and Shirley, *Love Tricks* (1625), I.i, on
the trade of newsmongering: 'It has been a great profession; marry, most
commonly they are soldiers . . . will write you a battle in any part of Europe at
an hour's warning, and yet never set foot out of a tavern . . . nothing destroys
them but want of a good memory, for if they escape contradiction they may be
chronicled' (*Works* 1833, I.8–9).
   27–8.] News is vividly associated with a familiar context of subversive talk.
On taverns as centres of radical thought and the exchange of information,
see Valerie Pearl, *London and the Outbreak of the Puritan Revolution* (1961),
pp. 233–4.
   28. *As fain*] being obliged.
   29. *politic*] artfully contriving. The line is a foot short (see collation) but
nothing has obviously dropped out.
   30. *dish out*] perhaps in the modern sense, but Fitton may be ironically
implying that pre-Staple news was doctored to make it more appealing to
readers (*O.E.D.* v.2, to dress up, present (attractively) for acceptance).
   32. *How . . . there*] *H.&S.* retain *F*'s punctuation (see collation), detecting
an allusion to Edmund Howes, who continued Stow's *Annales of England*, and
cite *S.W.*, II.v.124–5, where Morose imagines 'when . . . (*How* do you call
him) the worst reveller in the towne is taken'. Jonson's attitude to the chronicler's labours is more clearly suggested in *N.N.W.*, 21–31. Howes's plodding
dedication to his task apparently attracted considerable ridicule, and Jonson
seems to have been alert to the potential denigration of historical writing into
mere gossip.
   33. *gentle reader*] The newsbook prefaces were careful to use this conventional address to their public.

Cymbal.   Yes, dedicated to him –
Fitton. Or rather prostituted –
P. Junior.   You are right, sir.   35
Cymbal. – No more shall be abused, nor country parsons
 O'the inquisition, nor busy justices
 Trouble the peace, and both torment themselves
 And their poor ign'rant neighbours with enquiries
 After the many and most innocent monsters,   40
 That never came i'th'counties they were charged with.
P. Junior. Why, methinks, sir, if the honest common people
 Will be abused, why should not they ha' their pleasure
 In the believing lies are made for them,
 As you i'th'Office, making them yourselves?   45
Fitton. O sir, it is the printing we oppose.
Cymbal. We not forbid that any news be made
 But that't be printed; for when news is printed,
 It leaves, sir, to be news. While 'tis but written –
Fitton. Though it be ne'er so false, it runs news still.   50
P. Junior. See divers men's opinions! Unto some,
 The very printing of them makes them news,
 That ha' not the heart to believe anything
 But what they see in print.
Fitton.   Ay, that's an error
 Has abused many; but we shall reform it,   55
 As many things beside (we have a hope)
 Are crept among the popular abuses.

---

35. *prostituted*] i.e. because writers pander to popular taste.
36–40. *Nor ... monsters*] Reports of prodigies and monsters in the provinces were very common; several occur in Stow, and pamphlets appeared
regularly to document the latest sensation, frequently in the shape of ballads
illustrated with woodcuts and sometimes accompanied by the names of witnesses. One from Southampton dated 1602 'is verified by the magistrats and
officers of the same towne, witnesses of this most fearefull sight' (*Shirburn
Ballads*, ed. A. Clark, p. 293). Shaaber, *Forerunners of the English Newspaper*,
pp. 151–6, discusses other examples including the famous 'serpent of *Sussex*'
in *N.N.W.*, 48.
42–61.] Much of this debate is adapted from *N.N.W.*, 52–67.
45.] i.e. just as you in the office get pleasure from the actual invention of
those lies.
52–4. *The ... print*] Cf. Mopsa in *Wint.*, IV.iv.261–2: 'I love a ballad in
print, a life, for then we are sure they are true.'

Cymbal. Nor shall the stationer cheat upon the time
    By buttering over again –
Fitton.   Once in seven years,
    As the age dotes –
Cymbal.   And grows forgetful o'them,   60
    His antiquated pamphlets, with new dates.
    But all shall come from the mint –
Fitton.   Fresh and new stamped –
Cymbal. With the Office seal: Staple Commodity.
Fitton. And if a man will assure his news, he may.
    Twopence a sheet he shall be warranted   65
    And have a policy for't.
P. Junior.   Sir, I admire
    The method o'your place. All things within't
    Are so digested, fitted and composed,
    As it shows Wit had married Order.
Fitton.   Sir –
Cymbal. The best we could to invite the times.

58–9. *Nor . . . again*] Evidently a common practice, although topical news
stories were presumably less easy to re-hash than the popular tales of calamities
and monsters. *H.&S.* cite an example of the latter in which a 1613 pamphlet,
The Miracle of Miracles (see p. 21), recounting the antics of a headless bear,
was reissued in 1641 with altered details and a new title-page (*Most Fearefull
and Strange Newes*). The pamphlet was itself a reworking of a 1584 publication
(*S.T.C.* 5681). There is no evidence that Butter engaged in such deceptions,
although in his issue of 2 October 1623 he published a letter from a reader who
complained that an earlier report about 'the strange birth of Antichrist' was
simply 'an old tale new furbusht' (pp. 20–1).

62.] Cf. Brathwaite, 'A Corranto-Coiner': 'his owne *Genius* is his intelligencer. His *Mint* goes weekly and he *coines* monie by it' (*Whimzies*, p. 15).
Although Brathwaite is referring to printed news, his image resembles Jonson's
in suggesting a process of lucrative forgery.

64. *assure*] feel certain of.

65.] Folke Dahl, *Bibliography of English . . . Newsbooks*, p. 153, records that
'ij^d.' is written in a contemporary hand on the one surviving copy of the issue
for 8 June 1627, adding: 'This is most probably the original price of the newsbook. In 1632 the price had been raised to 3d.'

66. *policy*] written guarantee.

69. *Wit . . . Order*] Edd. compare the play-titles *The Marriage of Wit and
Science* (c. 1569) and *The Marriage of Wit and Wisdom* (c. 1579). For Jonson's
use of the morality tradition in the play, see Introduction, p. 11, and the notes
to the second Interman.

Fitton.   It has   70
    Cost sweat and freezing.
Cymbal.   And some broken sleeps
    Before it came to this.
P. Junior.   I easily think it.
Fitton. But now it has the shape –
Cymbal.   And is come forth.
P. Junior. A most polite neat thing! With all the limbs
    As sense can taste!
Cymbal.   It is, sir, though I say it,   75
    As well-begotten a business and as fairly
    Helped to the world.
P. Junior.   You must be a midwife, sir!
    Or else the son of a midwife (pray you pardon me!) –
    Have helped it forth so happily. What news ha' you?
    News o'this morning? I would fain hear some   80
    Fresh from the forge (as new as day, as they say).
Cymbal. And such we have, sir.
Register. [*To Nathaniel.*]   Show him the last roll
    Of emissary Westminster's: 'The Heir'.
P. Junior. [*Calls.*] Come nearer, Tom.
                        [THOMAS BARBER *approaches.*]
Nathaniel. [*Reading.*]   There is a brave young heir

---

70. *invite the times*] i.e. become a centre for the day's news, a place of popular resort.
    74. *polite*] 'Trimme, fine, bright' (Cockeram, *English Dictionarie*, 1631).
    77. *You ... midwife*] Pennyboy's obtuseness is again underlined by his
insensitivity to language, as the childbirth metaphor begun in line 71 belated-
ly reveals itself to him. This is in striking contrast to the terse wit of 'man-
midwife, the Prologue' in the Induction (57–8); but repetition of the childbirth
metaphor assists the juxtaposition of theatre and news office, poet and journalist, that is Jonson's major concern in the play. Cf. the epigraph to *N.N.W.*,
Nascitur è tenebris ..., which *H.&S.* translate as 'It is a world springing from
darkness and asserting itself'.
    81. *as ... day*] probably a hawker's cry; in *N.I.*, IV.iii.31, Latimer remarks
on Pinnacia's use of the phrase that 'She answers like a fishwife'. *H.&S.* compare a song in the *Shirburn Ballads* (ed. Clarke, p. 338): 'New place, new, as
new as the daye; / New whitings, new, here haue yow maye.' Fish peddlers
were regarded as gossips; cf. Chapman, *The Widow's Tears*, I.iii.128–30: 'pray
heaven the Oister-wives have not brought the newes of my woing hether
amongst their stale Pilcherds' (Holaday, p. 491).

Is come of age this morning, Master Pennyboy.
P. Junior. (*rejoiceth that he is in.*)   That's I!   85
Nathaniel. His father died on this day seven-night.
P. Junior.   True.
Nathaniel. At six o'the clock i'the morning, just a week
    Ere he was one and twenty.
P. Junior. [*Pointing to the roll.*] I am here, Tom!
    [*To Nathaniel.*] Proceed, I pray thee.
Nathaniel. [*Reading.*]   An old canting beggar
    Brought him first news, whom he has entertained   90
    To follow him since.
P. Junior.   Why, you shall see him. [*Calls.*] Founder,
    Come in. [CANTER *approaches.*] No follower, but com-
        panion:
    I pray thee, put him in, friend. There's an angel –
                        He gives the clerk [*a coin*].
    Thou dost not know, he's a wise old fellow
    Though he seem patched thus and made up o'pieces.   95
                        [*Exit* NATHANIEL.]
    Founder, we are in, here, in – i'the News Office!
    In this day's roll, already! I do muse
    How you came by us, sirs.
Cymbal.   One Master Picklock
    A lawyer, that hath purchased here a place
    This morning of an emissary under me –   100
Fitton. Emissary Westminster.
Cymbal.   Gave it into th'Office–

---

84. S.D.s] *This ed.; Enter* Barber Gifford (*after 83*).   S.H. Nathaniel]
Gifford; CLA. *F (passim).*   85. S.D. *rejoiceth*] Peny *reioyceth* F.   86.
seven-] *F3;* seventh- *F.*   88. S.D.] *This ed.; F margin: Tels* Thom: *of it.*
91. S.D.] *F3; F margin: Call in the* Canter.   93.1. *a coin*] Kifer.

---

86. *seven-night*] See collation. F's *seventh-*, a use of ordinal for cardinal, is
very unusual (*O.E.D.* cites one other example) and the only instance of it in
Jonson; 'probably a printer's error', as Partridge says (*Accidence*, p. 120).
    88. *here*] i.e. in the news roll.
    89. *canting*] whining.
    90. *entertained*] employed.
    95. *patched*] See note to I.iii.0.1–2. Canter is noticeably silent for the next
fifty lines as he observes his son's garrulous self-importance.
    102. *piece*] masterpiece, in its original sense of the *essay* or piece of work by

Fitton. For his essay, his piece.
P. Junior.   My man o'law!
He's my attorney and solicitor, too;
A fine pragmatic! What's his place worth?
Cymbal. A *nemo-scit*, sir.
Fitton.   'Tis as news come in –   105
Cymbal. And as they are issued. I have the just moiety
For my part; then the other moiety
Is parted into seven. The four emissaries,
Whereof my cousin Fitton here's for Court,
Ambler for Paul's, and Buz for the Exchange,   110
Picklock for Westminster, with the Examiner
And Register: they have full parts. And then one part
Is under-parted to a couple of clerks,
And there's the just division of the profits.
P. Junior. Ha' you those clerks, sir?
Cymbal.   There is one desk empty,   115
But it has many suitors.
P. Junior.   Sir, may I
Present one more and carry it, if his parts
Or gifts (which you will, call 'em) –
Cymbal.   Be sufficient, sir.
P. Junior. What are your present clerk's abilities?
How is he qualified?
Cymbal.   A decayed stationer   120

---

which a craftsman gained the title of master in his guild. At V.i.103 Picklock
himself uses the word in its modern sense, seeking to turn his original essay
into a masterpiece of deception.
    104. *pragmatic*] man of business.
    105. nemo-scit] literally, 'nobody knows', since the job is paid on a per-
centage basis; the phrase is meant to imply considerable potential earnings.
Cymbal deflects P. Junior's question about price into talk of what the job is
worth to its holder.
    '*Tis as*] depending on what.
    106. *moiety*] half.
    113. *under-parted*] subdivided.
    116. *But ... suitors*] P. Junior is easily gulled by this old ploy to push up the
price, as the succeeding conversation shows.
    117. *carry*] win; but perhaps also with a suggestion of 'carry the cost'.
    119. *your ... clerk's*] i.e. Nathaniel. See note to I.iv.13.
    120–1. *A ... 'em*] The joke against Butter – that he has come down in the
world and been given a lowly job in the Staple – is carried through to the
closing lines of III.iii.

He was, but knows news well, can sort and rank 'em.
Fitton. And for a need can make 'em.
Cymbal.   True Paul's bred,
    I'the Churchyard.
P. Junior. [*Indicating Tom.*] And this at the West Door,
    O'th'other side. He's my barber Tom,
    A pretty scholar and a Master of Arts   125
    Was made, or went out Master of Arts in a throng,
    At the University; as before, one Christmas,
    He got into a masque at Court, by his wit
    And the good means of his cittern, holding up thus
                    [*Strumming an imaginary instrument.*]
    For one o'the music. He's a nimble fellow,   130
    And alike skilled in every liberal science,
    As having certain snaps of all; a neat
    Quick vein in forging news, too. I do love him,
    And promised him a good turn, and I would do it.
    What's your price? The value?
Cymbal.   Fifty pounds, sir.   135
P. Junior. Get in, Tom. Take possession. I install thee.
    [*He pays Cymbal.*] Here, tell your money. Give thee joy,

---

137. S.D.] *This ed.; F margin (137–40): Hee buyes* Thom *a* Clerkes place.

122–3. *True . . . Door*] A large number of stationers' shops were situated in
the walled churchyard of St Paul's; advertisements for employment were
posted on the West Door of the Church.
    126. *Master . . . throng*] When James I paid state visits to Oxford in 1605
and Cambridge in 1615, degrees were conferred on his retinue. Kifer cites
an account of the latter occasion in Nichols's *Progresses of James I*, III.61:
'Degrees were vilely prostituted to mean persons, such as apothecaries and
barbers'; and *H.&S.* quote from an eye-witness account at Oxford, where the
king's followers 'pressed in so thick, that . . . so they looked like gentlemen, &
had gotten on a gown and a hood, they were admitted' (*Harl.* MS.7044. f.105b).
    129–30. *cittern . . . music*] Citterns, wire-strung instruments of the guitar
type, were commonly kept in barbers' shops for apprentices and waiting
customers to play. Cf. *S.W.*, III.v.64–5. Tom Barber improves on the efforts
of Robin Goodfellow in *Love Restored*, who tried to get access to the masque at
court: 'I pretended to be a musician, mary, I could not shew mine instrument,
and that bred a discord' (95–7).
    132. *snaps*] scraps, oddments; with a pun on the habit characteristic amongst
barbers of snapping their fingers as they worked. The practice is burlesqued
in Beaumont's *Knight of the Burning Pestle*, III.249–51.
    133. *forging*] Jonson's trenchant pun neatly caps the exposition of Staple
methods and tactics in this scene.
    137. *tell*] count.

good Tom,
And let me hear from thee every minute of news,
While the new Staple stands or the Office lasts,
Which I do wish may ne'er be less, for thy sake.   140

[*Re-enter* NATHANIEL.]

Nathaniel. [*To Cymbal.*] The emissaries, sir, would speak with
    you
And Master Fitton. They have brought in news,
Three bale together.
Cymbal. [*To P. Junior.*] Sir, you are welcome here.
Fitton. So is your creature.
Cymbal.   Business calls us off, sir,
That may concern the Office.
P. Junior.   Keep me fair, sir,   145
Still i'your Staple. I am here your friend,
On the same floor.
Fitton.   We shall be your servants.

They [CYMBAL, FITTON *and* Register] *take leave of*
PENNYBOY [JUNIOR] *and* [PENNYBOY] CANTER.

P. Junior. How dost thou like it, Founder?
P. Canter.   All is well,
But that your man o'law methinks appears not
In his due time. – O, here comes master's worship.   150

ACT I   SCENE vi

[*Enter*] PICKLOCK

[*Picklock.*] How does the heir, bright Master Pennyboy?
Is he awake yet in his one and twenty?

---

144. *creature*] creation; one who 'owes his position to a patron' (*O.E.D.* 5).
Cf. Cotgrave, '*Creature* . . . a thing made of nothing'.

I.vi.1–2.] Picklock's opening words recapitulate the start of I.iii, consolidat-
ing the play's exposition or *protasis*. The introduction of Pecunia's name and
reputation in 28f. is the signal for the beginning of an intrigue which will draw
together the plot elements of prodigal, Staple and money, forming the play's
epitasis.

Why this is better far than to wear cypress,
Dull smutting gloves or melancholy blacks,
And have a pair of twelvepenny broad ribbons   5
Laid out like labels.
P. Junior.   I should ha' made shift
To have laughed as heartily in my mourner's hood
As in this suit, if it had pleased my father
To have been buried with the trumpeters.
Picklock. The Heralds of Arms, you mean.
P. Junior.   I mean   10
All noise that is superfluous.

I.vi.0.1.] *Gifford;* PICKLOCK. PENI-BOY. IV./P. CANTER. *F.*

3. *cypress*] a light, transparent material of silk and linen, so called after its
place of origin (Linthicum, p. 119). Its black variety was often employed in
mourning, perhaps through association with the cypress tree (a traditional
symbol of grieving) and because being transparent it could be used to veil and
subdue fine clothes without totally concealing them. Linthicum says that
cypress went out of fashion at the end of James's reign.
    4. *smutting*] from v. *smut*, to blacken. *O.E.D.* has 'making black or gloomy',
citing this passage: its only example in this sense.
    5. *twelvepenny . . . ribbons*] the widest ribbon available, here used for a
hatband; 'pennybredth', or the width of an English penny, was a standard
measure of ribbon width (Linthicum, p. 283). Ribbons were associated with
festivity, and extravagantly used by gallants.
    6. *labels*] The narrow strips of cloth hanging on either side of a bishop's
mitre were known as *infulae* or labels; the word also described the ribbon
carrying the seal on a document.
    made shift] managed successfully (Kifer).
    8–11. *if . . . superfluous*] A. H. Nason (*Heralds and Heraldry*, p. 106) ex-
plicates this reference to the process technically called being 'buried with
heralds': 'To superintend the burial of nobility and gentry, to marshal the
"hatchment" of the deceased, to act as master of ceremonies at his funeral, and
to record at the Heralds' Office his name, titles, descent, marriage, and issue,
was one of the most important duties of the officers of arms. For these services,
their fees and their incidental perquisities were large, and their monopoly was
jealously guarded.' By the later years of James's reign many families were
resisting the crippling expense of such funerals; in 1604, in *Westward Ho!*,
I.ii.50–2, Dekker had made the pointed reference: 'he will follow me when he
thinks I have mony, and . . . prey upon me as Heraldes do upon Funerals'
(Bowers II.327).
    10–11.] a tetrameter followed by an alexandrine; possibly the words 'All
noise' belong to the previous line, and were misplaced by a compositor.
    11–12. *All . . . tombstone*] a sentiment that is superbly expressed by Sir
Thomas Browne in *Hydriotaphia*, Ch. V (*Works*, ed. Keynes, I. 165–6), and in
George Herbert's poem 'Church Monuments'.

Picklock.   All that idle pomp
And vanity of a tombstone, your wise father
Did by his will prevent. Your worship had –
P. Junior. A loving and obedient father of him,
I know it: a right kind-natured man   15
To die so opportunely.
Picklock.   And to settle
All things so well, compounded for your wardship
The week afore, and left your state entire
Without any charge upon't.
P. Junior.   I must needs say,
I lost an officer of him, a good bailiff,   20
And I shall want him. But all peace be with him;
I will not wish him alive again, not I,
For all my fortune. Give your worship joy
O'your new place, your emissaryship
I'the News Office.
Picklock.   Know you why I bought it, sir?   25
P. Junior. Not I.
Picklock.   To work for you and carry a mine
Against the master of it, Master Cymbal,
Who hath a plot upon a gentlewoman
Was once designed for you, sir.
P. Junior.   Me?
Picklock.   Your father,
Old Master Pennyboy of happy memory,   30

---

15. I know it;] *F;* I know it [I] *Gifford.*   a right] *Gifford;* a right, *F.*

15.] Gifford and *H.&S.* compensate for the defective second foot in this line
by inserting a bracketed [I] after *I know it.* It is possible that the comma after
right in *F* is a printer's sophistication designed to steady the line; Jonson
generally employs *right* as an adverbial intensifier when in conjunction with an
adjective (as in *M.L.*, II.iii.49). But it can also appropriately mean 'upright,
righteous'; and cf. the usage at II.Int.62.

   17. *compounded . . . wardship*] made you an allowance during your minority.

   20. *officer . . . bailiff*] P. Junior already sees his father's death as the loss of a
loyal administrator on his personal estate.

   21. *want*] miss.

   22–3. *I . . . fortune*] Cf. *The London Prodigal*, II.i.104–6: 'God be praised,
he is far enough. / He is gone a pylgrimage to Paradice, / And left me to cut a
caper against care' (*Shakespeare Apocrypha*, ed. Tucker Brooke, p. 199).

   23. *Give*] God give.

   26. *carry a mine*] work a stratagem. Cf. I.iii.30 note.

And wisdom too, as any i'the county,
Careful to find out a fit match for you
In his own lifetime (but he was prevented)
Left it in writing in a schedule here,
To be annexèd to his will, [*Shows him the document.*] that
    you,   35
His only son, upon his charge and blessing
Should take due notice of a gentlewoman
Sojourning with your uncle, Richer Pennyboy.
P. Junior. A Cornish gentlewoman, I do know her,
Mistress Pecunia Do-all.
Picklock.   A great lady   40
Indeed she is, and not of mortal race,
Infanta of the Mines: her grace's grandfather
Was duke, and cousin to the King of Ophir,
The Subterranean; let that pass. Her name is,
Or rather her three names are (for such she is)   45
Aurelia Clara Pecunia, a great princess
Of mighty power, though she live in private
With a contracted family. Her secretary –

---

34. *schedule*] codicil.
39–42. *Cornish ... Mines*] Fynes Moryson (*Itinerary*, 1617) says of Cornwall: 'The inward parts abound with a rich vaine of Metalls ... not onely
Tinne, but Gold and Silver with it, and Dyamonds formed into Angles by
nature it selfe' (p. 136). The presence of precious minerals in Cornwall was
often exaggerated; G. Abbot in *A Briefe Description of the Whole World* (1605)
judiciously explains that there is no gold there because 'the countrie standeth
too cold, neither hath it sufficient force of the Sunne to concoct and digest that
Metall' (sig. N). In *Alch.*, II.i.35–6 (Revels), Mammon resolves to use the
philosopher's stone to 'purchase Devonshire, and Cornwall, / And make them
perfect Indies!'.
40. *Pecunia Do-all*] proverbial (Tilley M1084: 'Money will do anything').
Cf. R. Barnfield, 'The Encomion of Lady Pecunia' (1598), lines 7–8: 'Goddesse
of Golde, great Empresse of the Earth, / O thou that canst doe all Thinges
under Heaven' (*Poems*, ed. Arber, p. 85).
42–4. *her ... Subterranean*] a pedigree which links Spanish riches with
mythological sources. The *King* of line 43 suggests Solomon, who fetched gold
from Ophir in I Kings, xi.28. His name was subsequently the focus of a magi-
cal tradition, and this Biblical exploit was turned into a piece of alchemical
lore, transforming base metal into gold. Ophir has been uncertainly located in
South-west Arabia, where gold mines were worked in ancient times, but the
name came to be a generalised symbol of riches.
45–6. *her ... Pecunia*] E. B. Partridge translates them as 'Golden Bright
Money' (*The Broken Compass*, p. 181). On the contemporary allusion to the
Spanish Infanta, see II.Int.24–5 note.

P. Canter. Who is her gentleman-usher too –
Picklock.   One Broker;
   And then two gentlewomen, Mistress Statute   50
   And Mistress Band, with Wax the chambermaid,
   And Mother Mortgage the old nurse, two grooms,
   Pawn and his fellow. You have not many to bribe, sir.
   The work is feasible and th'approaches easy,
   By your own kindred. Now, sir, Cymbal thinks –   55
   The master here and governor o'the Staple –
   By his fine arts and pomp of his great place
   To draw her. He concludes, she is a woman,
   And that so soon as sh'hears of the new Office
   She'll come to visit it, as they all have longings   60
   After new sights and motions. But your bounty,
   Person and bravery must achieve her.
P. Canter.   She is
   The talk o'the time! Th'adventure o'the age!
Picklock. You cannot put yourself upon an action
   Of more importance.
P. Canter.   All the world are suitors to her. 65
Picklock. All sorts of men and all professions!
P. Canter. You shall have stall-fed doctors, crammed divines
   Make love to her, and with those studièd
   And perfumed flatteries, as no room can stink

48–9. *Her ... Broker*] Jonson's allegory runs on traditional lines; cf.
Dekker, *Newes from Hell* (1606): 'of Brokers, theres a longer line of them in
hell, than there is in *London*. Marry for opening shop, & to keepe a Bawdy
house for Lady *Pecunia*' (Grosart II.137). Cf. *E.M.I.*, III.v.31–8.
   53. *Pawn ... fellow*] Who is Pawn's fellow?
   61. *motions*] shows. The word usually describes a puppet-show, or a literal
or figurative puppet. It recurs frequently in Jonson's crusade against the
mechanical parade of human folly.
   62. *bravery*] finery.
   63. *adventure*] venture.
   65. *All ... her*] Cf. the description of Lady Pecunia in William Basse,
A Helpe to Discourse (1620): 'Shee is a Lady of most matchlesse carriage, /
Wedded to none, though sought of all in marriage' (p. 256).
   66–84.] Cf. Dekker's description of 'the entertainment and receiving of
Money into the Cittie [of London], whose presence all the Citizens day and
night thirsted to behold' (*Worke for Armourours*, Grosart IV.136).
   67. *stall-fed*] i.e. fed at a trough or manger; overfed, corpulent. But Jonson
may also be satirising the pretence to erudition implied by such phrases as
'stall-learning' – knowledge acquired by the perusal of books on a stationer's

More elegant than where they are.
Picklock.   Well chanted,   70
    Old Canter, thou singst true.
P. Canter.   And (by your leave)
    Good master's worship, some of your velvet coat
    Make corpulent curtsies to her till they crack for't.
Picklock. There's Doctor Almanac woos her, one of the jeerers,
    A fine physician.
P. Canter.   Your sea-captain, Shunfield,   75
    Gives out he'll go upon the cannon for her –
Picklock. Though his loud mouthing get him little credit.
P. Canter. Young Master Piedmantle, the fine herald,
    Professes to derive her through all ages,
    From all the kings and queens that ever were.   80
Picklock. And Master Madrigal, the crownèd poet
    Of these our times, doth offer at her praises
    As fair as any, when it shall please Apollo
    That wit and rhyme may meet both in one subject.
P. Canter. And you to bear her from all these, it will be –   85
Picklock. A work of fame –
P. Canter.   Of honour –

---

76. her –] *Kifer; her. F.*

stall – to reinforce the contemptuous reference to *doctors* (i.e. academics).
There is also a glance at the process by which dignitaries (especially divines)
were 'stalled' (installed) in their official positions.
    crammed divines] Cf. Dekker, *Worke for Armorours*, p. 139: 'Some ran out of
the Church to see her, with greater devotion following her all the way she
went, then the former deitie they worshipped.' Jonson uses the same epithet in
N.I., V.i.18, 'a good crammed divine!' (Revels); de Winter argues (p. lvii) that
it is a burlesque of George Wither's satire 'Of Covetousness': 'How many also
of our grave Divines, / That should seeke treasure not in earthly Mines, /
Descend to basenesse' (*Juvenilia*, I.90; see note to line 81). Jonson's line is a
characteristically pungent version of Wither's pious thought.
    72. *some ... coat*] i.e. well-dressed lawyers.
    76. *go upon*] attack, lead an assault on. Cf. *Cat.*, I.140–3: 'bold CETHEGUS
... prais'd so into daring, as he would / Goe upon the gods'; and for the construction, cf. *T.G.V.*, II.iv.109: 'I'll die on him that says so.'
    81–4. *Madrigal ... rhyme*] De Winter suggests that here Jonson is follow-
ing up his portrayal of George Wither as Chronomastix the ambitious satirist in
the masque *Time Vindicated* (1624) with another burlesque in the shape of the
poetaster Madrigal. But Wither is only glanced at here (cf. IV.iv.168).
    84. *wit*] understanding, judgement.
    86–9. *A ... do it*] A subtle counterpoint: Picklock, stressing fame and

Picklock.   Celebration –
P. Canter. Worthy your name.
Picklock.   .   The Pennyboys to live in't.
P. Canter. It is an action you were built for, sir.
Picklock. And none but you can do it.
P. Junior.   I'll undertake it –
P. Canter. And carry it.
P. Junior.   Fear me not, for since I came   90
    Of mature age, I have had a certain itch
    In my right eye – this corner here, do you see? –
    To do some work, and worthy of a chronicle. [*Exeunt.*]

        The first Intermean after the first Act.

Mirth. How now, gossip: how does the play please you?
Censure. Very scurvily, methinks, and sufficiently naught –
Expectation. As a body would wish! Here's nothing but a
    young prodigal come of age, who makes much of the
    barber, buys him a place in a new Office, i'the air, I know   5
    not where; and his man o'law to follow him, with the
    beggar to boot, and they two help him to a wife.
Mirth. Ay, she is a proper piece, that such creatures can broke
    for!
Tattle. I cannot abide that nasty fellow, the beggar. If he had   10
    been a court-beggar in good clothes, a beggar in velvet, as

1–79.] *Italic in F.*

---

reward, anticipates the catastrophe of broken expectations, while Canter's en-
thusiasm urges P. Junior to the humiliation out of which will come repentance
and renewal.
    91–2. *I . . . eye*] P. Junior's absurdity is highlighted in an adroit recollec-
tion of Theocritus, *Idylls*, iii.37–8: 'My right eye twitches; shall I see her?' (A.
S. F. Gow, *The Greek Bucolic Poets*, p. 16) (*H.&S.*).

    I.Int.8. *piece*] (1) piece of money (as Lady Pecunia) – cf. *Lord Piece* at
II.iv.107; (2) woman. In *Volp.*, I.ii.18–19, Nano describes the transmigration
of the soul: 'From Pythagore, she went into a beautiful piece / Hight Aspasia,
the *meretrix*' (Revels). The word can mean simply 'person', but tends to have
sexual innuendo. Mirth adopts the attitude of a respectable matron to a woman
of doubtful reputation.
    broke] See note to I.vi.48–9.
    11. *a beggar in velvet*] a courtier seeking favour or employment from the
King; cf. Dekker, *The Belman of London*: 'To be a *Begger* is to be a *Braveman*,

they say, I could have endured him.

Mirth. Or a begging scholar in black; or one of these beggarly
poets, gossip, that would hang upon a young heir like a
horseleech.	15

Expectation. Or a threadbare doctor of physic, a poor quacksalver.

Censure. Or a sea-captain, half-starved.

Mirth. Ay, these were tolerable beggars, beggars of fashion.
You shall see some such anon.	20

Tattle. I would fain see the fool, gossip. The fool is the finest
man i'the company, they say, and has all the wit. He is the
very justice o'peace o'the play, and can commit whom he
will, and what he will – error, absurdity, as the toy takes
him – and no man say black is his eye, but laugh at him.	25

Mirth. But they ha' no fool i'this play, I am afraid, gossip.

Tattle. It's a wise play, then.

Expectation. They are all fools the rather in that.

Censure. Like enough.

Tattle. My husband Timothy Tattle (God rest his poor soul)	30
was wont to say, there was no play without a fool and a

---

because tis now in fashion for very brave [i.e. well dressed] men to *Beg'*
(Grosart III.88–9). But see also IV.Int.51 note.

16–17. *quacksalver*] Cf. Dekker on '*Quack-salving Empericks*, who . . .
clappe up their *Terrible Billes*, in the Market-place, and filling the Paper with
such horrible names of *diseases*, as if every disease were a Divell, and that they
could conjure them out of any Towne at their pleasure. Yet these Beggerly
Mountibancks are meare Coozeners, and have not so much skill as *Horseleeches'*
(*Lanthorne & Candle-Light*, Grosart III.293). Quacks were often compared to
horseleeches, and Mirth's preceding speech perhaps prompts Expectation's
remark.

18.] An Act of 1597–8 decreed that 'all seafaring men pretending losses of
their shippes or goods on the sea going about the Country begging' would be
banished or sent to the galleys (39 *Eliz.*, cap. 4).

21–2. *fool . . . wit*] Though no specific reference need be intended, it is
possible that Tattle alludes to William Rowley, who specialised in clown-roles
for the King's Men from 1624 until his death in February 1626 (the same
month as the first performance of *Staple*: see Bentley II.556–7). See III.ii.205–
6 note. Mirth, better informed than Tattle, might find in Rowley's demise an
explanation as to why there is no fool in the play.

24. *toy*] whim.

25. *no . . . eye*] proverbial (Tilley E252): 'you cannot say black is his eye'; de
Winter glosses from Ray's *Collection of English Proverbs*: 'you can find no fault
in him, charge him with no crime.'

devil in't; he was for the devil still, God bless him. The
devil for his money, would he say, 'I would fain see the
devil.' 'And why would you so fain see the devil?' would I
say. 'Because he has horns, wife, and may be a cuckold as   35
well as a devil,' he would answer. 'You are e'en such
another, husband,' quoth I; 'was the devil ever married?
Where do you read the devil was ever so honourable to
commit matrimony?' 'The play will tell us that,' says he.
'We'll go see't tomorrow: *The Devil is an Ass.* He is an   40
arrant learn'd man that made it, and can write, they say,
and I am foully deceived but he can read too.'
Mirth. I remember it, gossip, I went with you. By the same
    token, Mistress Trouble-truth dissuaded us, and told us he
    was a profane poet and all his plays had devils in them.   45
    That he kept school upo' the stage, could conjure there,

31–2. *no ... in't*] Gifford cites John Gee, *The Foot out of the Snare* (1624),
p. 68: 'It was wont, when an Enterlude was to bee acted in a Countrey-Towne,
the first question that an Hob-naile Spectator made, before hee would pay his
penny to get in, was, *Whether there bee a Divell and a foole in the play?* And if
the Foole get upon the Divels backe, and beate him with his Cox-combe til he
rore, the play is compleate.' Cf. the prologue to Shirley's *The Doubtful Heir*,
which mocks the unsophisticated Globe audience by pointing out that the play
has 'No clown, no squibs, no Devill in't; oh now / You Squirrels that want
Nuts, what will you do?' (*Works* 1833, IV.279).
    35–9. *Because ... matrimony*] In all likelihood the gossips would know of
the devil's matrimonial adventures from the play *Grim the Collier of Croydon*
(*c.* 1600), in which a junior fiend named Belphagor is sent from Hell to investi-
gate the conduct of women, makes a disastrous marriage, and returns below
to be asked 'what new shapes are those upon thy Head?' Pluto thenceforth
decrees that 'All Devils shall, as thou dost like horns wear' (*Tudor Facsimile
Texts*, 37, 1912, pp. 56–7). The story was Italian in origin, was popularised by
Machiavelli, and reappears in *The Thomason Tracts* for 1647 (E.408); it was
doubtless part of an earlier pamphlet literature in England.
    40. *We'll ... Ass*] Cf. *D.A.*, I.iv.21–2. Being also a proverbial expression
(Tilley D242), the title of Jonson's play is redolent of a traditional popular
drama favoured by the gossips.
    42. *he ... too*] perhaps a wry recollection of Tucca's gibe at Horace-Jonson
in Dekker's *Satiromastix*: 'read, *lege*, save thy selfe and read' (IV.i.136; Bowers
I.351), which in turn alludes to Jonson's escape from hanging in 1598, after
killing his fellow-actor Spencer, by pleading benefit of clergy. Several references to this episode in Dekker's play probably helped to make it standard
popular gossip about Jonson.
    44. *dissuaded us*] discouraged us from going.
    46–7. *kept ... Westminster*] This allusion to boy-actors is clarified in
III.Int.42–7.

above the School of Westminster and Doctor Lamb too.
Not a play he made but had a devil in it. And that he would
learn us all to make our husbands cuckolds at plays. By
another token, that a young married wife i'the company   50
said she could find in her heart to steal thither and see a
little o'the vanity through her mask, and come practise at
home.
Tattle. O, it was Mistress –
Mirth. Nay, gossip, I name nobody. It may be 'twas myself.   55
Expectation. But was the devil a proper man, gossip?
Mirth. As fine a gentleman of his inches as ever I saw trusted to
the stage, or anywhere else, and loved the commonwealth
as well as e'er a patriot of 'em all. He would carry away the
Vice on his back quick to hell in every play where he came,   60
and reform abuses.
Expectation. There was the Devil of Edmonton: no such man, I
warrant you.
Censure. The conjurer cozened him with a candle's end. He
was an ass.   65

---

47. *Doctor Lamb*] an astrologer of considerable notoriety at this time. In
1608 he was gaoled for 'damnable invocation and worship of evill Spirits'
(p. 3), but allowed to receive his clients in prison, which led to a conviction for
child-rape in 1623. Pardoned and released, he was savagely attacked by a
London mob in June 1628 and died the following day (*A Briefe Description of
. . . John Lambe* (1628), *S.T.C.* 15177).

49–53. *learn . . . home*] a standard argument against dramatic representation; cf. Prynne, *Histriomastix*, Part I, p. 386: 'Hee who shall but seriously
consider those amorous smiles . . . adulterous kisses and embracements . . .
which attend and set out Stage-playes; must needs acknowledge; that they are
. . . *the occasions of real* whoredoms, incests, adulteries'.

57. *gentleman . . . inches*] upstanding fellow.

59. *patriot*] 'pejorative name for a shifting group of members of Parliament
who were critics or opponents of the Crown and active champions of liberties'
(Kifer).

62. *Devil of Edmonton*] The hugely popular anonymous comedy *The Merry
Devil of Edmonton* went into a fourth edition in 1626.

64. *conjurer . . . end*] This incident does not occur in the extant (1608) version of the play, but its survival in a prose version by T. Brewer, *The Life and
Death of the Merry Devill of Edmonton* (entered 1608) suggests that it was
originally part of the Faustian pact with which the play opens. Peter Fabel the
conjurer agrees to let the devil have his soul when a candle-end in his study
burns down; he then extinguishes the candle and pockets it for safe keeping
(sig. A4v-B).

Mirth. But there was one Smug, a smith, would have made a
   horse laugh and broke his halter, as they say.

Tattle. O, but the poor man had got a shrewd mischance one
   day.

Expectation. How, gossip?   70

Tattle. He had dressed a rogue jade i'the morning that had the
   staggers, and had got such a spice of 'em himself by noon
   as they would not away all the play time, do what he could
   for his heart.

Mirth. 'Twas his part, gossip. He was to be drunk by his part.   75

Tattle. Say you so? I understood not so much.

Expectation. Would we had such another part and such a man
   in this play. I fear 'twill be an excellent dull thing.

Censure. Expect, intend it.

   66–7. *Smug ... laugh*] the tippling clown of *The Merry Devil*, who in the
prose version is 'of many set by for my mirth' (sig. A3).

   72. *staggers*] disease of domestic animals of which a staggering gait is a
symptom (*O.E.D.*).

   spice] dose. 'This reeling infirmity, threw poore *Smug* from poste to poste
and from wall to wall ... till halfe the wilde blood in his body, was runne out
at his nose' (*Life and Death*, B4v).

   73. *all ... time*] throughout the performance.

   79. *intend*] attend to. Censure sees the actors coming on again.

Act II

[*Enter*] PENNYBOY SEN[IOR], PECUNIA, MORTGAGE, STATUTE, BAND
[*and*] BROKER.

[*P. Senior.*] Your grace is sad, methinks, and melancholy.
You do not look upon me with that face
As you were wont, my goddess, bright Pecunia.
Although your grace be fall'n off two i'the hundred
In vulgar estimation, yet am I   5
Your grace's servant still, and teach this body
To bend and these my aged knees to buckle
In adoration and just worship of you. [*He kneels.*]
Indeed, I do confess, I have no shape
To make a minion of, but I'm your martyr,   10
Your grace's martyr. I can hear the rogues,
As I do walk the streets, whisper and point,
'There goes old Pennyboy, the slave of money,
Rich Pennyboy, Lady Pecunia's drudge,
A sordid rascal, one that never made   15

II.i] *A Room in* Pennyboy *senior's House. Gifford.*   4. fall'n off] *Gifford;*
falne, of *F*.

II.i.2. *face*] punning on the obverse or head of a coin, and hence a slang
expression for the coin itself. (Queen Money is 'brightest-facde Lady' in
Dekker's *Worke for Armorours*; Grosart IV.135). The play's idiosyncratic brand
of dramatic allegory is immediately arresting.
    4.] The old maximum interest rate of 10 percent was cut to 8 percent in
1624, in response to arguments like Culpeper's *A Tract against Usurie* (1621)
that 'the high rate of Usury' discouraged trade (unprofitable because it paid no
more than the standard rate of interest) and put England at a disadvantage with
foreign neighbours whose rate was rarely more than 6 percent.
    10. *minion*] favourite, lover. Pecunia's ability to enslave rich old men is a
commonplace of moralistic literature at this time (e.g. Barnfield, *Encomion of
Lady Pecunia*: 'Shee, loves olde men; but young men she rejects; / Because to
her, their Love is quicklie colde' (*Poems*, p. 86). But Jonson is careful to avoid
committing her to voluntary participation in an unattractive liaison.
    15–16. *one ... sleep*] De Winter detects an allusion to 'the old saying' that
'beggars and misers may feast in their dreams'; I have not traced the proverb in
this form, but cf. Tilley D589, 'Golden dreams make men wake hungry'.

Good meal in his sleep but sells the acates are sent him,
Fish, fowl and venison, and preserves himself,
Like an old hoary rat, with mouldy pie crust.'
This I do hear, rejoicing I can suffer
This, and much more, for your good grace's sake.   20
Pecunia. Why do you so, my guardian? I not bid you.
Cannot my grace be gotten, and held too,
Without your self-tormentings and your watches,
Your macerating of your body thus
With cares and scantings of your diet and rest?   25
P. Senior. O no! Your services, my princely lady,
Cannot with too much zeal of rites be done:
They are so sacred.
Pecunia.   But my reputation
May suffer, and the worship of my family,
When by so servile means they both are sought.   30
P. Senior. You are a noble, young, free, gracious lady,
And would be everybody's in your bounty;
But you must not be so. They are a few
That know your merit, lady, and can value't.
Yourself scarce understands your proper powers.   35
They are almighty, and that we, your servants,
That have the honour here to stand so near you,
Know, and can use too. All this nether world

---

16. Good ... sells] *F*; Good meal but in his sleep, sells *conj. Nares, cited by*
H.&S.

---

16. *acates*] delicacies, dainty provisions.
16–18. *but ... crust*] Gifford thought that Pope, in his *Imitation of Horace,*
Sat. II.ii.51–2, 'has very happily transferred this (for he did not find it in
Horace) to the character of Avidienus', the miser who with his wife 'Sell their
presented Partridges, and Fruits, / And humbly live on rabbits and on roots'
(*Poems*, ed. Butt, IV.59). But it is possible that another classical source lies
behind both passages.
22. *grace*] favour. Pecunia's admonishment infuses didactic vigour into her
otherwise static and emblematic role.
24. *macerating*] wasting.
35. *proper*] inherent, native.
36–9. *They ... yours*] Cf. *Volp.*, I.i.21–7 (Revels), and Parsimonie's address to Queen Money in Dekker's *Worke for Armorours*: 'O Sacred *Money!*
Queene of Kingdomes, Mistres over the mines of Gold and Silver, Regent of
the whole world' (Grosart IV.135).
38. *use*] exploit (with a pun on 'usury').

Is yours, you command it and do sway it,
The honour of it and the honesty,   40
The reputation – ay, and the religion
(I was about to say, and had not erred)
Is Queen Pecunia's. For that style is yours
If mortals knew your grace, or their own good.
Mortgage. Please your grace to retire.
Band.   I fear your grace   45
Hath ta'en too much of the sharp air.
Pecunia.   O no!
I could endure to take a great deal more
(And with my constitution) were it left
Unto my choice. What think you of it, Statute?
Statute. A little now and then does well, and keeps   50
Your grace in your complexion.
Band.   And true temper.
Mortgage. But too much, madam, may increase cold rheums,
Nourish catarrhs, green sicknesses and agues,
And put you in consumption.
P. Senior.   Best to take
Advice of your grave women, noble madam.   55
They know the state o'your body, and ha' studied
Your grace's health.
Band.   And honour: here'll be visitants

40–3. *The* ... *Pecunia's*] H.&S. cite Horace, *Epistles*, I.vi.36–7: 'Of
course a wife and dowry, credit and friends, birth and beauty, are the gift of
Queen Cash [*regina Pecunia donat*]' (Loeb ed., p. 289); and Gifford found a
parallel in Aristophanes' *Ploutos*, 141–6, where the god of money is told of his
importance. The latter parallel is not very exact, however, and there is a considerable difference in tone. When Burton talks of 'the goddess we adore *Dea
Moneta*, Queen Money', he refers back to Sallust, *The War with Jugurtha*:
'only a few hold their honour dearer than gold' (Loeb ed., p. 169; *Anat. of
Melancholy*, Everyman ed., I.65).
    41. *religion*] perhaps recalling the word's original sense of a 'bond', that
which holds society together.
    43. *style*] title.
    51. *complexion*] good health.
    52. *increase* ... *rheums*] give you a cold (*rheums* = discharges).
    53. *green sicknesses*] anaemic disorder to which young unmarried women
were thought especially prone. But Pecunia's robustness is apparent from her
demeanour, and we quickly associate such maladies not with exposure but
rather with the miser's reluctance to let her circulate.
    agues] fevers.

Or suitors by and by, and 'tis not fit
They find you here.
Statute.   'Twill make your grace too cheap
To give them audience presently.
Mortgage. [*Leading Pecunia away.*]   Leave your secretary   60
To answer them.
Pecunia.   Wait you here, Broker.
Broker.   I shall, madam,
And do your grace's trusts with diligence.
[*Exeunt all but* BROKER.]

ACT II   SCENE ii

[*Enter*] PIEDMANTLE

[*Piedmantle.*] What luck's this? I am come an inch too late.
[*Seeing Broker.*] Do you hear, sir? Is your worship o'the
family
Unto the lady Pecunia?
Broker.   I serve her grace, sir,
Aurelia Clara Pecunia, the Infanta.
Piedmantle. Has she all those titles, and 'her grace' besides?   5
I must correct that ignorance and oversight
Before I do present. Sir, I have drawn
A pedigree for her grace, though yet a novice
In that so noble study.

II.ii.0.1.] *Gifford;* PYED-MANTLE. BROKER. / PENI-BOY. SEN. *F.*   2.
S.D.] *This ed.*

60. *presently*] immediately. Cf. Nathaniel's counsel at I.iv.20, promoting
the interests of the News Staple. Pecunia, like news, is being made the creature of a public relations outfit dedicated to profit, but her attendants are less
obviously disreputable, and, as purely allegorical characters, representative of
processes that may be turned to good later in the play.

II.ii.7. *present*] appear, present myself; with a suggestion perhaps of 'give
her (the pedigree)'. Jonson's only other absolute use of *present* is in *Volp.*,
III.v.12 (Revels): 'Has she presented?', where Mosca asks Volpone if Lady
Politic has made him a gift before leaving.
9. *noble study*] Jonson's knowledge of and reverence for heraldry are well
known, but here he is also attacking its considerable abuse under James I.
Henry Peacham wrote in 1622: 'the most common and worst of all, is in all
places the ordinary purchasing of Armes and Honors for Money, very pre-

Broker.   A Herald at Arms?
Piedmantle. No, sir, a pursuivant. My name is Piedmantle.   10
Broker. Good Master Piedmantle.
Piedmantle.   I have deduced her –
Broker. From all the Spanish mines in the West Indies,
  I hope, for she comes that way by her mother.
  But by her grandmother she's Duchess of Mines.
Piedmantle. From man's creation I have brought her.
Broker.   No further?   15
  Before, sir, long before: you have done nothing, else.
  Your Mines were before Adam. Search your office,
  Roll five and twenty, you will find it so.
  I see you are but a novice, Master Piedmantle,
  If you had not told me so.

  [*Enter* PENNYBOY SENIOR *behind, concealing himself.*]

Piedmantle.   Sir, an apprentice   20
  In armory. I have read *The Elements*

20. S.D.] *This ed.*

---

judiciall to true Nobilitie' (*The Compleat Gentleman*, p. 16). See note to lines
21–2 below. In Jonson's play money itself acquires a pedigree.
    10. *Piedmantle*] The burlesque of 'Blue Mantle' (see *Persons of the Play*,
note 10) clearly calls for a motley costume.
    11. *deduced her*] traced her lineage. Cf. Earle, *Microcosmographie*, 'A Herald':
'He seemes very rich in discourse, for he tels you of whole fields of Gold and
Silver, O'r & Argent, worth much in French, but in English nothing' (sig.
M10). In these spurious demonstrations of Pecunia's name and fame Jonson
capitalises on contemporary hostility to Spanish wealth (and to the recent plan
to marry Prince Charles to the Spanish Infanta); but once again his original
inspiration is Horace's comment on worldly vanity: *genus et formam regina
Pecunia donat* (see II.i.40–3 note).
    17. *Your ... Adam*] a common idea, expressed by Thomas Tymme in his
Dialogue Philosophicall (1612): 'the Earth ... hath ... minerals, and mettals
in such plenty, that it may seeme a store-house of infinite riches, ordained by
God, for man, for whom he prepared this habitacle before he created him'
(p. 57). A more ambivalent view emerges from *Helicon Reformed* (1617), describing the Creation: 'Mettals and gemms under each shore and hill, / Thou
close did couch, for use to the world's end, / When man would more on meanes
then God depend' (p. 6).
    Mines] Broker's fancy transforms the mines into a family dynasty.
    18. *Roll ... twenty*] i.e. of the records of the College of Heralds. Broker's
precise reference is clearly facetious, and used by Jonson to contrive a mis-
chievous parallel to the 'rolls and files' (I.v.5) of the news office.
    20. S.D.] This may be unnecessary; P. Senior's eavesdropping does not

And *Accidence* and all the leading books,
And I have now upon me a great ambition
How to be brought to her grace to kiss her hands.
Broker. Why, if you have acquaintance with Mistress Statute   25
Or Mistress Band, my lady's gentlewomen,
They can induce you. One is a judge's daughter
But somewhat stately; th'other, Mistress Band,
Her father's but a scrivener, but she can
Almost as much with my lady as the other,   30
Especially if Rose Wax the chambermaid
Be willing. Do you not know her, sir, neither?
Piedmantle. No, in troth, sir.
Broker.   ·   She's a good pliant wench
And easy to be wrought, sir. But the nurse,
Old Mother Mortgage, if you have a tenement   35
Or such a morsel? – Though she have no teeth,

---

have to be known to the audience before he 'leaps out' at line 63, presumably
from behind the hangings in the centre doorway. But see 40–1 note.

21. *armory*] 'that division of the science of heraldry that deals with the
blazoning and marshalling of arms' (Nason, *Heralds & Heraldry*, p. 108).

21–2. The ... Accidence] The former volume, *The Elements of Armories*,
was by Jonson's friend Edmund Bolton; published in 1610, it carried a com-
mendatory preface by Camden. Of the latter, *The Accidence of Armory* by
Gerard Leigh, which went through seven editions from 1562 to 1612, Nason
claims that 'for the spirit of the heraldry of Jonson's day, its mystery, its sham,
its learned ignorance, we need seek no more representative work' (p. 12).

23–4. *ambition / How*] The construction is intelligible but awkward; Jonson
may have had in mind the specialised sense derived from Lat. *ambire*, to go
round or about (see *O.E.D.* headnote). The herald turns over in his mind all
possible ways of gaining an audience; he may also attempt a bribe at this point:
see lines 40–1 below.

26. *Band*] i.e. a legal deed or agreement, duly sealed (see lines 31–2); cf.
the modern 'bond'.

27. *induce*] introduce.

28. *stately*] standoffish, haughty. Not otherwise used by Jonson in this
sense.

29. *can*] i.e. exert influence.

31. *Rose Wax*] alluding to the normal colour of sealing wax (de Winter).

35. *tenement*] strictly, 'a portion of a house tenanted as a separate dwelling'
(*O.E.D.*); although it is a suitable bribe for Mortgage, the mention of property
rather labours the allegory. Perhaps it is intended to underline Broker's mock-
ingly formal treatment of the herald in this scene.

36–8.] Jonson vividly associates Mortgage's decrepitude with moral pli-
ability and a vulgar lack of discrimination.

She loves a sweetmeat, anything that melts
In her warm gums. She could command it for you
On such a trifle, a toy. Sir, you may see
How for your love, and this so pure complexion	40
(A perfect sanguine) I ha' ventured thus,
The straining of a ward, opening a door
Into the secrets of our family.
Piedmantle. I pray you let me know, sir, unto whom
I am so much beholden; but your name?	45
Broker. My name is Broker. I am secretary
And usher to her grace.
Piedmantle. [*Bowing to him.*] Good Master Broker!
Broker. Good Master Piedmantle!
Piedmantle. [*Hinting.*]	Why, you could do me,
If you would now, this favour of yourself.
Broker. Truly, I think I could. But if I would,	50
I hardly should, without or Mistress Band
Or Mistress Statute please to appear in it,
Or the good nurse I told you of, Mistress Mortgage.
We know our places here. We mingle not
One in another's sphere, but all move orderly	55
In our own orbs; yet we are all concentrics.

40–1. *this . . . sanguine*] Much discussed; the best explanation is by L. L. Mills (*N.&Q.* 212 (1967), 208–9), who argues that Broker's helpfulness at this point is the direct result of a bribe, and that the phrase *A perfect sanguine*, coupled with the indicative *this* (line 40) refers to a coin, which has perhaps changed hands at lines 23–4 as Piedmantle solicits information: Broker holds it up and points out that he has given solid advice for it. (The word *complexion* is used in its modern sense of 'tinge'; pure gold was often referred to as 'red' in Jonson's day, and Mills compares the phrase 'the colour of your money'.) The rather cryptic quality of Broker's speech might be explained by his catching sight of Pennyboy Senior as the latter hides himself (at line 20 in this ed.) to eavesdrop on the conversation. Thus Broker is playing a dangerous double game, accepting Piedmantle's bribe whilst appearing to shun his advances, for which, ironically, he is congratulated by the usurer at line 64.

42. *straining . . . ward*] stretching a point (being so open about matters within my charge); *ward* can mean 'guardianship' or simply 'care', and it also implies a space or boundary to be protected. The hint of fortification and relaxed defences recalls I.iii.26–31.

45. *but . . . name*] do tell me your name.

56. *are . . . concentrics*] all revolve around Pecunia (Kifer).

Piedmantle. Well, sir, I'll wait a better season.
Broker.   Do,
    And study the right means. Get Mistress Band
    To urge on your behalf, or little Wax.
        Broker makes a mouth at him.
Piedmantle. I have a hope, sir, that I may by chance   60
    Light on her grace as she's taking the air.
Broker. That air of hope has blasted many an aerie
    Of kastrils like yourself, good Master Piedmantle.
            He jeers him again. [*Exit* PIEDMANTLE.]
            Old Pennyboy leaps [*out.*]
P. Senior. Well said, Master Secretary. I stood behind
    And heard thee all. I honour thy dispatches.   65
    If they be rude, untrainèd in our method
    And have not studied the rule, dismiss 'em quickly.
    Where's Lickfinger my cook, that unctuous rascal?
    He'll never keep his hour, that vessel of kitchen stuff!

---

62. aerie] ayrie *F;* aiery *Whalley.*   63. kastrils] Castrills *F;* kestrels *Kifer.*

59.1. *makes a mouth*] pulls a face, silently jeers. Perhaps Broker combines
his 'mouth' with his last two words, implying that Piedmantle must stoop low
for assistance.
    61. *Light on*] chance on, happen to meet; but Broker takes the phrase in a
predatory sense.
    62. *aerie*] nest of bird of prey (Jonson's spelling 'ayrie' puns on 'ayre' in the
same line in *F*). See collation. Cf. III.iv.43–4, and for another perspective on
hawking, see *Ep.* 85, 'To Sir Henry Goodyere', where it is a lesson to men in
how 'to strike ignorance' and 'make the fool their quarry' (7, 10). In *Staple*,
however, as often in his plays, Jonson relies on fools and knaves to prey on
each other.
    63. *kastrils*] small hawks – but also used contemptuously of persons (per-
haps with a pun on 'coistrel', a cowardly knave). *O.E.D.* gives the word only
as the obsolete form of 'kestrel', but I have retained the old spelling since in
Jacobean parlance it commonly identifies a troublemaker, like Kastril the
'angry boy' in *Alch.,* or those referred to in *S.W.,* IV.iv.192–3: 'What a cast of
kastrils are these, to hawke after ladies, thus?'.
    65. *honour . . . dispatches*] i.e. I approve of the way you get rid of them.
    68. *unctuous*] greasy, fat (used of meat). Cf. *Alch.,* II.ii.83–4: 'the swelling
unctuous paps / Of a fat pregnant sow' (Revels ed.).
    69. *kitchen stuff*] dripping; general refuse from cooking. The allusion is
obviously to Lickfinger's girth.

ACT II SCENE iii

[*Enter*] LICKFINGER

[*Broker.*] Here he is come, sir.
P. Senior.   Pox upon him, kidney,
   Always too late!
Lickfinger.   To wish 'em you, I confess,
   That ha' them already.
P. Senior.   What?
Lickfinger.   The pox!
P. Senior.   The piles,
   The plague and all diseases light on him
   Knows not to keep his word. I'd keep my word sure!   5
   I hate that man that will not keep his word.
   When did I break my word?
Lickfinger.   Or I, till now?
   And 'tis but half an hour.
P. Senior.   Half a year,
   To me that stands upon a minute of time.
   I am a just man. I love still to be just.   10
Lickfinger. Why, do you think I can run like light-foot Ralph,

---

II.iii.0.1.] *Gifford;* BROKER. PENY-BOY. SE. / LICK-FINGER. *F.*

II.iii.1–2. *Pox* . . . *'em*] The plural agrees with 'pocks' – usually referring to
the ravages of syphilis, and thus a term for the disease itself. It could also
appropriately describe the effects of smallpox.
   kidney] A common term for 'disposition' or 'temperament' (cf. *Wiv.*,
III.v.105: 'a man of my kidney'), which underlines Lickfinger's associations
with the kitchen.
   5. *sure*] without fail.
   9. *stands upon*] attaches great importance to, sets store by. Cf. *Cor.*,
IV.vi.97–9, where Menenius derides the tribunes 'that stood so much / Upon
the voice of occupation'.
   10. *just*] exact (as at I.v.106); but also anticipating his claim at line 45 to be
'for justice'.
   still] always.
   11. *light-foot Ralph*] *H.&S.* compare Lady Bedford's runner Ralph, 'The
Countess's man who won the race', in *U.V.* 47 (marginal note); Donaldson
cites Aubrey: 'The king was mighty inquisitive to know who this Ralph was:
Ben told him 'twas the drawer at the Swan tavern by Charing Cross, who drew
him good Canary. For this drollery his majesty gave him an hundred pounds'
(*Brief Lives*, ed. Dick, p. 179).

Or keep a wheelbarrow with a sail in town here
To whirl me to you? I have lost two stone
Of suet i'the service posting hither.
You might have followed me like a watering pot   15
And seen the knots I made along the street.
My face dropped like the skimmer in a fritter pan,
And my whole body is yet (to say the truth)
A roasted pound of butter with grated bread in't!
        He sweeps his face.
P. *Senior.* Believe you he that list. You stayed of purpose,   20
To have my venison stink and my fowl mortified,
That you might ha' 'em –
Lickfinger.   A shilling or two cheaper:
That's your jealousy.
P. *Senior.*   Perhaps it is.
Will you go in, and view and value all?
Yonder is venison sent me, fowl, and fish,   25

13–16. *I . . . street*] Cf. Ursula in *B.F.*, II.ii.51–2, 'I do water the ground in
knots as I go', and 80–1, 'I feel myself dropping already . . . two stone o'suet
a day is my proportion' (Revels). Also Dekker, *The Wonderfull Yeare*: 'My
gorbelly Host . . . out of the house he wallowed presently, being followed with
two or three dozen of napkins to drie up the larde, that ranne so fast downe his
heeles, that all the way he went, was more greazie than a kitchin-stuffe-wifes
basket' (Grosart I.140).

17. *dropped . . . skimmer*] i.e. ran with sweat just as a skimmer drips oil.
A *skimmer* was a shallow utensil, usually perforated, used to skim liquids
(*O.E.D.*).

19.] 'To roast a pound of Butter curiously and well, you shall take a pound
of sweet Butter and beate it stiffe with sugar, and the yolkes of egges; then clap
it round-wise about a spit, and lay it before a soft fire; and presently dredge it
with . . . fine bread crummes, currants, sugar and salt mixt together . . . till the
butter be overcommed and no more wil melt . . .; then roast it browne . . . and
serve it out' (G. Markham, *Country Contentments* (1615), p. 58).

19.1. *sweeps*] wipes.

20. *list*] chooses.

21. *mortified*] decayed. To 'mortify' a bird was to hang it until it is tender
and thus more appetising, but P. Senior is blind to such gastronomic subtle-
ties, which Fynes Moryson, *Itinerary* (1617), III.iii.2, says are a French preserve: 'the French alone delight in mortified meates' (p. 134).

23. *jealousy*] suspicion.

25–6.] P. Senior's lack of vigorous appetite makes a simple point about his
miserliness, but the repeated abhorrence of this *senex iratus* to game meats and
fowl may have a point of reference in Elyot's *The Castel of Helth* (1541 – 44? –
ed.): 'To them whiche be coleryke, being in there natural temperature . . .

THE STAPLE OF NEWS

In such abundance I am sick to see it!
I wonder what they mean; I ha' told 'em of it.
To burden a weak stomach, and provoke
A dying appetite, thrust a sin upon me
I ne'er was guilty of. Nothing but gluttony,   30
Gross gluttony, that will undo this land!
Lickfinger. And 'bating two i'the hundred.
P. Senior.   Ay, that same's
A crying sin, a fearful damned device
Eats up the poor, devours 'em –
Lickfinger.   Sir, take heed
What you give out.
P. Senior.   Against your grave great Solons?   35
Numae Pompilii, they that made that law
To take away the poor's inheritance?
It was their portion: I will stand to't.
And they have robbed 'em of it, plainly robbed 'em.
I still am a just man, I tell the truth.   40
When monies went at ten i'the hundred, I,
And such as I, the servants of Pecunia,
Could spare the poor two out of ten, and did it.
How say you, Broker?

---

32. 'bating] *Kifer;* bating *F.*

grosse meates moderately taken, be more convenient, than the meates that be
fyne, and better shal they digest a piece of good biefe, than a chickens legge'
(fol. 72r).
   32. *'bating*] abating, reducing.
   33–4. *a . . . poor*] The objection that reducing the interest rate would mean
'that money will bee harder to come by' had been anticipated by Culpeper (*A
Tract against Usurie*): 'it were true, if the high rate of Usurie did increase
money within this Land; but the high rate . . . doth inrich onely the Usurer,
and impoverish the Kingdome . . . ; and it is the plenty of money within the
Land that maketh money easie to be borrowed' (pp. 10, 14).
   35. *give out*] say aloud, broadcast. P. Senior's complaint strikes a quasi-
populist note which would not go down well with the authorities.
   Solons] Solon was the lawgiver of Athens in the fifth century B.C.; his name
became synonymous with wise legislation and rule.
   36. *Numae Pompilii*] According to legend, Numa Pompilius succeeded
Romulus as king of Rome; his name became a byword for wise and stable
government. P. Senior's disparaging of authority becomes in Jonson's scheme
a comment on his lack of the civic virtues.
   38. *portion*] due.

Lickfinger. [*Aside.*]   Ask your echo.
Broker.   You did it.
P. Senior. I am for justice. When did I leave justice?   45
We knew 'twas theirs, they'd right and title to't.
Now –
Lickfinger. You can spare 'em nothing.
P. Senior.   Very little . . .
Lickfinger. As good as nothing.
P. Senior.   They have bound our hands
With their wise solemn act, shortened our arms.
Lickfinger. Beware those worshipful ears, sir, be not shortened,   50
And you play crop i'the Fleet if you use this licence.
P. Senior. What licence, knave? [*Threatening him.*] Informer?
Lickfinger.   I am Lickfinger,
Your cook.
P. Senior.   A saucy Jack you are, that's once.
What said I, Broker?
Broker.   Nothing that I heard, sir.
Lickfinger. I know his gift. He can be deaf when he list.   55
P. Senior. Ha' you provided me my bushel of eggs
I did bespeak – I do not care how stale
Or stinking that they be, let 'em be rotten –
For ammunition here to pelt the boys
That break my windows?
Lickfinger.   Yes, sir, I ha' spared 'em   60
Out of the custard politic for you, the Mayor's.
P. Senior. 'Tis well. Go in, take hence all that excess,

44. *Aside* . . . echo.] *Kifer;* (Ask your *Eccho*) *F.*   46. they'd] they'had *F.*
52. S.D.] *This ed.*

---

48. *As* . . . *nothing*] Lickfinger's satiric prodding is remorseless, establishing
him as a significant opponent and antithesis to the miser.
    51. *play* . . . *Fleet*] have your ears cropped in the Fleet Prison. Jonson him-
self was supposedly threatened with this punishment in 1605 for satirising the
King in *E.H.*
    53. *Jack*] knave. A pun on 'Jack Sauce' (a glutton) may be intended; *H.&S.*
compare *T.T.*, III.iii.47. Cf. John Taylor, *Jacke-a-Lent*: 'Jack Sawce (the
worst knave amongst the pack.)' (*Workes* 1630, L3).
    that's once] that settles it.
    56. *bushel*] eight gallon measure of capacity, used for corn, fruit etc.
(*O.E.D.*).
    61. *custard* . . . *Mayor's*] It was the custom at the Lord Mayor's feast in
London for a jester to leap into an enormous bowl of custard. Cf. *D.A.*, I.i.97.

Make what you can of it, your best. And when
I have friends that I invite at home, provide me
Such, such and such a dish, as I bespeak;   65
One at a time, no superfluity.
Or if you have it not, return me money.
You know my ways.
Lickfinger.   They are a little crooked.
P. Senior. How, knave?
Lickfinger.   Because you do indent.
P. Senior.   'Tis true, sir.
I do indent you shall return me money.   70
Lickfinger. Rather than meat, I know it. You are just still.
P. Senior. I love it still. And therefore if you spend
The red-deer pies i'your house, or sell 'em forth, sir,
Cast so that I may have their coffins all
Returned here and piled up. I would be thought   75
To keep some kind of house.
Lickfinger.   By the mouldy signs?

---

63. your] *F;* you're *Kifer.*   76. signs?] *F;* signs! *Gifford.*

63. *your best*] See collation. Kifer's modernisation (which in effect emends the text) is perfectly defensible, and in keeping with P. Senior's admonitory tone: 'you'd better produce something worthwhile'. But *your best* is a familiar enough idiom (see *O.E.D.* 8, examples from this period) and appends a laconic and hard-bitten demand to the speech, one which acknowledges Lickfinger's talents in a suitably terse, grudging manner.

69. *indent*] 'A pun on the toothed or wavy line which 1) marked off the two halves of a legal document drawn up in duplicate, 2) formed the cut edge of two such separate documents: hence the use to express drawing up the documents, and finally to enter upon an agreement' (*H.&S.*).

71. *You . . . still*] a telling riposte to P. Senior's earlier claim (line 40) to be generous in his dealings.

72. *spend*] consume.

74. *Cast*] arrange it.

coffins] crusts of pies. The comparison between pie and sepulchre was fairly common, as Anne Lancashire points out in her Revels ed. of *The Second Maiden's Tragedy*, note to IV.iii.129–33, where it is used to make the same point as Jonson's. Cunningham cites a story about Queen Elizabeth at table ridiculing this use of 'coffin', but Markham (*Country Contentments*, p. 65) perhaps throws light on the origins of the comparison when he says that red deer venison should be 'bak't in a moist, thicke, tough, course and long lasting crust'.

76. *mouldy*] punning on 'mould' as (*a*) the moulded pie-crust, and (*b*) the earth of a grave; Lickfinger asks, in effect, 'are you going to advertise the fact that your house is a sepulchre?'

P. Senior. And then remember meat for my two dogs:
　　Fat flaps of mutton, kidneys, rumps of veal,
　　Good plenteous scraps. My maid shall eat the relics.
Lickfinger. When you and your dogs have dined! – A sweet
　　reversion.　　　　　　　　　　　　　　　　　80

　　　[*Enter*] FITTON, ALMANAC, SHUNFIELD [*and*] MADRIGAL.

P. Senior. Who's here? My courtier, and my little doctor?
　　My muster-master? [*Sees Madrigal.*] And what plover's
　　　that
　　They have brought to pull?
Broker.　　　　　　　　I know not; some green plover.
　　I'll find him out.
P. Senior.　　　　　Do, for I know the rest.
　　They are the jeerers, mocking, flouting Jacks.　　85

　　　　　　　ACT II　SCENE iv

[*Fitton.*] How now, old money-bawd? W'are come –
P. Senior.　　　　　　　　　　　　To jeer me
　　As you were wont, I know you.
Almanac.　　　　　　　　　　No, to give thee
　　Some good security, and see Pecunia.
P. Senior. What is't?
Fitton.　　　　　Ourselves.
Almanac.　　　　　We'll be one bound for another.

　　　Madrigal steps aside with Broker.

80.1.] Gifford (*after* out *in line 84*); *after* II.iv *in* F (subst.).　　II.iv.] FITTON.
PENI-BOY.　SE.　ALMANACH. / SHVNFIELD.　MADRIGAL.　LICK- / FINGER.
BROKER. F.

---

　　77. *remember meat*] a timely reminder on the verge of Lent; cf. *Vox Graculi*
(1622), p. 24: 'Butchers dogs shall make Libels against *Lent*, for affording no
better diet then Herring-cobs, for their slabbring Chappes.'
　　79. *relics*] leftovers.
　　80. *reversion*] remnant, leavings.
　　81. *courtier*] i.e. Fitton.
　　82. *muster-master*] officer responsible for the accuracy of the muster-roll, the
official list of officers and men in an army or ship's company (*O.E.D.*).
　　plover] dupe. Madrigal is clearly distinguished from his companions by a
general air of unworldliness.
　　83. *pull*] pluck, i.e. cheat.

Fitton. This noble doctor here.
Almanac.   This worthy courtier.   5
Fitton. This man o'war, he was our muster-master.
Almanac. But a sea-captain now, brave Captain Shunfield.
     He [Pennyboy Senior] holds up his nose.
Shunfield. You snuff the air now, as the scent displeased you.
Fitton. [*To P. Senior.*] Thou needst not fear him, man; his
     credit is sound.
Almanac. And seasoned too since he took salt at sea.   10
P. Senior. I do not love pickled security.
     Would I had one good fresh man in for all,
     For truth is, you three stink.
Shunfield.   You are a rogue.
P. Senior. I think I am, but I will lend no money
     On that security, captain.
Almanac.   Here's a gentleman,   15
     A freshman i'the world, one Master Madrigal.
                    [*Exeunt* BROKER *and* MADRIGAL.]
Fitton. Of an untainted credit. What say you to him?
Shunfield. He's gone, methinks. Where is he? Madrigal?
P. Senior. H'has an odd singing name. Is he an heir?

4.] *Two lines in* F, *divided at* Ourselves.   4.1.] *F margin next to* 17–20.
8. as] *F;* has *1716.*   16.1.] *Gifford subst. (after* 17*); F margin:* Madrigall
steps aside with Broker.

II.iv.7 .1. *sea-captain* ... nose] apparently a familiar reaction; for an
account of it more sympathetic to seamen, cf. John Taylor, *Faire and Fowle
Weather* (1615): 'Whole spawnes of Land-sharks ... / Will hold their noses
and cry fogh and fye, / When serviceable Marriners passe by' (sig. B4).
   8. *snuff*] sniff.
   10. *took ... sea*] took to being a sailor. In later usage a *salt* is an experienced
seaman.
   11. *pickled*] Cf Overbury's *Characters* (1618 ed.), E4*v*: 'A Saylor ... is part
of his owne Provision, for he lives ever pickled.'
   15. *Here's a gentleman*] The preliminary skirmish over, Almanac produces
the latest pawn in the jeerers' search for quick profit.
   16. *freshman*] novice, a raw, unsophisticated fellow.
   18.] Shunfield is disconcerted by the suddenness of Madrigal's departure,
spirited away by Broker with an invitation to visit the ladies (see line 127).
   19. *heir*] with a pun on 'air' in the musical sense; a similar pun occurs in
Lyly's *Mother Bombie*, II.ii.24–6: 'Ile let him take the aire, ... if he meane
to be my heire.' The pun indicates that Madrigal's *full hopes* do not extend
beyond an insubstantial poetic fortune (as P. Senior is quick to realise in lines
22–3).

Fitton. An heir to a fair fortune –
Almanac.   And full hopes;   20
    A dainty scholar and a pretty poet.
P. Senior. Y'ave said enough. I ha' no money, gentlemen,
    An' he go to't in rhyme once, not a penny.
                              He snuffs again.
Shunfield. Why, he's of years though he have little beard.
P. Senior. His beard has time to grow. I have no money.   25
    Let him still dabble in poetry. No Pecunia
    Is to be seen.
Almanac.   Come, thou lov'st to be costive
    Still i'thy court'sy; but I have a pill,
    A golden pill, to purge away this melancholy.
Shunfield. 'Tis nothing but his keeping o'the house here   30
    With his two drowsy dogs.
Fitton.   A drench of sack
    At a good tavern, and a fine fresh pullet
    Would cure him.
Lickfinger.   Nothing but a young 'are in white broth;
    I know his diet better than the doctor.

33. 'are] *This ed.;* Haire *F;* Heir *F3;* hare *Kifer.*

---

23. *once*] ever.
27. *costive*] (1) stingy; (2) constipated.
29. *pill . . . melancholy*] 'Pills to purge melancholy' was a proverbial expression, and was adopted as the title of a famous eighteenth century collection of ballads. Possibly Almanac too has a musical offering from Madrigal in mind.
30. *'Tis . . . but*] It's entirely caused by.
31. *drench*] drink.
33. *'are*] Modernisation poses difficulties here in preserving the effect of Jonson's pun. On the page, *F*'s *Haire* could represent either 'heir' or 'hare', and these two words were sometimes (though not always) pronounced alike, without aspiration. Kifer supports her reading (see collation) with a gloss to the effect that 'hare' and 'heir' were homophones in Jacobean times; but if so, the pun depends on 'hare' – the literal meaning in this context – not overwhelming but rather assisting the implied sense of 'heir', an effect that is lost in the modern divergence of pronunciation. Thus, *F3*'s *Heir* may be not a misreading but an attempt to retain, as far as standardised spelling allows, the satiric point of Jonson's wordplay. Here the pun is preserved by a Cockney idiom which might well suit Lickfinger's characterisation in a modern performance.
34. *his diet*] Cf. *Vox Graculi* (1622), p. 28, forecasting a new kind of famine for 1623: 'men shall turne *Omaphagi*, and devoure one another . . . Usurers shall cramme downe young Heires, as if they were pickled greene Geese, or bakt Woodcockes.'

Shunfield. What, Lickfinger, mine old host of Ram Alley!   35
    You ha' some market here?
Almanac.   Some dosser of fish
    Or fowl to fetch off?
Fitton.   An odd bargain of venison
    To drive?
P. Senior.   Will you go in, knave?
Lickfinger.   I must needs.
    You see who drives me, gentlemen.
                        Pennyboy [Senior] thrusts him in.
Almanac.   Not the devil.
Fitton. He may be in time; he is his agent now.   40
P. Senior. You are all cogging Jacks, a covey o'wits,
    The jeerers, that still call together at meals;
    Or rather an aerie, for you are birds of prey
    And fly at all: nothing's too big or high for you.
    And are so truly feared, but not beloved   45
    One of another, as no one dares break
    Company from the rest, lest they should fall
    Upon him absent.
Almanac.   O, the only oracle
    That ever peeped or spake out of a doublet.

---

37. off] *F3; of F.*   39. S.D.] *F margin next to 44–5.*

---

35. *Ram Alley*] one of the more notorious places of disrepute in Jacobean London; as an engaging appendix to the last two notes, it still exists as Hare Place, 47 Fleet Street. According to Lording Barry's play *Ram-Alley* (1611) the vicinity 'stinks with cooks and ale' (Dodsley, 10.292).

36. *dosser*] basketful. A *dosser* was a pannier or basket carried on the back.

38–9. *I ... devil*] proverbial: 'He must needs go that the devil drives' (Tilley D278).

39. thrusts him in] perhaps through the door opposite to that used by Broker and Madrigal at line 16.1, the one leading to the living quarters, the other to the kitchen (and the street).

40. *his agent*] The usurer's diabolical associations are a common theme; cf. line 201 note.

41. *cogging*] cheating.
    covey] set, gaggle (deriving from the original meaning 'a family of partridges').

42. *call together*] assemble (*O.E.D.* records only the sense of 'summon to assemble'); the idea of *call* meaning 'jeer' may also be present, anticipating IV.i.

43–8. *you ... absent*] Cf. Barnabe Rich, *Faultes ...* (1606), c2*v*: 'I am pestered with a finicall companie that comes in now all together, throwing upon mee, birdes of a wing, and it is fittest for them to flie together'.

Shunfield. How the rogue stinks, worse than a fishmonger's
    sleeves!   50
Fitton. Or currier's hands!
Shunfield.   And such a parboiled visage!
Fitton. His face looks like a dyer's apron, just!
Almanac. A sodden head, and his whole brain a posset curd!
P. Senior. Ay, now you jeer; jeer on. I have no money.
Almanac. I wonder what religion he's of.   55
Fitton. No certain species sure. A kind of mule,
    That's half an Ethnic, half a Christian!
P. Senior. I have no money, gentlemen.
Shunfield.   This stock,
    He has no sense of any virtue, honour,
    Gentry or merit.
P. Senior.   You say very right,   60
    My meritorious captain (as I take it!).
    Merit will keep no house nor pay no house rent.
    Will Mistress Merit go to market, think you,
    Set on the pot, or feed the family?
    Will Gentry clear with the butcher or the baker,   65
    Fetch in a pheasant or a brace of partridges
    From goodwife Poulter for my lady's supper?
Fitton. See, this pure rogue.

---

49. *peeped*] squeaked; *O.E.D. peep* = 'to speak in a weak, querulous, shrill
tone'. Whalley and subsequent edd. compare Isaiah, viii.19 on the ventriloqu-
ism of ancient priests 'that peepe and that mutter'; but Jonson's verb merely
underlines the incongruity of the miser attempting the role of moral scourge.

51. *currier's*] of one who grooms horses.

51-2. *such ... apron*] Presumably the idea is that P. Senior's face is blotchy
(stained different colours, like the apron).

52. *just*] exactly.

53. *posset curd*] a drink made of hot milk, curdled with ale or wine, to which
sugar and spice were added.

57. *Ethnic*] heathen.

58. *stock*] block, stupid fellow.

61. *meritorious*] Jonson contrives a recondite classical pun on *meritorious* =
earning money (by prostitution): *O.E.D.* 5. Cf. *Disc.*, 317-8: 'Some love any
Strumpet (be shee never so shop-like, or meritorious) in good clothes.' This
usage was probably intelligible to Jonson's audience through its resemblance to
such Latin words as *meretrix* meaning a prostitute, which Jonson uses in *Volp.*,
I.ii.19 (see note to I.Int.8), and which was popularised in puns like the subtitle
of Barry's *Ram-Alley, or Merry Tricks*.

68. *pure*] utter.

P. Senior.   This rogue has money, though.
My worshipful brave courtier has no money.
No, nor my valiant captain.
Shunfield.   Hang you, rascal!   70
P. Senior. Nor you, my learned doctor. I loved you
   While you did hold your practice and kill tripe-wives,
   And kept you to your urinal; but since your thumbs
   Have greased the ephemerides, casting figures,
   And turning over for your candle-rents,   75
   And your twelve houses in the zodiac,
   With your almutens, almacantaras,
   Troth, you shall cant alone for Pennyboy.
Shunfield. I told you what we should find him, a mere bawd.
Fitton. A rogue, a cheater.
P. Senior.   What you please, gentlemen.   80
   I am of that humble nature and condition
   Never to mind your worships, or take notice
   Of what you throw away thus. I keep house here

81. I am] *F;* I'm *Whalley.*

---

72. *hold . . . kill*] The word *practice* had already acquired the connotation of professional activity in medicine, and P. Senior anticipates Canter's dismissal of the doctor's speculative pursuits at IV.iv.159–65. Cf. Brathwaite, *Whimzies,* 'An Almanack-maker': 'He ha's some small scruple of Physitian in him, and can most *Empyrically* discourse of the state of your Body: but had he store of *Patients,* hee would slaughter more than a *Pestilence*' (p. 5).
   tripe-wives] women who prepare and sell tripe.
73. *urinal*] i.e. the vessel for analysing urine to diagnose disease.
74. *ephemerides*] almanacs containing astrological predictions.
75. *turning over*] i.e. the pages of almanacs (*H.&S.*).
   candle-rents] 'rent or revenue derived from house property' (which like a candle continually deteriorates with use) – *O.E.D.*
76. *twelve houses*] See J. Melton, *Astrologaster* (1620), p. 35: 'These twelve Houses are the Tenements most commonly . . . Astrologers . . . doe let out to simple people, whereby they purchase to themselves much Money, and to their Tenants much sorrow . . . these Twelve Signes, placed in their Twelve Houses, are like a Jury that sit upon the life and death of Mortalitie.'
77. *almutens*] ruling planets in horoscopes.
   almacantaras] parallels of altitude on an astrological chart, with the horizon reckoned as the first almacantar (*O.E.D.*).
78. *alone*] in vain.
79. *mere*] absolute.
83–4. *keep . . . cobbler*] 'A cobbler is a king at home' was apparently a proverbial saying (*Lean's Collectanea* (1902), III.380).

Like a lame cobbler, never out of doors,
With my two dogs, my friends; and (as you say)   85
Drive a quick pretty trade still. I get money.
And as for titles, be they rogue or rascal
Or what your worships fancy, let 'em pass
As transitory things. They're mine today
And yours tomorrow.
Almanac.   Hang thee, dog!
Shunfield.   Thou cur!   90
P. Senior. You see how I do blush and am ashamed
Of these large attributes? Yet you have no money.
Almanac. Well, wolf, hyena, you old pocky rascal,
You will ha' the hernia fall down again
Into your scrotum, and I shall be sent for.   95
I will remember then that, and your fistula
In ano I cured you of.
P. Senior.   Thank your dog-leechcraft!
They were wholesome piles afore you meddled with 'em.
Almanac. What an ungrateful wretch is this!
Shunfield.   He minds
A courtesy no more than London Bridge   100
What arch was mended last.

92. you have] *F*; you've *1716*.   97. dog-leechcraft] *This ed.*; dog-leech
craft *F*.

92. *large*] gross (Kifer).
96–7. *fistula / In ano*] anal (pipe-like) ulcer, common in Jonson's day.
97. *dog-leechcraft*] Previous edd. have concentrated on deriving this from
the 'leaches' who controlled the dogs used at bull and bear-baiting, and compare Face's abusing of Subtle (*Alch.*, I.i.103) as *dog-leech*, which F. H. Mares
in his Revels ed. glosses as 'veterinary'. These explanations are fanciful. The
term *leechcraft* was commonly applied to medical practice, and *dog* was such
a universal term of abuse that it would easily attach itself to *leechcraft* as an
epithet for quackery. Cf. the attack on 'learned doctors' like Subtle and
Almanac in Melton's *Astrologaster*: 'I shall be in more danger of death by taking
your Potions, then I shall be of the Disease . . . and in this you and all other
Medicasters and Dog-leaches are happy, because . . . the Earth covers all your
ignorances' (p. 17).
98. *piles*] Contemporary treatment for piles was a gruesome process, including the application of leeches and severing of veins in the ankle; it presumably carried with it a high risk of complication.
100–1. *London . . . last*] The state of the only bridge crossing the Thames in
this period exercises several contemporary writers, and even in 1816 Gifford
was moved in his note on this line to denounce it as a 'pernicious structure'.
Middleton complained that 'what the advantage of one tide performs comes

Fitton.   He never thinks,
More than a log, of any grace at court
A man may do him, or that such a lord
Reached him his hand.
P. Senior.   O yes: if grace would strike
The brewer's tally, or my good lord's hand   105
Would quit the scores. But sir, they will not do it.
(*He shows a piece* [*of gold*].) Here's a piece. My good Lord
Piece doth all:
Goes to the butcher's, fetches in a mutton,
Then to the baker's, brings in bread, makes fires,
Gets wine, and does more real courtesies   110
Than all my lords, I know. My sweet Lord Piece,
You are my lord; the rest are cogging Jacks,
Under the rose.
Shunfield.   Rogue, I could beat you now.
P. Senior. True, captain, if you durst beat any other,
I should believe you. But indeed you are hungry;   115
You are not angry, captain, if I know you
Aright, good captain. No Pecunia
Is to be seen, though Mistress Band would speak
Or little Blushet-Wax be ne'er so easy.
I'll stop mine ears with her against the Sirens   120
Court and philosophy. God be wi' you, gentlemen.
Provide you better names, Pecunia is for you.   [*Exit.*]

---

another tide presently and washes away' (*The Blacke Book* (1604), Bullen 8.22,
quoted by *H.&S.*).

102–4. *any . . . hand*] a veiled allusion to the proverb 'A Friend in court is
worth (is better than) a penny in purse' (Tilley F687) – a sentiment which P.
Senior proceeds to discredit.

104. *strike*] cancel.

106. *quit the scores*] settle the bill.

113. *Under the rose*] between you and me, in confidence (proverbial: Tilley
R185). P. Senior's communion is all with the coin he is holding.

118. *though*] even if.

119. *Blushet*] blushing.

easy] (1) persuadable; (2) workable, like wax which has been warmed to
make a seal. The hint of autonomy amongst Pecunia's attendants momentarily
enlivens Jonson's rather stiff allegory.

122. *Provide . . . names*] i.e. than Fitton, Shunfield etc., with all they express of your characters; but P. Senior is also looking back to lines 91–2 and
saying, 'when you learn to be more ingratiating . . .'.

Fitton. What a damned harpy it is. Where's Madrigal?
Is he sneaked hence?

MADRIGAL *returns* [*with* BROKER].

Shunfield.   Here he comes with Broker,
Pecunia's secretary.
Almanac.   He may do some good   125
With him perhaps. Where ha' you been, Madrigal?
Madrigal. Above with my lady's women, reading verses.
Fitton. That was a favour! [*To Broker.*] Good morrow, Master
Secretary.
Shunfield. Good morrow, Master Usher.
Almanac. [*Bowing.*]   Sir, by both
Your worshipful titles, and your name Mas Broker,   130
Good morrow.
Madrigal.   I did ask him if he were
Amphibion Broker.
Shunfield.   Why?
Madrigal.   A creature of two natures
Because he has two offices.
Broker.   You may jeer,
You ha' the wits, young gentlemen. But your hope
Of Helicon will never carry it here   135
With our fat family. We ha' the dullest,
Most unbored ears for verse amongst our females.
I grieved you read so long, sir. Old Nurse Mortgage,

132. S.H. *Madrigal*] *Whalley;* ALM. *F.*

127. *Above ... verses*] Pecunia's women are perhaps visible in this scene sitting in the gallery above the stage. Pecunia herself should not be, as this would reduce the impact of her appearance in the next scene.
130. *Mas*] shortened form of Master.
131. *did ask*] Prompted by Almanac's facetiousness, Madrigal feebly essays the jeerers' idiom for the first time; he is completely at home with it by line 168.
135. *Helicon*] the mountain sacred to the Muses in Greek mythology, and so associated with poetic inspiration.
136. *fat*] dull, slow-witted.
137. *unbored*] unenlightened. *O.E.D.*'s only figurative sense.
138–41.] Jonson seems almost to invite speculation about the quality of attention which another quartet of female characters – the gossips sitting on the stage – give to the play itself. Cf. II.Int.1.

She snored i'the chair, and Statute (if you marked her)
Fell fast asleep; and Mistress Band, she nodded,   140
But not with any consent to what you read.
They must have somewhat else to chink than rhymes.
If you could make an epitaph on your land
(Imagine it on departure), such a poem
Would wake 'em, and bring Wax to her true temper.   145
Madrigal. I'faith, sir, and I will try.
Broker.   'Tis but earth,
Fit to make bricks and tiles of.
Shunfield.   Pox upon't,
'Tis but for pots, or pipkins at the best.
If it would keep us in good tobacco pipes –
Broker. 'Twere worth keeping.
Fitton.   Or in porc'lain dishes,   150
There were some hope.
Almanac.   But this is a hungry soil
And must be helped.
Fitton.   Who would hold any land
To have the trouble to marl it?
Shunfield.   Not a gentleman.
Broker. Let clowns and hinds affect it, that love ploughs
And carts and harrows, and are busy still   155
In vexing the dull element.
Almanac.   Our sweet songster
Shall rarify't into air.

146.] *As F;* I'll try. *It is* Gifford.

142. *chink*] i.e. as Money's agents. Broker probably rubs thumb and finger
together in an expressive gesture.
143. *land*] i.e. Madrigal's supposed inheritance.
144. *Imagine ... departure*] imagine yourself losing it. Broker slyly invites
Madrigal to inspire his own downfall.
146–56. *'Tis ... element*] an elaborate skirmish which becomes less obscure
in the light of the story recorded in Thomas Plume's notebook about Jonson's
acquisition of the nickname 'Wise-acres': 'Ben Jonson said he should rather
have an acre of wit than of land' (*H.&S.*, I 187, n.16).
148. *pipkins*] small earthenware or (at this time) metal pots, mainly used in
cooking.
153. *marl*] fertilise (with marl, a type of clayey soil).
154. *Let ... it*] Let rustics and labourers seek such work.
156. *dull element*] i.e. earth, which Madrigal will transpose into the 'higher'
element of air (see next line).

Fitton. [*Confidentially.*]   And you, Mas Broker,
     Shall have a feeling.
Broker.   So it supple, sir,
     The nerves.
Madrigal.   O, it shall be palpable,
     Make thee run through a hoop or a thumb-ring,   160
     The nose of a tobacco pipe, and draw
     Thy ductile bones out like a knitting needle
     To serve my subtle turns.
Broker.   I shall obey, sir,
     And run a thread like an hourglass.

                    [*Re-enter* PENNYBOY SENIOR.]

P. Senior.   Where is Broker?
     Are not these flies gone yet? [*To the jeerers.*] Pray quit my
          house;   165
     I'll smoke you out else.
Fitton.   O, the prodigal!
     Will you be at so much charge with us, and loss?
Madrigal. I have heard you ha' offered, sir, to lock up smoke
     And caulk your windows, spar up all your doors,

---

157. S.D.] *This ed.*   165. Pray quit] pray'quit *F.*   168. I have] *F;* I've
1716.   offered] *F3 (offer'd);* offerèd *F.*   169. windows] windores *F.*

---

158. *feeling*] tip, bribe (Kifer). Cf. *D.A.*, III.iii.78–80: 'they must have a
feeling, / . . . the hand-gout / Be oyled'. Fitton puns on 'you'll sense how good
he is'.
     supple] gratify (lit. 'soften').
     160. *hoop*] ring.
     160–3. *thumb-ring . . . turns*] Falstaff in *1H4* claims that when he was young
'I could have crept into any alderman's thumb-ring' (II.iv.326–7) (*H.&S.*).
There is an allusion here to the superstition of keeping a 'familiar' or attendant
spirit in a ring; cf. *D.A.*, Prologue, 5–6: 'Though you presume *Satan* a subtill
thing, / And may have heard hee's worne in a thumbe-ring'.
     161. *nose*] presumably the hole in the mouth-piece; cf. line 174.
     162. *ductile*] flexible.
     164. *run . . . hourglass*] i.e. like a trickle of sand.
     167.] Fitton plays straight man to Madrigal, setting up the conceit that
follows.
     168–72.] adapted from Plautus' *Aulularia* ('The Pot of Gold'), 297–301, on
the miserly habits of Euclio (*H.&S.*).
     169. *spar up*] bolt.

Thinking to keep it a close prisoner wi' you,   170
And wept when it went out, sir, at your chimney.
Fitton. And yet his eyes were drier than a pumice.
Shunfield. A wretched rascal, that will bind about
The nose of his bellows, lest the wind get out
When he's abroad.
Almanac.   Sweeps down no cobwebs here   175
But sells 'em for cut fingers; and the spiders,
As creatures reared of dust and cost him nothing,
To fat old ladies' monkeys.
Fitton.   He has offered
To gather up spilled water, and preserve
Each hair falls from him to stop balls withal.   180
Shunfield. A slave and an idolator to Pecunia!
P. Senior. You all have happy memories, gentlemen,
In rocking my poor cradle. I remember, too,
When you had lands and credit, worship, friends,
Ay, and could give security. Now you have none,   185
Or will have none right shortly. This can time
And the vicissitude of things. I have
All these and money too, and do possess 'em,
And am right heartily glad of all our memories
And both the changes.
Fitton.   Let us leave the viper.   190

180. withal] *F3*; with all *F*.

173–5. *A ... abroad*] Cf. *Aulularia*, 304–5: 'I suppose he plugs up the pipe
at his lower end so he won't lose any wind while he sleeps' (*Six Plays*, ed. L.
Casson, p. 83).
    175–6. *Sweeps ... fingers*] suggested by *Aulularia*, 87; cf. Bottom's 'good
Master Cobweb: if I cut my finger, I shall make bold with you' (*M.N.D.*,
III.i.175–7). Cobwebs were used as adhesives to stop bleeding.
    176–8. *spiders ... monkeys*] There is much incidental satire in plays of the
period on the habit of keeping pet monkeys, and their spider-diet is frequently
noticed; *H.&S.* compare Cartwright, *The Siege*, 545–7 (II.ii): 'What doe you
else but feel the Monky's pulse, / And cater Spiders for the queasie Creature /
When it refuseth Comfits?' (*Plays & Poems*, ed. Blakemore Evans, p. 381).
    179–80. *preserve ... withal*] a variation on *Aulularia*, 312–13; but Jon-
son more closely echoes Dekker's description of Covetousness in *Worke for
Armorours* (Grosart IV.129): 'Hee ... shaved his owne head and beard himselfe, and when it came to wey a pound, hee sold it to a Frenchman to stuffe
tennis balles.' P. Senior is described as 'old Covetousness' in II.Int.8.
    186. *can*] can bring about.

[*Exeunt all but* PENNYBOY SENIOR *and* BROKER.]
P. Senior. He's glad he is rid of his torture, and so soon.
Broker, come hither. Up, and tell your lady
She must be ready presently, and Statute,
Band, Mortgage, Wax. My prodigal young kinsman
Will straight be here to see her; top of our house,   195
The flourishing and flaunting Pennyboy.
We were but three of us in all the world;
My brother Francis, whom they called Frank Pennyboy,
Father to this: he's dead. This Pennyboy
Is now the heir. I, Richer Pennyboy,   200
Not Richard, but old Harry Pennyboy,
And (to make rhyme) close, wary Pennyboy –
I shall have all at last, my hopes do tell me.
Go, see all ready; and where my dogs have faulted,
Remove it with a broom, and sweeten all   205
With a slice of juniper – not too much, but sparing.
We may be faulty ourselves else, and turn prodigal
In entertaining *of* the prodigal.   [*Exit* BROKER.]

[*Enter*] PENNYBOY JU[NIOR, PENNYBOY] CANTER
[*and*] PICKLOCK.
Here he is! And with him – what? A clapper-dudgeon!

---

195. top] *Whalley;* 'top *F, F3, 1716.*   196. flaunting] flanting *F.*

195. *top*] See note to II.v.93.
201. *old Harry*] 'one of the popular names of the Devil' (Brand, *Popular Antiquities*, III.54).
202.] a recurring motif in the play: cf. I.i.22 and III.Int.9–11.
206. *slice*] Kifer interprets this as 'fire-shovel', which is supported by *O.E.D.* and by the likelihood that juniper was burned (see next note) on a shovel inserted into the fire. But it is more likely to mean simply 'piece'.
  juniper] juniper wood and berries were burned to purge the air; cf. Middleton, *The Mayor of Queenborough*, V.i.61–3: 'burn a little juniper in the hall-chimney: / Like a beast as I was, I pissed out the fire last night, and never dreamt of the king's coming' (Bullen II.91). Jonson's attitude towards the practice may be shown by a remark in *C.R.*, II.iv.74–5: 'this mixing in fashion I hate it worse, then to burne juniper in my chamber'.
208–11.] If Broker meets the new arrivals at the door, the ensuing courtesies will provide time for P. Senior's observations.
209. *clapper-dudgeon*] Dekker, *O per se O*, Nv: 'A *Clapperdogeon* is in English a Begger borne'; but the origin of the phrase remains obscure. Previous ·edd. record Collier's suggestion that it refers to the beggar's knocking

That's a good sign, to have the beggar follow him   210
So near at his first entry into fortune.

ACT II   SCENE v

[*P. Junior.*] How now, old uncle? I am come to see thee
    And the brave lady here, the daughter of Ophir,
    They say thou keepst.
P. Senior.   Sweet nephew, if she were
    The daughter o'the sun, she's at your service,
    And so am I, and the whole family   5
    Worshipful nephew.
P. Junior.   Sayst thou so, dear uncle?
    Welcome my friends then. Here is Domine Picklock,
    My man o'law, solicits all my causes,
    Follows my business, makes and compounds my quarrels
    Between my tenants and me, sows all my strifes   10
    And reaps them too, troubles the country for me
    And vexes any neighbour that I please.

II.v.] PENY-BOY. IV. PENI-BOY. SEN. PICLOCK. / CANTER.) BROKER.
PECVNIA. STATVTE. / BAND. WAX. MORTGAGE. *hid in the study. F.*

with a *dudgeon* (name for the wood from which knife-handles were made, and
thus shorthand for the handle itself) on the wooden clap-dish which he carried.
    210-11.] To be followed by a beggar and relieve him is a proverbial sign of
good fortune (*Lean's Collectanea*, II.15); cf. Dekker & Massinger, *The Virgin-
Martyr*, II.i.194-7: 'I comming / Forth of the temple, heard my begger-boy, /
. . . crave an almes, / Which with glad hand I gave, with lucky hand' (Bowers
III.398).

    II.v.o.1.] *F*'s S.D. (see collation) is as Gifford says 'evidently the prompter's
call on the actors required for the ensuing scene'.
    2. *Ophir*] See I.vi.42-4 note.
    3-4. *if . . . sun*] Pecunia does in fact claim later that 'by the father's side I
come from Sol' (IV.iv.11: see note). Cf. *Volp.*, I.i.10 (Revels).
    7. *Domine*] 'used in respectful address to . . . members of learned profes-
sions' (*O.E.D.*).
    8-12.] in Jonson's epigrammatic 'character' vein: cf. *M.L.*, I.ii.15f., and
reminiscent of Overreach's troublemaking 'with the favour of my man of Law'
in *New Way to Pay Old Debts*, II.i.34-48 (*E.& G.* II.315-16). Cf. also Webster, *The Devil's Law-Case*, II.i.108-10: 'he is the very myracle of a lawyer, /
One that perswades men to peace, & compounds quarrels / Among his neighbours, without going to law' (Lucas II.254).
    9. *compounds*] settles.

P. Senior. Bur ⁻ ⁺h commission?

P. Junior.   Under my hand and seal.

P. Senior. A worshipful place!

Picklock.   I thank his worship for it.

P. Senior. But what is this old gentleman?

P. Canter.   A rogue,   15
A very canter I, sir, one that maunds
Upon the pad. We should be brothers, though,
For you are near as wretched as myself.
You dare not use your money, and I have none.

P. Senior. Not use my money, cogging Jack? Who uses it   20
At better rates, lets it for more i'the hundred
Than I do, sirrah?

P. Junior.   Be not angry, uncle.

P. Senior. What, to disgrace me with my queen, as if
I did not know her value?

P. Canter.   Sir, I meant
You durst not to enjoy it.

P. Senior.   Hold your peace,   25
You are a Jack.   (*Young Pennyboy is angry.*)

P. Junior.   Uncle, he shall be a John!
And, you go to that, as good a man as you are.

26. S.H. *P. Junior.*] *F3*; P. SE. *F.*   27–8. And .... / An'] *F*; An' ...: /
An' *Whalley*; An ...: / And *Gifford.*

---

14. *worshipful*] honourable.

15. *rogue*] vagrant.

16–17. *maunds ... pad*] a slang phrase meaning 'begs on the highway'
(*H.&S.*). Cf. *The Roaring Girl*, V.i.127–31: 'I am ... a maunderer upon the
pad I confesse, and ... instructed in the rudaments of roguery' (Bowers
III.85).

17–18. *We ... myself*] Canter's moral design upon his brother becomes
evident for the first time, and an audience alert to the convention of virtuous
authority in disguise perhaps has a hint of his identity.

23. *queen*] In this protestation from 'old money-bawd' (II.iv.1) we inevitably hear a pun on 'quean', a prostitute, anticipating lines 98–100. Pecunia is
the honest whore of the play.

26. *a John*] a servant to me (Kifer); cf. *T.T.*, IV.i.57–8: 'All Constables are
truly Iohn's for the King, / What ere their names are'.

27. *you ... that*] what's more, for all that. *F*'s *And* preceding this phrase
could mean 'if', as some edd. have thought (see collation), but this would
obscure P. Junior's improvisatory train of thought, and it involves explaining
why the compositor set *And* followed by the abbreviated form *An'* in the very
next line.

An' I can make him so, a better man.
Perhaps I will too. [*To Canter and Picklock.*] Come, let
  us go.
P. Senior.   Nay, kinsman,
  My worshipful kinsman and the top of our house,   30
  Do not your penitent uncle that affront,
  For a rash word to leave his joyful threshold
  Before you see the lady that you long for,
  The Venus of the time and state, Pecunia!
  I do perceive your bounty loves the man   35
  For some concealèd virtue that he hides
  Under those rags.
P. Canter.   I owe my happiness to him,
  The waiting on his worship since I brought him
  The happy news welcome to all young heirs.
P. Junior. Thou didst indeed, for which I thank thee yet.   40
  Your fortunate princess, uncle, is long a-coming.
P. Senior. She is not rigged, sir; setting forth some lady
  Will cost as much as furnishing a fleet.

  The study is opened where she [PECUNIA] *sits in state*
  [*attended by* BROKER, STATUTE, BAND, WAX *and*
  MORTGAGE].

  Here she's come at last, and like a galley
  Gilt i'the prow.

42. S.H.] *conj. de Winter;* P. CA. F.

---

41. *fortunate*] i.e. bringing good fortune. Mention of one auspicious visit (in
lines 38–9) prompts thoughts of the next.
42–3.] a common trope: cf. John Taylor, *A Navy of Land Ships,* 'The Lady-
Ship ... a very comely Ship to the eye, set out with most excessive and superfluous cost, she was most richly adorned ... there was more time spent in
rigging of her, then in all the rest of the Fleete' (*Workes* 1630, L5). The comparison can be traced back to Proverbs, xxxi.14, but it usually has a critical
edge in an age of ostentatious dress and equally elaborate preparations for
voyages (Kifer suggests a topical allusion to Buckingham's heavy expenditure
on the fleet sent to attack Cadiz in 1625).
43.1. The study] Jonson's direction in the margin; *H.&S.* compare *Catiline,*
I.15, also a marginal note (V 435). Some kind of discovery space is clearly
used, perhaps a curtained booth placed against one of the doors, or else the
central doorway in the façade (also curtained). The unveiling of Pecunia can
be compared to Volpone's 'Open the shrine that I may see my saint' (I.i.2,
Revels), but its overtly ceremonial quality creates a more complex effect.

P. Junior.   Is this Pecunia?   45
                    [*She rises and comes forward.*]
P. Senior. Vouchsafe my toward kinsman, gracious madam,
     The favour of your hand.
Pecunia.   Nay, of my lips, sir,
     To him. (*She kisseth him.*)
P. Junior.   She kisses like a mortal creature.
     Almighty madam, I have longed to see you.
Pecunia. And I have my desire, sir, to behold   50
     That youth and shape which in my dreams and wakes
     I have so oft contemplated and felt
     Warm in my veins and native as my blood.
     When I was told of your arrival here,
     I felt my heart beat as it would leap out   55
     In speech, and all my face it was a flame;
     But how it came to pass I do not know.
P. Junior. O, beauty loves to be more proud than nature,
     That made you blush. I cannot satisfy
     My curious eyes, by which alone I'm happy,   60

45.1.] *This ed.*   60. I'm] I'am *F.*

46. *toward*] promising, eligible.

47. *hand ... lips*] a provocative reminder of Doll's insistence to Mammon:
'my lip to you, sir' (*Alch.*, IV.i.35, Revels) – especially in view of Mammon's
opinion (line 56) that she resembles 'One o'the Austriac princes'. *H.&S.*, in
discussing the *Alch.* passage (X 99), cite James Howell's comment on the
Infanta whom Charles sought in marriage: 'She is full and big-lipp'd; which is
held a Beauty ... in the Austrian Family' (*Familiar Letters*, I.3.ix). In his
devious way Jonson seems to be courting Censure's accusation in II.Int.21–5
(see notes).

50–7.] Gifford detected an allusion to a passage 'descriptive of the rising
passion of Medea' in the *Argonautica* by Apollonius of Rhodes (III.286–90).
Medea falls in love with Jason in his quest for the golden fleece, and so aids
him in his appointed labours to win it. With this exotic and sympathetic gloss
on the present situation, compare the satirical sketch in *C.R.*, plainly recalled
here, in which 'Cupid strikes *monie* in love with the *prodigall*, makes her dote
upon him' (Induction, 76–7).

52. *contemplated*] accented on the second syllable.

55–6. *heart ... speech*] i.e. straining against the bounds of decorum (especially for women) which observed the dictum found in Ecclesiasticus, xxi.26:
'The heart of fooles is in their mouth: but the mouth of the wise is in their
heart.' Cf. *Tw.N.*, II.iv.111–19.

58–9. *beauty ... blush*] i.e. your beauty thinks itself above natural reactions
like blushing.

In my beholding you. (*He kisseth her.*)
P. *Canter.*   They pass the compliment
     Prettily well.
Picklock.   Ay, he does kiss her. I like him.
P. *Junior.* My passion was clear contrary and doubtful.
     I shook for fear, and yet I danced for joy.
     I had such motions as the sunbeams make   65
     Against a wall or playing on a water,
     Or trembling vapour of a boiling pot –
P. *Senior.* That's not so good. It should ha' been a crucible
     With molten metal, she had understood it.
P. *Junior.* I cannot talk, but I can love you, madam.   70
     Are these your gentlewomen? I love them too.
                              [*He kisses them in turn.*]
     And which is Mistress Statute? Mistress Band?
     They all kiss close. The last stuck to my lips.
Broker. It was my lady's chambermaid, soft Wax.
P. *Junior.* Soft lips she has, I am sure on't. [*Hesitates.*] Mother
     Mortgage ...   75
     I'll owe a kiss till she be younger. Statute,
     Sweet Mistress Band, and honey, little Wax,
     We must be better acquainted.

          He doubles the compliment to them all.

Statute.   We are but servants, sir.
Band. But whom her grace is so content to grace,
     We shall observe –
Wax.   And with all fit respect –   80
Mortgage. In our poor places –
Wax.   Being her grace's shadows.
P. *Junior.* A fine, well-spoken family. What's thy name?
Broker. Broker.
P. *Junior.* [*Aside to him.*] Methinks my uncle should not need thee,

---

64–7.] derived from Virgil's *Aeneid*, viii.19–25: 'magno curarum ...
laquearia tecti' (Gifford). But the antithesis of line 64 is apparently unVirgilian,
and belongs to the conventions of Elizabethan love poetry; cf. Sidney's 'I waile
for want, and yet am chokte with store' (*Poems*, ed. W. A. Ringler, p. 41).
     78.1. doubles ... all] kisses Statute, Band and Wax again.

Who is a crafty knave enough, believe it.
Art thou her grace's steward?
Broker.   No, her usher, sir.   85
P. Junior. What, o'the hall? Thou hast a sweeping face.
Thy beard is like a broom.
Broker.   No barren chin, sir.
I am no eunuch though a gentleman-usher.
P. Junior. Thou shalt go with us. Uncle, I must have
My princess forth today.
P. Senior.   Whither you please, sir,   90
You shall command her.
Pecunia.   I will do all grace
To my new servant.
P. Senior.   Thanks unto your bounty.
He is my nephew, and my chief, the point,
Tip, top and tuft of all our family!
But sir, conditioned always you return   95
Statute and Band home, with my sweet, soft Wax,
And my good nurse here, Mortgage.
P. Junior.   O, what else?
P. Senior. By Broker.
P. Junior.   Do not fear.
P. Senior.   She shall go wi' you
Whither you please, sir, anywhere.
P. Canter. [*Aside to Picklock.*]   I see
A money-bawd is lightly a flesh-bawd too.   100

93–7.] *F margin: Old* Peny-boy *thankes her, but makes his condition.*

83–4.] P. Junior seizes on the nearest proverb ('A crafty knave needs no
broker': Tilley K122) as an occasion for some typically jejune rib-digging.
Jonson quotes the proverb in *E.M.I.*, III.v.33–4 (*H.&S.*).
    86. *sweeping*] passing with stately movement (*O.E.D.*); cf. Brathwaite, *A
Boulster Lecture*, p. 163: 'this *Gentleman-Usher* must show himselfe rough, that
he may get his Lady better roome . . . He must puffe and looke big, and swell
like a pageant of State.' Brathwaite's typical specimen sports a 'wild-luxurious
beard' (p. 165).
    93. *chief*] Nason, *Heralds and Heraldry*, p. 114, suggests that 'Jonson is here
punning upon the heraldic word 'chief' [which] consists of the upper third,
that is, of the *top* of the escutcheon.'
    point] acme.
    94. *tuft*] chief – a nonce usage, for the alliteration (*O.E.D.*).
    100. *lightly*] commonly.

Picklock. [*To Canter.*] Are you advised? [*Aside.*] Now o'my
    faith, this Canter
    Would make a good grave burgess in some barn.
P. Junior. Come, thou shalt go with us, uncle.
P. Senior.   By no means, sir.
P. Junior. We'll have both sack and fiddlers.
P. Senior.   I'll not draw
    That charge upon your worship.
P. Canter.   He speaks modestly,   105
    And like an uncle.
P. Senior.   But Mas Broker here,
    He shall attend you, nephew, her grace's usher;
    And what you fancy to bestow on him,
    Be not too lavish, use a temperate bounty,
    I'll take it to myself.
P. Junior.   I will be princely   110
    While I possess my princess, my Pecunia.
P. Senior. Where is't you eat?
P. Junior.   Hard by, at Picklock's lodging;
    Old Lickfinger's the cook, here in Ram Alley.
P. Senior. He has good cheer. Perhaps I'll come and see you.
P. Canter. [*Taking P. Junior aside.*] O fie! An alley, and a
    cook's shop, gross!   115
    'Twill savour, sir, most rankly of 'em both.
    Let your meat rather follow you to a tavern.
Picklock. A tavern's as unfit too for a princess.

---

103. S.H. *P. Senior.*] *Whalley;* P. CA. *F.*   115. S.D.] *This ed.; The* Canter
takes him aside, and perswades him, F margin (116–8).

    101. *Are ... advised?*] Have you finally grasped that? Gifford thought that
Picklock is sounding 'a gentle note of admiration', but presumably it is sarcasm at Canter's apparent slowness to realise the situation, and perhaps a
scoffing at his moralistic tone.
    102. *burgess ... barn*] 'an allusion to the custom of beggars gathering in
barns, which served them as inns, or hostelries' (de Winter).
    112–13. *Picklock's ... Alley*] In Barry's *Ram-Alley*, the lawyer Throat
declares that 'there's many a worthy lawyer's chamber, / 'Buts upon Ram-
Alley' Dodsley, 10.292). The alley was 'conveniently located for access to the
Devill Tavern, St. Paul's, and other "business" locales mentioned in the play'
(F. C. Chalfant, *Ben Jonson's London*, p. 147).
    115–16. *alley ... both*] implying that flesh is available there both in cook-
shops and through prostitution.

P. Canter. No, I have known a princess, and a great one,
Come forth of a tavern.
Picklock.   Not go in, sir, though.   120
P. Canter. She must go in if she came forth. The blessèd
Pocahontas (as the historian calls her)
And great king's daughter of Virginia
Hath been in womb of a tavern. And besides,
Your nasty uncle will spoil all your mirth   125
And be as noisome.
Picklock.   That's true.
P. Canter.   No, faith,
Dine in Apollo with Pecunia,
At brave Duke Wadloe's, have your friends about you
And make a day on't.
P. Junior.   Content, i'faith:
Our meat shall be brought thither. Simon the king   130

120. of a tavern] *F;* of tavern *Whalley.*   126. That's] *F;* That is *Whalley.*
No, faith,] No'faith, *F.*

121–3. *The ... Virginia*] Capt. John Smith, in the Dedication to *The Generall Historie of Virginia* (1624) records how 'blessed Pokahontas, the great Kings daughter of *Virginia*, oft saved my life' (*H.&S.*). Pocahontas was captured by the English in 1612, converted and baptised, and subsequently married an Englishman, John Rolfe. She visited England in 1616, and made a great impression at court (where she saw Jonson's *Christmas his Masque*), but died as she was about to board ship to return to Virginia.

124. *Hath ... tavern*] Pocahontas stayed in two taverns: first, the Bell Savage Inn 'without' Ludgate (which later gave rise to the tradition that it was named after her). When the London air proved too much for her, she removed to an inn across the river at Brentford, where she was visited by various notables including Jonson himself. G. S. Woodward, giving no source for the story, relates that Jonson met her 'in the inn parlor' and 'questioned her rapidly for five minutes and then for the next forty-five minutes sat staring at her curiously until Pocahontas finally withdrew silently to her quarters upstairs, leaving Jonson to his bottle of sherry' (*Pocahontas*, 1969, p. 179). Jonson's memory of this occasion may have associated her indelibly with the tavern and somehow engendered the curious phrase *in womb of.*

127. *Apollo*] the Apollo Room in the Devil Tavern at Temple Bar, Fleet Street. The tribe of Ben met regularly there, and Jonson's *Leges Conviviales* were inscribed over the chimney.

128. *Duke Wadloe's*] Simon Wadloe was innkeeper at the Devil Tavern until 1627.

130. *Simon the king*] alluding to the ballad 'Old Simon the King' whose host-figure displays, appropriately, his 'ale-dropt hose, & his malmsey nose' (Kifer). The ballad was reprinted in *Pills to Purge Melancholy*, III.143, and the Bishop Percy *Folio*, ed. Furnivall, p. 124.

Will bid us welcome.
Picklock.   Patron, I have a suit.
P. Junior. What's that?
Picklock.   That you will carry the Infanta
    To see the Staple. Her grace will be a grace
    To all the members of it.
P. Junior.   I will do it,
    And have her arms set up there with her titles,   135
    Aurelia Clara Pecunia, the Infanta.
    And in Apollo. Come, sweet princess, go.
P. Senior. Broker, be careful of your charge.
Broker.   I warrant you.
                                                    [*Exeunt.*]

            The second Intermean after the second Act.

Censure. Why, this is duller and duller, intolerable, scurvy!
    Neither devil nor fool in this play! Pray God some on us be
    not a witch, gossip, to forespeak the matter thus.
Mirth. I fear we are all such, an' we were old enough; but we
    are not all old enough to make one witch. How like you the   5
    Vice i'the play?
Expectation. Which is he?
Mirth. Three or four: old Covetousness, the sordid Pennyboy,
    the money-bawd who is a flesh-bawd too, they say.

1–69.] *Italic in* F.   4. an'] *1716; and* F.

___

135.] Gifford compares *Disc.*, 199–201, and comments: 'It was the custom
for foreign princes and noblemen of high rank or office, to *set up* their arms
and titles in the places through which they passed, or the inns in which they
lodged.'
    136.] See note to II.Int.24–5.

II.Int.3. *forespeak*] make predictions about. Censure is thinking of their
discussion in the First Intermean and jokingly suggests that their accurate
guess that the play wouldn't have a devil or a fool in it might be taken to prove
they are witches.
    4–5 *we ... witch*] our combined ages are not sufficient to make one witch.
Witches were not necessarily old, but the popular stereotype of the withered
hag probably lies behind Mirth's remark. Cf. Sir John Harington's report of
an interview with James I in 1604: 'His Majesty ... askede me, with much
gravitie, if I did trulie understande why the Devil did worke more with ancient
women than others?' (*Shakespeare's England*, I.540).
    8. *old Covetousness*] a recognisable morality type: cf. *Respublica* (1553),

Tattle. But here is never a fiend to carry him away! Besides, he   10
has never a wooden dagger. I'd not give a rush for a Vice
that has not a wooden dagger to snap at everybody he
meets.

Mirth. That was the old way, gossip, when Iniquity came in
like Hocus Pocus in a juggler's jerkin, with false skirts,   15
like the Knave of Clubs. But now they are attired like men
and women o'the time, the Vices male and female! Prodigality like a young heir, and his mistress Money (whose
favours he scatters like counters), pranked up like a prime
lady, the Infanta of the Mines.   20

Censure. Ay, therein they abuse an honourable princess, it is
thought.

---

where Avarice resolves that 'to work my feat, I will ... call my name Policy
instead of Covetise' (ed. Farmer, p. 183).

  10.] See note to I.Int.31–2.

  11. *wooden dagger*] the traditional accoutrement of the Vice-figure in morality drama. In *The Trial of Treasure* (1567), Inclination threatens Sapience and
Just: 'Back, I say, or my dagger shall about your pate, / ... I'll make your
bones sore' (Dodsley III.278). This *old way* is often alluded to in later Tudor
and earlier Stuart drama. See next note.

  14–15. *Iniquity ... jerkin*] Iniquity is the Vice in *D.A.* and Tudor interludes like *Nice Wanton* and *King Darius*; his dexterity and showmanship in the
earlier drama were probably recalled for Jacobean audiences by the conjurers
and jugglers at fairs and similar events. Prominent amongst the latter was 'one
man more excelling in that craft than others, that went about in King *James* his
time, and long since, who called himself, *The Kings Majesties most excellent
Hocus Pocus*, and so was he called ... at the playing of every Trick, he used to
say, *Hocus Pocus, toxtus talontus* ... a dark composure of words, to blinde the
eyes of the beholders' (T. Ady, *A Candle in the Dark* (1655), p. 29).

  16. *like ... Clubs*] Efforts have been made to fix the origin of this simile,
but R. C. Jones (*Y.E.S.*, 3 (1973), 74–7) is probably right to stress that the
card knaves 'were common enough emblems of vices in general' and occur in
Jacobean pamphlet literature; although Jones also proposes a specific source
in Fulwell's *Like Will to Like* (1568), at the start of which Newfangle enters
'laughing, and hath a knave of clubs in his hand' (Dodsley III.309). The court
card is clearly a ready symbol for knavery, distinctively attired (these cards
were originally known as *coat* cards); cf. *N.I.*, I.iii.104–5: 'Some may be
coats, as in the cards; but then / Some must be knaves' (Revels). In *D.A.*,
I.i.85, the devil refers to Vice and 'his long coat', and Samuel Rowlands (*The
Knave of Harts*, 1612) shows that *false skirts* retained their emblematic significance into the Jacobean period: 'Others that *Clubs* and *Spades* apparrel notes,
/ Because they both are in side-guarded Coates, / Tearme them two Usurers,
villanous rich' (sig. B2).

  21–3.] Mirth's first question ('By ... thought?') is not answered, but

Mirth. By whom is it so thought? Or where lies the abuse?

Censure. Plain in the styling her 'Infanta' and giving her three
names.   25

Mirth. Take heed it lie not in the vice of your interpretation.
What have Aurelia, Clara, Pecunia to do with any person?
Do they any more but express the property of money,
which is the daughter of earth, and drawn out of the
mines? Is there nothing to be called Infanta but what is   30
subject to exception? Why not the Infanta of the Beggars,
or Infanta o'the Gypsies, as well as King of Beggars and
King of Gypsies?

Censure. Well, an' there were no wiser than I, I would sew him
in a sack and send him by sea to his princess.   35

Mirth. Faith, an' he heard you, Censure, he would go near to
stick the ass's ears to your high dressing, and perhaps to all
ours for hearkening to you.

34, 36. an'] *1716;* and *F.*

Jonson is probably alluding to the 'sinister interpretation' of which he speaks
in 'To the Readers' following this scene, lines 3–4 (cf. I.iv.8 note). Given
the general opinion of Spanish royalty in England at this time, it is an open
question whether Censure thinks Pecunia or the Infanta more abused by the
association.

24–5. *Plain ... names*] suspecting an allusion to Isabella Clara Eugenia,
daughter of Philip II of Spain and ruler of the Netherlands, who was aunt to
the Infanta sought by Charles in marriage (Cunningham).

27–8. *What ... money*] De Winter, comparing I.vi.45, sees a reference to
the Paracelsian doctrine, held by the alchemists, that 'Gold is in its Essence
threefold: Celestial ... Elementary ... Metallic' (*Coelum Philosophorum*, ed.
A. E. Waite, I.11). See next note.

29. *daughter of earth*] an idea commonly invoked to disparage mineral wealth
and destroy the mystique of money, which 'brags that she is the daughter to
the Sun' but is in fact 'of base birth bred, and begotten onely of the earth'
(Dekker, *Worke for Armorours*, Grosart IV.151). But Jonson's moralising in
this play shuns naive abuse, and Mirth's common sense echoes more closely
the dispassionate tone of Tymme's *Dialogue Philosophicall*: 'the matter of one
Element cannot suffice to the begetting of mixed and compound bodies ...
gold ... and all metalls ... tooke their originall not from one Element alone,
but from all foure in mixture; or rather if you will from the earth, as from their
mother' (p. 3).

30–1. *but ... exception*] without it arousing objections; or possibly, except
things or people which stand out in the public eye. Mirth is voicing Jonson's
usual objection to those who find personal allusions in his satire.

34. *an' ... I*] i.e. if there weren't wiser folk around like you to advise me
against it.

37. *ass's ears*] as a punishment for stupidity. Lyly uses a similar image in

Tattle. By'r Lady, but he should not to mine. I would hearken
and hearken, and censure if I saw cause, for th'other   40
princess' sake – Pocahontas, surnamed the blessèd, whom
he has abused indeed – and I do censure him and will
censure him: to say she came forth of a tavern was said like
a paltry poet.

Mirth. That's but one gossip's opinion, and my gossip Tattle's   45
too! But what says Expectation here? She sits sullen and
silent.

Expectation. Troth, I expect their Office, their great Office, the
Staple, what it will be! They have talked on't, but we see't
not open yet. Would Butter would come in and spread   50
itself a little to us.

Mirth. Or the butter-box, Buz the emissary.

Tattle. When it is churned and dished, we shall hear of it.

Expectation. If it be fresh and sweet butter; but say it be sour
and wheyish?   55

Mirth. Then it is worth nothing, mere pot butter, fit to be
spent in suppositories or greasing coach wheels, stale
stinking butter, and such I fear it is, by the being barrelled
up so long.

Expectation. Or rank Irish butter.   60

Censure. Have patience, gossips. Say that contrary to our
expectations it prove right, seasonable, salt butter.

Mirth. Or to the time of year, in Lent, delicate almond butter!

Midas, IV.i.174–5: 'having here the eares of an asse, it wil be told, all my
haires are asses eares' (Bond III.144).

high dressing] i.e. hair worn up in an elaborate style. Middle-class women
had abandoned the hood by Charles's reign and cultivated more ostentatious
fashions, like those satirised by Massinger in *The City Madam*, IV.iv.103–5:
'your borrow'd hair / Powder'd, and curl'd, was by your dressers art / Form'd
like a Coronet, hang'd with diamonds' (*E.&G.* IV.82–3). The quotation suggests that wigs frequently assisted the effect. For a *high dressing* somewhat
resembling an ass's ears, see the illustration (6) facing p. 31 in the Revels
Volpone, ed. R. B. Parker.

52. *butter-box*] See I.ii.70–1. Fynes Moryson, *Itinerary*, III.iii.3, says that
the Dutch 'carry with them . . . boxes of butter for their foode, whereupon
in like sort strangers call them Butter boxes'; it seems to have been a general
term of contempt. Cf. *E.M.I.*, III.iv.43–4. Here it is also a witty way of saying
'Butter's agent'.

62. *seasonable*] well seasoned, properly preserved.

63. *almond butter*] a Lent substitute for dairy products made from almonds,

I have a sweet tooth yet, and I will hope the best, and sit
down as quiet and calm as butter, look as smooth and soft   65
as butter, be merry and melt like butter, laugh and be fat
like butter – so butter answer my expectation and be not
mad butter. If it be, it shall both July and December see. I
say no more, but – *Dixi.*

---

sugar and rose-water, according to a sixteenth century recipe; later concoctions
use cream and white of egg (*O.E.D.*).

66. *laugh* . . . *fat*] proverbial (Tilley L91). Cf. *E.M.O.*, III.i.10.

68. *mad* . . . *see*] alluding to the proverb 'Butter is mad twice a year' (Tilley
B772), i.e. in July, when it is too soft, and in December, when it is too hard
(Gifford).

69. Dixi] the advocate's formal conclusion: 'there I rest my case' (literally, I
have spoken).

To the Readers

In this following Act, the Office is opened and shown to the
prodigal and his princess Pecunia, wherein the allegory and
purpose of the author hath hitherto been wholly mistaken, and
so sinister an interpretation been made, as if the souls of most
of the spectators had lived in the eyes and ears of these ridicu-   5
lous gossips that tattle between the Acts. But he prays you thus
to mend it. To consider the news here vented to be none of his
news, or any reasonable man's, but news made like the time's
news (a weekly cheat to draw money) and could not be fitter
reprehended than in raising this ridiculous Office of the Staple,   10
wherein the age may see her own folly, or hunger and thirst

1.] In performance Mirth's last speech is immediately followed by the entry
of Fitton and Cymbal (I am assuming that at Blackfriars the Intermeans replaced the customary musical interludes); an interval might conceivably
occur here, but would fall more logically after Act III. Jonson's statement that
'the Office is opened' may imply the use of a booth whose curtains are drawn at
this point, or the stage could have been set for the Staple scenes during the
preceding Intermean. Possibly a booth contained the clerks' desks and some
semblance of a filing system; other furniture, like the table specified in I.i and
I.iv and mentioned again at III.i.40, has probably been onstage throughout
Act II.

8–9. *news . . . money*] Cf. Donald Lupton, *London . . . Carbonadoed* (1632),
'Currantoes or weekly News', pp. 140–2: 'they use to lye (as weather-beaten
Souldiers) upon a *Booke-binders* stall, they are new and old in six dayes . . .
No Pope, Emperour, or King, but must bee touched by their pen . . . these
are all conceites ordinarily, which their owne idle braine, or busy fancies,
upon the blockes in *Paules*, or in their Chambers invented: They have used
this trade so long, that now every one can say, its even as true as a *Currantoe*,
meaning that it's all false.' But the dilemma of newsmen who were committed
to publish reports they could not verify is clearly set out in several newsbook
prefaces. In one the editor addresses himself to 'a question which was lately
made unto mee, *viz.* wherefore I would publish any tydings which were only
rumored without any certainty: I will answer . . . that I rather will write true
tidings only to be rumoured, when I am not fully sure of them, then to write
false tidings to bee true, which will afterwards prove otherwise' (*Late Newes*,
3 Ju y 1624, pp. 1–2). In another, he acknowledges that many are sceptical
abou t the validity of reports, but is resolved to 'go forward in the progression
of tl ese matters . . . I cannot use a better method' (*First from Constantinople*,
2 D :cember 1623, p. 2).

after published pamphlets of news, set out every Saturday but
made all at home, and no syllable of truth in them; than which
there cannot be a greater disease in nature, or a fouler scorn
put upon the times. And so apprehending it, you shall do the   15
author and your own judgement a courtesy, and perceive the
trick of alluring money to the Office and there cozening the
people. If you have the truth, rest quiet, and consider that
        Ficta voluptatis causa, sint proxima veris.

---

12. *set ... Saturday*] Publication on a fixed day of the week did not actually
begin until 1641; before then newsbooks were printed according to the avail-
ability of news, though it was obviously in the trade's interest to achieve a
regular issue. Jonson's remark may reflect a practice of releasing new material
at the weekend, when it would attract the greatest number of customers.

    18. Ficta ... veris] Jonson translates as '*Poet* never credit gain'd / By
writing truths, but things (like truths) well fain'd', in *S.W.*, 2nd Prologue,
9–10.

Act III

[*Enter*] FITTON [*and*] CYMBAL.

[*Fitton.*] You hunt upon a wrong scent still, and think
The air of things will carry 'em, but it must
Be reason and proportion, not fine sounds,
My cousin Cymbal, must get you this lady.
You have entertained a pettifogger here,   5
Picklock, with trust of an emissary's place,
And he is all for the young prodigal.
You see he has left us.
Cymbal.   Come, you do not know him
That speak thus of him. He will have a trick
To open us a gap by a trap-door   10
When they least dream on't. Here he comes.

[*Enter* PICKLOCK.]
                                                     What news?
Picklock. Where is my brother Buz, my brother Ambler?
The Register, Examiner and the clerks?
Appear, and let us muster all in pomp,
For here will be the rich Infanta presently   15
To make her visit. Pennyboy the heir,
My patron, has got leave for her to play
With all her train, of the old churl her guardian.
Now is your time to make all court unto her,

III.i.o.i.] *Kifer;* FITTON. CYMBAL, *to them* PICKLOCKE. / REGISTER. CLERKE.
THO: BARBER. *F.*

III.i.2. *air*] outward appearance; punning on 'musical air', as the next line
shows, and alluding to Cymbal's name. Fitton reminds him that a good confidence trick requires more than specious display.
    5. *pettifogger*] junior lawyer who conducts petty cases.
    10. *trap-door*] O.E.D. has no figurative usage in this sense before 1648;
since Jonson's stage used a trap, the metaphor may be inspired by theatrical
practice.

154

That she may first but know then love the place,   20
And show it by her frequent visits here;
And afterwards, get her to sojourn with you.
She will be weary of the prodigal quickly.
Cymbal. Excellent news!
Fitton.   And counsel of an oracle!
Cymbal. How say you, cousin Fitton?
Fitton.   Brother Picklock,   25
I shall adore thee for this parcel of tidings.
It will cry up the credit of our Office
Eternally, and make our Staple immortal!
Picklock. Look your addresses then be fair and fit,
And entertain her, and her creatures too,   30
With all the migniardise and quaint caresses
You can put on 'em.
Fitton.   Thou seemst by thy language
No less a courtier than a man o'law.
I must embrace thee.
Picklock.   Tut, I am Vertumnus,
On every change or chance, upon occasion,   35
A true chameleon. I can colour for't.
I move upon my axle like a turnpike,
Fit my face to the parties, and become
Straight one of them. [*He and Fitton embrace.*]

[*Enter* NATHANIEL, THOMAS BARBER *and* REGISTER.]

Cymbal.   Sirs, up into your desks,
And spread the rolls upon the tables, so.   40
  Is the Examiner set?

39. S.D. *He . . . embrace.*] *This ed.*

_____

27. *cry up*] proclaim.
31. *migniardise*] *H.&S.* cite Cotgrave's definition (1611): 'quaintnesse, neatnesse, daintinesse, delicacie, wantonnesse; smooth or fair speech, kind usage'; it was probably a fashionable word in court circles.
34. *Vertumnus*] the Roman god of change, who wooed Pomona in a succession of guises. Fitton's eager capitulation to the man he previously suspected is ironically placed by Picklock's suave assurance that he is not what he seems.
36. *colour*] i.e. change colour, adjust my appearance and manner to suit.
37. *turnpike*] turnstile (horizontal bar turning on a vertical pin).
41. *Examiner*] See I.v.4 and notes. Perhaps this character, who never makes

Register.   Yes, sir.
Cymbal.   Ambler and Buz
     Are both abroad now.
Picklock.   We'll sustain their parts.
     No matter, let them ply the affairs without.
     Let us alone within, I like that well.
     On with the cloak, and you with the Staple gown,   45

     Fitton puts on the office cloak, and Cymbal the gown.

     And keep your state, stoop only to the Infanta.
     We'll have a flight at Mortgage, Statute, Band,
     And hard, but we'll bring Wax unto the retrieve.
     Each know his several province, and discharge it.
Fitton. I do admire this nimble engine, Picklock.
Cymbal.   Cuz,   50
     What did I say?
Fitton.   You have rectified my error!

                    ACT III   SCENE ii

[*Enter*] PENNYBOY JU[NIOR], P[ENNYBOY] CANTER, PECU-
NIA, STATUTE, BAND, MORTGAGE, WAX [*and*] BROKER.

[*P. Junior.*] By your leave, gentlemen, what news? Good?
     Good still?
     I'your new Office? Princess, here's the Staple.
     This is the governor: kiss him, noble princess,
     For my sake.   [*Pecunia kisses Cymbal.*]
             Tom! How is it, honest Tom?

50–1.] F *margin:* Fitton *is brought about.*   III.ii.0.1–2.] F *adds:*
CVSTOMERS.

---

an explicit appearance, is meant to be visible 'within' to visiting customers,
thereby reinforcing the illusion of a busy news office.
     44.] Picklock is quick to assert his position as a Staple executive.
     46. *keep . . . state*] observe the pomp and ceremony befitting a high position;
behave in a dignified manner (*O.E.D.*).
     47. *a flight*] i.e. as birds of prey; cf. II.iv.43–4. Picklock might illustrate
using the loose folds of his own gown (he is *gownèd vulture* at V.ii.93).
     48. *And . . . but*] and with a bit of luck.
     retrieve] recovery of game which has been once sprung (*H.&S.*).
     50. *engine*] strategem.
     50–1. brought about (F margin)] brought round, persuaded.

How does thy place, and thou? My creature, princess,   5
This is my creature. Give him your hand to kiss.
                    [*Tom kisses Pecunia's hand.*]
He was my barber, now he writes *Clericus!*
I bought this place for him and gave it him.
P. Canter. He should have spoke of that, sir, and not you.
Two do not do one office well.
P. Junior.   'Tis true,   10
But I am loath to lose my courtesies.
P. Canter. So are all they that do them to vain ends.
And yet you do lose when you pay yourselves.
P. Junior. No more o'your sentences, Canter, they are stale.
We come for news, remember where you are.   15
I pray thee, let my princess hear some news,
Good Master Cymbal.
Cymbal.   What news would she hear?
Or of what kind, sir?
P. Junior.   Any, any kind,
So it be news, the newest that thou hast;
Some news of state, for a princess.
Cymbal.   Read from Rome there.   20
Thomas. [*Reading.*] They write, the King of Spain is chosen
            Pope.

5–7.] *F margin: Hee tells* Pecunia *of* Thom.   20–1.] *F margin: Newes from*
Rome.

III.ii.7. *writes*] signs himself.
    11. *lose . . . courtesies*] miss out on the credit due to me for my kind act; or
possibly, go without the obeisances a grateful inferior should pay me.
    12–13.] a traditional sentiment; cf. Proverbs, xxvii.2: 'Let another man
praise thee, and not thine owne mouth; a stranger, and not thine owne lips.'
(See also Tilley P547, C554, M476.)
    20. *from Rome*] In the sixteenth century Italy was a prime centre for news-
gathering, and even after the focus shifted to Amsterdam (which James Howell
called 'a great Staple of News', *Familiar Letters*, p. 9), it was conventional to
begin newsbooks and corantos with reports 'from Italy' or 'from Rome'.
    21–2. *King . . . Emperor*] a conflation which parodies a standard view of the
Catholic alliance in the Thirty Years War (1618–48). Cf. the partisan editorial
in *The Newes and Affaires of Europe* (6 March 1624), alerting readers to the
intention of 'the Pope, the Emperour, and the King of *Spaine*, to runne (as it
were) one course for their owne glories, and encrease of dominion' (p. 1). In
1621 the House of Commons urged James I to the Protestant war effort with
the claim that Philip IV of Spain 'affects the Temporall Monarchie of the
whole earth' (*Proceedings in . . . Parliament*, p. 29, Burney I), and three years

P. Junior. How!

Thomas. And Emperor too, the thirtieth of February.

P. Junior. Is the Emperor dead?

Cymbal.   No, but he has resigned
And trails a pike now under Tilly.

Fitton.   For penance.

P. Junior. These will beget strange turns in Christendom!   25

Thomas. [*Reading.*] And Spinola is made General of the
      Jesuits.

P. Junior. Stranger!

Fitton.   Sir, all are alike true and certain.

Cymbal. All the pretence to the Fifth Monarchy
      Was held but vain until the ecclesiastic
      And secular powers were united thus   30
      Both in one person.

23–4.] *F margin: Newes of the* Emperor, *and* Tilly.   26–7.] *F margin:
Newes of* Spinola.   28–33.] *F margin: The fifth* Monarchy, *vniting the*
Ecclesiasticke *and* Secular *power.*

---

later Thomas Scott published his pamphlet *The Spaniards perpetuall designes to
an universall monarchie* (1624).

    23. *the Emperor*] Ferdinand II, Holy Roman Emperor from 1619 to 1637.

    24. *trails a pike*] serves as a common soldier (*H.&S.*). When marching the
pike was 'trailed', i.e. held by the side in a sloping position with the butt just
above the ground.

    Tilly] Johann Tzerclaes, Count of Tilly, general of the army of the Catholic
alliance until 1632. He figures prominently in the newsbooks.

    26. *Spinola ... Jesuits*] See I.iv.6 note. *H.&S.* wonder if Jonson is exploit-
ing a popular confusion between the famous general Ambrogio di Spinola and
Father Spinola the Jesuit, martyred at Nagasaki in 1622. Such mistakes were
no doubt common (another potential source of confusion is the report in *Weekly Newes*, 14 March 1623, p. 1, that '*Signeur Philippo Spinola* the Sonne of the
Marquis, is become a Jesuite'). But the point here is the widespread English
conviction that all Jesuits are political agitators; in his *The Unmasking of all
popish monks* (1628), Lewis Owen retails a story, no doubt already in circulation, of how in 1606 the Jesuits 'procured the King of *Spaine* ... to send
Spinola with an army to take *Weesell*, one of the *Hans* Cities [which] is now
beggerd by meanes of the *Jesuites* and *Spaniards* their protectors' (p. 117).

    28. *Fifth Monarchy*] Christ's kingdom on earth, which according to Daniel's
prophecy was to succeed the imperial monarchies of Assyria, Persia, Greece
and Rome. It became a popular concept with millenarian religious sects in
England, but earlier attempts by Catholic Europe to discern its fulfilment in
the Holy Roman Empire foundered on the growing discord between Pope and
Emperor, the spiritual and temporal powers.

Fitton.   'T has been long the aim
  Of the house of Austria.
Cymbal.   See but Maximilian
  His letters to the Baron of Bouttersheim
  Or Scheiter-huyssen.
Fitton.   No, of Liechtenstein:
  Lord Paul, I think.
P. Junior.   I have heard of some such thing.   35
  Don Spinola made General of the Jesuits!
  A priest!
Cymbal.   O no, he is dispensed withal,
  And the whole Society, who do now appear
  The only engineers of Christendom.
P. Junior. They have been thought so long, and rightly too.   40
Fitton. Witness the engine that they have presented him
  To wind himself with up into the moon,

34–6.] F margin: *A plot of the house of* Austria.   37.] *F margin: More of*
Spinola.   39. engineers] *F3;* Enginers *F.*

---

32. *Maximilian*] Duke of Bavaria (Bavier) and founder of the Catholic league, who drove Frederick V, Elector-Palatine out of Bohemia in 1620, and was subsequently rewarded by Ferdinand II with the Electorate of Bavaria.

33–4. *Bouttersheim ... Scheiter-huyssen*] coinages redolent of Rabelais and such works as Joseph Hall's *Mundus Alter et Idem* (1605). The first name, despite its Teutonic suffix, satirises the Dutch love of butter (Holland was loosely identified with much of northern Germany at this time), and the second is cognate with the English (shit-house). Cf. *Ep.* 107, 'To Captain Hungry', 25–6.

34. *Liechtenstein*] Karl von Liechtenstein was Ferdinand's appointed governor of Bohemia from after the expulsion of Frederick, until 1625, and presided over the country's official conversion to Catholicism. *Lord Paul* appears to be a piece of inaccurate name-dropping by Fitton.

37. *dispensed*] released from his vows.

39. *engineeers*] (1) schemers; (2) inventors of ingenious machines and devices (so Kifer). *F*'s *Enginers* underlines the double meaning, and there is a case for preserving this archaism (cf. *pioners* at I.iii.30); but the modern form can also suggest contrivance or subversion as well as mechanical construction, and in this case it assists the metre (cf. IV.ii.35).

41–2.] This was a popular fantasy in the early seventeenth century, following recent advances in astronomy; but in satirising the vogue Jonson's inspiration (as in *N.N.W.*) is probably the moon-voyages in Lucian's *True History* and *Icaromenippus*. The idea serves to burlesque Spinola's prowess as an inventor of war machines, which Jonson had already mocked in *Volp.*, II.i.51 (Revels) in the shape of 'Spinola's whale', designed to drown London with its spouting.

And thence make all his discoveries!

Cymbal. [*To Thomas.*]   Read on.

Thomas. And Vitellesco, he that was last General,

  Being now turned cook to the Society,   45

  Has dressed His Excellence such a dish of eggs –

P. Junior. What, poached?

Thomas.   No, powdered.

Cymbal.   All the yolk is wildfire,

  As he shall need beleaguer no more towns

  But throw his egg in.

Fitton.   It shall clear consume

  Palace and place, demolish and bear down   50

  All strengths before it.

Cymbal.   Never be extinguished

  Till all become one ruin.

Fitton. [*Prompting.*]   And from Florence –

Thomas. They write, was found in Galileo's study

46.] *F margin: His* Egges. 47.] *Two lines in F, divided at 'powdered'.*
52. S.D.] *This ed.* 54.] *F margin:* Galilæo's *study.*

---

44. *Vitellesco*] Mutius Vitelleschi, general of the Society of Jesus from 1615 to 1645.

46. *His Excellence*] Spinola.

47. *powdered*] seasoned – sprinkled with salt or spice.

powdered ... wildfire] i.e. filled with a compound of gunpowder and chemicals, extremely difficult to extinguish once ignited (*O.E.D.*).

48–9. *As ... in*] The newsbooks for 1624–5 had been full of Spinola's protracted and costly siege of Breda; casualties and deserters were numerous, and by April 1625 Spinola had resolved to 'use all his power and industry to make himself master of [the city] ... and thereupon was great store of Fireballs sent to the Spanish Campe [and] a skilful Enginer who hath undertaken to fire *Breda* with his devices and instruments' (*The Continuation of our Weekely Newes*, 14 April 1625, p. 14).

53. *Galileo*] *H.&S.* point out that this is Jonson's only reference to Galileo. See next note.

54. *burning glass*] F. A. Pottle ('Two Notes', *M.L.N.*, 40, 223–6) compares the patent taken out by William Drummond of Hawthornden in September 1626 for a set of 'Burning Glasses' capable of igniting objects out of firing range on land or sea. Jonson might have heard of this scheme at an earlier stage from Drummond himself, in time for its use in the play; but there were other such proposals in the air at this time. An MS document of 1596 written by John Napier the mathematician and entitled 'Secrett inventionis ... for defence of this Iland' describes a burning mirror which would consume an enemy's ships 'at whatever appointed distance' (*Napier Memorial Volume*, ed. C. G. Knott, p. 47). And in 1623 Cornelius Drebbel (see note to line 59) sought funds to

A burning glass (which they have sent him too)
To fire any fleet that's out at sea –   55
Cymbal. By moonshine, is't not so?
Thomas.   Yes, sir, i'the water.
P. Junior. His strengths will be unresistible if this hold!
Ha' you no news against him, on the contrary?
Nathaniel. Yes, sir. They write here, one Cornelius-Son
Hath made the Hollanders an invisible eel   60
To swim the haven at Dunkirk and sink all
The shipping there.
P. Junior.   Why ha' not you this, Tom?
Cymbal. Because he keeps the Pontificial side.

56–8.] *F margin: The burning glasse, by Moon-shine.*   59–60.] *F margin: The Holanders Eele.*

---

construct a solar energy plant, using mirrors to concentrate the sun's rays, which would supply London's fuel needs (L. E. Harris, *The Two Netherlanders*, pp. 189–91). The connection between these fanciful projects and Galileo's experiments is pure invention by Jonson, although in a letter of 1609 Galileo does remark on the potential usefulness of the telescope 'in naval and military operations' (see J. J. Fahie, *Galileo His Life and Work* (1903), p. 77).

56. *moonshine . . . water*] 'Moonshine in the water' was proverbial for something insubstantial or unreal (cf. the modern use of 'moonshine' to mean imaginary nonsense). Cf. Burton, *Anatomy of Melancholy*, I.36: 'we spend our days in unprofitable questions and disputations . . . about moonshine in the water' (Everyman ed.).

59. *Cornelius-Son*] corruption of Dutch 'Cornelissen': Cornelius Drebbel, an engineer and inventor who in 1621 constructed some kind of underwater vessel in which he sailed from Westminster to Greenwich. Jonson may be thinking more specifically of his employment by naval officials as an explosives expert, responsible 'for the making of dyvers watermines, water petards, forged cases to be shot with fireworks, and boats to goe under water' (quoted by Harris, p. 195). But in *Harl.* MS 383, fol. 39, one Robb. Gett, writing to Joseph Mead in August 1626, retails a story about Sir Henry Mannering (Manwaring?) who 'bought an old keel . . . to try an experiment upon; which was, to blow it up, by means of a shipp artificially made to goe underwater'. Spectators beheld 'the vessel tost farr above water, and with great violence and noyse broken in pieces . . . it may prove an instrument of notable mischief to the enemy.'

61–2. *swim . . . there*] Just before *Staple*'s first performance, a Butter newsbook for 18 January 1626 carried a Dutch report that 'The *Duynkerkers* are againe at Sea, and doe great hurt both to the *English* and our Nation' (p. 11). In the previous year Buckingham had tried to organise a direct attack on Dunkirk, to quell the pirates and establish a bridgehead for the relief of the Palatinate, but the plan was dropped for lack of support.

63.] Cymbal is careful to maintain an appearance of balanced news coverage.

P. Junior. How! Change sides, Tom. 'Twas never in my
    thought
    To put thee up against ourselves. Come down,   65
    Quickly.
Cymbal.   Why, sir?
P. Junior.   I ventured not my money
    Upon those terms. If he may change, why so.
    I'll ha' him keep his own side, sure.
Fitton.   Why, let him.
    'Tis but writing so much over again.
P. Junior. For that I'll bear the charge. There's two pieces.   70
Fitton. [*To Cymbal.*] Come, do not stick with the gentleman.
Cymbal.   I'll take none, sir;
    And yet he shall ha' the place.
P. Junior.   They shall be ten then.
    Up, Tom; and th'Office shall take 'em. Keep your side,
    Tom. [*Tom changes sides with Nathaniel.*]
    Know your own side; do not forsake your side, Tom.
Cymbal. Read.
Thomas.   They write here, one Cornelius-Son   75
    Hath made the Hollanders an invisible eel
    To swim the haven at Dunkirk and sink all
    The shipping there.
P. Junior.   But how is't done?
Cymbal.   I'll show you, sir.
    It is an automa runs under water,

64–6.] *F margin:* Peny-boy *will haue him change sides:*   73.] *F margin:*
though hee pay for it.

In practice nearly all foreign news came from Protestant sources, and occasional attempts in the newsbooks to restore the balance are hardly an exercise in impartial journalism – as in the issue for 29 March 1625, with the somewhat satirical preface: 'To the indifferent Reader ... whereas we have hetherto printed (for the most part) the Occurrances which have come to our hands, from the Protestants side, which some have excepted against: wherefore to give them content, we purpose to publish ... such Relations as are printed at *Antwerp* [in the Spanish Netherlands], *Utopia,* or other such like places, that they may from time to time have somewhat to build their miraculous faith upon ... this we do not for profit, but to free ourselves from partiallity, and to make a destinction t'wixt each relation'.

    79. *automa*] 'erroneous singular of "automata"' (*O.E.D.*).

With a snug nose, and has a nimble tail   80
Made like an auger, with which tail she wriggles
Betwixt the coasts of a ship and sinks it straight.
P. Junior. Whence ha' you this news?
Fitton.   From a right hand, I assure you:
The eel boats here that lie before Queenhithe,
Came out of Holland.
P. Junior.   A most brave device   85
To murder their flat bottoms.
Fitton.   I do grant you.
But what if Spinola have a new project,
To bring an army over in cork shoes
And land them here at Harwich? All his horse
Are shod with cork, and fourscore pieces of ordnance,   90
Mounted upon cork carriages, with bladders
Instead of wheels, to run the passage over
At a spring tide.
P. Junior.   Is't true?
Fitton.   As true as the rest.
P. Junior. He'll never leave his engines. I would hear now
Some curious news.

87–9.] *F margin:* Spinola's *new proiect: an army in cork-shoes.*

---

80. *snug*] trim, neat, compact (*O.E.D.*).
tail] stern; not, as edd. claim, a propeller.
81. *auger*] boring tool.
82. *coasts*] ribs. Cf. Cotgrave: '*Les Costes* . . . wedge-like peeces of wood'.
83. *From . . . hand*] from a superior source.
84. *Queenhithe*] Queenhithe Dock near the Southwark bridge, where the Dutch ships unloaded fish during Lent in defiance of import restrictions (B. Johansson, *Religion and Superstition*, pp. 53–4). De Winter quotes *Westward for Smelts* (1620) to the effect that the eel-ships kept watch in Lent 'lest the inhabitants, contrarie to the Law, should spill the bloud of innocents, which would be greatly to the hinderance of these Butter-boxes' (A3).
87–9. *Spinola . . . Harwich*] In late 1625 a garrison of ten thousand men was stationed at Harwich on the Essex coast in expectation of an invasion by Spinola, whose fleet had just broken a blockade of Dunkirk by the English and Dutch, in the wake of Buckingham's disastrous expedition against Cadiz (Reade, *Sidelights on the Thirty Years War*, II.490).
88. *cork shoes*] Shoes with high cork soles were fashionable, and frequently derided as wanton. Linthicum thinks they may have originated with court-esans, and cites Porter, *The Two Angry Women of Abingdon*: 'maides that wear corke shooes may step awry' (line 676). Jonson's joke visualises not only a floating army but also the incongruous spectacle of mincing soldiers.

Cymbal.   As what?

P. Junior.   Magic, or alchemy   95
    Or flying i'the air, I care not what.

Nathaniel. [*Reading.*] They write from Leipzig (reverence to
        your ears),
    The art of drawing farts out of dead bodies
    Is by the Brotherhood of the Rosy Cross
    Produced unto perfection in so sweet   100
    And rich a tincture –

Fitton.   As there is no princess
    But may perfume her chamber with th'extraction.

P. Junior. There's for you, princess.

P. Canter.   What, a fart for her?

P. Junior. I mean the spirit.

P. Canter.   Beware how she resents it.

P. Junior. And what hast thou, Tom?

Thomas. [*Reading.*]   The perpetual motion   105
    Is here found out by an alewife in St Katherine's,
    At the sign o'the Dancing Bears.

P. Junior.   What, from her tap?
    I'll go see that, or else I'll send old Canter.

99.] *F margin: Extraction of farts*   104–5.] *F margin: The perpetuall Motion.*

---

95. *curious*] occult.

98. *farts ... bodies*] proverbial for the impossible: 'As soon may you get a
fart out of a dead man' (Tilley F63). Jonson uses it elsewhere in this general
sense, but the worldly twist he contrives here in allying it to the perfume trade
may be suggested by Rabelais, *Pantagruel*, Bk. V, 22: 'I saw a spodizator, who
very artificially got farts out of a dead ass, and sold them for five pence an ell'
(Urquhart-Le Motteux transl., Everyman II.302).

99. *Brotherhood ... Cross*] the German followers of Christian Rosencreutz,
the hero of two manifestoes which appeared in the early seventeenth century
and described the Order which he supposedly founded in the fifteenth. Jonson
was clearly well informed on the subject; see his masque *The Fortunate Isles*,
and Frances Yates, *The Rosicrucian Enlightenment* (Paladin ed., p. 182). See
also notes to line 129 and IV.ii.34.

104. *spirit*] i.e. the natural or vegetative spirit responsible for nourishment,
digestion and other functions of the lower body. The same pun is unconscious-
ly perpetrated by Thomas Tymme in his *Dialogue Philosophicall* (1612), p. 41:
'Spirit naturall, is an Æthereall substance, differing from the materiall body
and humors thereof ... the same hath a great force and passage, as hath the
winde.'

    resents] with a pun on 'smell out, detect' (*O.E.D.* 4, first example from
1641).

He can make that discovery.
P. Canter.   Yes, in ale. [*Noise without.*]
P. Junior. Let me have all this news made up and sealed.   110
Register. The people press upon us. Please you, sir,
Withdraw with your fair princess. There's a room
Within, sir, to retire to.
P. Junior.   No, good Register,
We'll stand it out here and observe your Office,
What news it issues.
Register.   'Tis the house of fame, sir,   115
Where both the curious and the negligent,
The scrupulous and careless, wild and staid,
The idle and laborious: all do meet
To taste the *cornucopiae* of her rumours,

---

109. S.D.] *Gifford.*   111–2.] *F margin: The* Register *offers him a roome.*
114–6.] *F margin: The* Office *call'd the house of fame.*   117. staid] *so Kifer;*
stay'd *F.*

105–7. *The . . . Bears*] Tymme, p. 60, describes and illustrates a *perpetuum mobile* which Cornelius Drebbel presented to King James. He 'extracted a fierie spirit, out of the minerall matter, joyning the same with his proper Aire, which encluded in the Axeltree, being hollow, carrieth the wheeles, making a continuall rotation or revolution'. Jonson refers satirically to it in *S.W.*, V.iii.63, and associates it here with perpetual motion of a different kind: in *The Masque of Augures* we hear of 'the three dancing Beares in *Saint Katherines* . . . which Alehouse is kept by a distressed lady', where drink is so plentiful that 'From morning to night, / And about to day-light, / They sit and never grudge it' (115–17, 208–10). The vicinity was largely inhabited by Drebbel's countrymen; cf. *D.A.*, I.i.61–2: 'to Saint *Kathernes*, / To drinke with the *Dutch* there' (*H.&S.*).

115. *house of fame*] perhaps glancing at Chaucer's poem, which describes not only the hilltop House of Fame but also that of Rumour 'in a valeye . . . faste by', which is 'full of rounynges and of jangles' (lines 1918–19, 1960, *Works*, ed. Robinson, p. 300). But both Chaucer and Jonson are indebted to a classical image of *Fama*, as described in *The Aeneid*, IV.181f., and more particularly to Ovid's satirical portrait of Rumour's house of sounding brass at the start of Book 12 of *Metamorphoses*, where a 'whole host . . . come and go, a shadowy throng, and a thousand rumours, false mixed with true, stray this way and that . . . each new teller adds something to what he has heard' (Penguin ed., transl. M. M. Innes, p. 269).

117. *staid*] serious, not capricious. The spelling 'stay'd' (see collation) is common before the nineteenth century; although Kifer was the first editor to modernise correctly, her reading *staid* is scarcely an emendation, as she suggests.

Which she, the mother of sport, pleaseth to scatter   120
Among the vulgar. Baits, sir, for the people!
And they will bite like fishes.

[*Enter three* Customers, *the first*] *a she Anabaptist.*

P. Junior.   Let's see't.
Dopper. Ha' you in your profane shop any news
          O' the saints at Amsterdam?
Register.   Yes, how much would you?
Dopper. Six pennyworth.
Register.   Lay your money down. Read, Thomas.   125
Thomas. The saints do write, they expect a prophet shortly,
          The prophet Baal, to be sent over to them
          To calculate a time, and half a time
          And the whole time, according to Naometry.

---

122. S.D.] *Kifer; F margin (123–4)*: I. *Cust. A she* Ana-baptist. *Some copies of*
F.   Let's see't] *F;* Let us see it *Whalley.*   127–8.] *F margin: Prophet*
Baal *expected in Holland.*

---

120. *she . . . sport*] i.e. Lady Fame.
123. Dopper] *F*'s DOP = Dopper, from the Dutch *dooper*, meaning a
dipper; the Anabaptists were so called because of their belief in adult baptism
by total immersion. It is likely, from line 111, that this character and the other
two customers who speak in the next fifty lines enter together, at or about line
122.
124. *saints*] Amsterdam tolerated a large number of radical Protestant sects,
including the Anabaptists. Cf. *Alch.*, II.iv.29–30: 'the holy brethren / Of
Amsterdam, the exil'd saints' (Revels).
127. *Baal*] punning on the name of John Ball, a tailor who 'put out mony
and Clocks, to be paid . . . when *King James* should be crowned in the *Pope's*
Chaire' (F. Osborne, *Traditionall Memoyres* (1658), p. 118, quoted by Gifford).
Cf. *The Fair Maid of the Inn*, V.ii.77: 'the very Ball of your false prophets'
(Lucas IV.216). See next two notes.
128–9. *time . . . time*] from Revelations, xii.14: 'And to the woman were
given two wings of a great Eagle, that shee might flee into the wildernesse into
her place, where she is nourished for a time, and times, and halfe a time, from
the face of the serpent.' Puritan fascination with millenarian texts encouraged
speculative enterprises like Ball's.
129. *Naometry*] referring to an unpublished treatise by the German mystic
Simon Studion, 'an apocalyptic-prophetic work of immense length, using
involved numberology based on Biblical descriptions of the measurements of
the Temple of Solomon and . . . leading up to prophecies about dates of future
events', including the overthrow of the Pope and Mahomet (F. Yates, *The*
Rosicrucian Enlightenment, p. 62). Yates calls it 'a basic source for the Rosi-

P. Junior. What's that?

Thomas.   The measuring o'the Temple, a cabal   130
  Found out but lately and set out by Archie,
  Or some such head, of whose long coat they have heard,
  And being black, desire it.

Dopper.   Peace be with them!

Register. So there had need, for they are still by the ears
  One with another.

Dopper.   It is their zeal.

Register.   Most likely.   135

Dopper. Have you no other of that species?

Register.   Yes,
  But dearer, it will cost you a shilling.

Dopper.   Verily,
  There is a ninepence, I will shed no more.

Register. Not to the good o'the saints?

Dopper.   I am not sure
  That man is good.

Register.   Read, from Constantinople,   140
  Nine penny'orth.

Thomas.   They give out here, the grand Signor
  Is certainly turned Christian, and to clear
  The controversy 'twixt the Pope and him,
  Which is the Antichrist, he means to visit
  The Church at Amsterdam this very summer,   145

132–4.] *F margin: Archie* mourn'd then.   141–2.] *F margin: The great* Turk *turn'd* Christian.

---

crucian movement' (p. 63), and although Jonson is most unlikely to have seen it, he was probably as well informed as anyone in England at that time about its general contents.

  130. *cabal*] secret.

  131. *Archie*] Archibald Armstrong, court fool to both James and Charles I. The marginal note 'Archie *mourn'd then*' and the black coat must refer to his mourning for James I in 1625–6; *H.&S.* suggest a source for lines 132–3 in an account of Archie's subsequent disgrace for speaking against the bishops, but this happened some years after the play's printing, in 1638.

  137. *a shilling*] See note to I.v.65. The Staple prices are greatly inflated (*ninepence* (138) = nine old pence, three-quarters of a shilling).

  141. *grand Signor*] the Sultan of Turkey, Mustapha II. In 1625 the Protestant coalition in Europe sought to enlist Turkish support for an offensive against Ferdinand.

And quit all marks o'the beast.

Dopper.   Now joyful tidings!
Who brought in this? Which emissary?

Register.   Buz,
Your countryman.

Dopper.   Now blessed be the man
And his whole family, with the nation.

Register. Yes, for Amboyna, and the justice there!   150
[*Aside to Thomas.*] This is a Dopper, a she Anabaptist.
Seal and deliver her her news: dispatch.

2 Customer. Ha' you any news from the Indies? Any miracles
Done in Japan by the Jesuits, or in China?

Nathaniel. No, but we hear of a colony of cooks   155
To be set ashore o'the coast of America
For the conversion of the cannibals,
And making them good, eating Christians.

153–4.] *F margin:* 2. *Cust.*   155–9.] *F margin:* A Coloney *oe* [sic] *Cookes
sent over to conuert the* Canniballs.   158. good,] *F;* good *F3.*

146. *marks . . . beast*] the distinguishing mark of the damned in Revelation,
xvi.2, routinely associated with Catholicism in Puritan thought.
150.] On 9 March 1623 (N.S.) ten Englishmen were executed after lengthy
torture had forced them to confess involvement in a conspiracy to seize the
Dutch castle of Amboyna in the Moluccas. The product of a long-standing
struggle between the rival East India companies for control of the spice trade,
this incident provoked bitter reaction in England and demands that those responsible be brought to justice. Nothing was done, but *A True Relation of the
unjust proceedings . . . at Amboyna* (1624) reported that *justice there* of a sort was
achieved: a 'newe sicknesse' carried off 1000 people, and 'At the instant of the
execution, there arose a great darkenesse, with a sudden and violent gust of
winde and tempest' (p. 29).
153–4. *miracles . . . China*] Accounts of Jesuit activity in the Far East at this
time tend to be graphic descriptions of martyrdom and endurance; but Jesuit
'miracles' nearer home are reported in numerous publications and are extensively derided by John Gee in his popular 1624 pamphlet *The Foot out of the
Snare* as 'old wonder-working Tales' (p. 33).
157–8.] See W. Wood, *New England's Prospect* (1634), pp. 75–6, on the
Mohawks: 'a cruel bloodie people . . . yea verie caniballs they were, sometimes
eating on a man, one part after another, before his face and while yet living . . .
They are so hardie that they can eat such things as would make other Indians
sick to look upon.' But despite this propaganda, North American Indians were
not known for cannibalism, and Jonson might have found an altogether more
apt subject for culinary conversion in Capt. John Smith's *The Generall Historie
of Virginia* (1624), describing 'the starving time' in Virginia in 1609, when the

[*Enter* LICKFINGER.]

Here comes the colonel that undertakes it.
3 Customer. Who, Captain Lickfinger?
Lickfinger.   News, news, my boys!   160
I am to furnish a great feast today,
And I would have what news the Office affords.
Nathaniel. We were venting some of you, of your new project –
Register. Afore 'twas paid for. You were somewhat too hasty.
P. Junior. What, Lickfinger, wilt thou convert the cannibals   165
With spit and pan divinity?
Lickfinger.   Sir, for that
I will not urge, but for the fire and zeal
To the true cause. Thus I have undertaken,
With two lay brethren to myself, no more –
One o'the broach, th'other o'the boiler –   170
In one six months, and by plain cookery,
No magic to't, but old Japhet's physic
(The father of the European arts)
To make such sauces for the savages,
And cook their meats with those enticing steams   175

---

160. S.H. *3 Customer.*] *F3*; C.2. *F (in F margin: 3 Cust.).*   161–2.] *F*
margin: By Colonel Lickfinger.   175. cook.] *1716;* cookes *F.*

---

colony was seriously declining and 'so great was our famine, that a Salvage we
slew, and buried, the poorer sort tooke him up againe and eat him, and . . .
divers one another boyled and stewed with roots and herbs' (pp. 105–6).
Jonson may also have in the back of his mind the incident in Rabelais where
Gargantua consumes 'six Pilgrims in a sallad' (*Gargantua*, Bk. I, 38; Everyman
I.88); de Winter notes that previous edd. delete 'the comma after *good*, thereby
hiding Jonson's jest'. See also notes to lines 166 and 176–9 below.
    159. *colonel*] 'trisyllabic at this date' (Kifer).
    166. *spit . . . divinity*] *H.&S.* compare Athenaeus, *Deipnosophistae*, xiv.660
(see Appendix A, and notes to IV.ii.5–40, 5–7). But cf. also the culinary war
in Rabelais where the enemies of Shrovetide are routed by Pantagruel and
Friar John 'armed with iron-spits . . . frying pans, kettles . . . oven-forks,
tongs, dripping pans' (*Pantagruel*, Bk. IV, 41; Everyman II.186).
    167–8. *for . . . cause*] parody of a puritan idiom; cf. *Alch.*, IV.v.33–4
(Revels).
    170. *broach*] spit.
    172. *Japhet's physic*] i.e. fire, brought down to earth by Prometheus, son
of Japetus. The latter was regularly confused with the Biblical Japhet, who
becomes easily associated with the art that Lickfinger holds a 'trade from
Adam' (III.iii.18). His *magic* is an art lawful as eating.

As it would make our cannibal-Christians
Forbear the mutual eating one another,
Which they do do more cunningly than the wild
Anthropophagi, that snatch only strangers,
Like my old patron's dogs there.
P. Junior.   O, my uncle's!   180
Is dinner ready, Lickfinger?
Lickfinger.   When you please, sir.
I was bespeaking but a parcel of news
To strew out the long meal withal, but 't seems
You are furnished here already.
P. Junior.   O, not half!
Lickfinger. What court news is there? Any proclamations   185
Or edicts to come forth?
Thomas.   Yes, there is one
That the king's barber has got, for aid of our trade,
Whereof there is a manifest decay:
A precept for the wearing of long hair,
To run to seed, to sow bald pates withal,   190
And the preserving fruitful heads and chins
To help a mystery almost antiquated.

189–92.] *F margin: To let long hayre runne to seed, to sow bald pates.*

176–9.] Cf. Robert Daborn, *A Christian turn'd Turke* (1612), C4, where
Rabshake the Turk expostulates: 'I turne Christian? they shall have more
charity amongst 'em first. They will devoure one-another as familiarly as Pikes
doe Gudgeons, and with as much facility as Dutchmen doe Flapdragons ...
you have an innocent Christian cal'd a Gallant, your Citie Christian will feed
upon no other meate by his good will.'

179. *Anthropophagi*] with the penultimate syllable stressed, as in the Greek
(*H.&S.*).

183. *strew out*] *O.E.D.* queries 'intersperse with' (citing only examples from
Jonson), but Lickfinger may mean he wants newsheets to display along the
dinner table for the amusement of guests. In *Ep.* 115, line 10, and *Und.* 47,
line 28, the phrase implies both 'occupy, fill up' and 'add spice and variety
to'; the link between news and fashionable banqueting is a persistent one in
Jonson's mind.

188.] *Vox Graculi* (1623) comments on 'The Pockes, a sharp shaver': 'There
are many also who are like to be troubled with such hote rheumes in their
heads, by walking the purlewes, that their haire shall fall off without the helpe
of a Barber' (sig. B).

189–90.] Jonson repeats the joke recorded by Drummond (*Conv. Drum.*,
486–9).

192. *mystery*] craft, trade.

Such as are bald and barren beyond hope
Are to be separated, and set by
For ushers to old countesses.
Lickfinger.   And coachmen,   195
To mount their boxes reverently and drive,
Like lapwings, with a shell upo' their heads,
Thorough the streets. Ha' you no news o'the stage?
They'll ask me about new plays at dinner-time,
And I should be as dumb as a fish.
Thomas.   O yes: 200
There is a legacy left to the King's Players,
Both for their various shifting of their scene
And dext'rous change o'their persons to all shapes
And all disguises, by the right reverend
Archbishop of Spalato.
Lickfinger.   He is dead   205
That played him!
Thomas.   Then h'has lost his share o'the legacy.

---

195. S.H. *Lickfinger.*] *F; Whalley gives 195–8 (And . . . streets.) to Thomas.*
201–3.] *F margin: Spalato's Legacy to the Players.*

194–5. *set . . . coachmen*] Cf. the exchange in *N.I.*, IV.i.15–18: 'my lady
. . . made me drive bare-headed i'the rain. / That she might be mistaken for a
countess?' (Revels). Nares remarks that 'It was a piece of state, that the servants of the nobility, particularly the gentleman-usher, should attend bare-
headed' (I.55). Jonson frequently satirises the practice.

197.] The lapwing leaves its nest within a few hours of being hatched; that it
does so with a shell on its head was proverbial (Tilley L69) for juvenile haste,
but Jonson is exploiting the image rather than the lore behind it.

202. *scene*] setting or location, rather than scenery (*H.&S.*). Cf. *Cat.*, I.185,
and *E.M.O.*, Induction, 277, where Jonson tilts at playwrights who 'lightly
alter the *Scene*' and fail to observe unity of place.

205. *Spalato*] Antonio de Dominis, Archbishop of Spalatro [sic] quarrelled
with the Pope and came to England in 1616 to promote his idea of a Universal
Church (*H.&S.*). He was well received by James I, but a Butter newsbook
reminded its readers of how 'he hath made very good use of *England* . . . as of
a Whoode, to keepe his head from a storme' (7 November 1622, p. 2). When
the scheme failed Spalato returned to Rome and Catholicism, but this *dext'rous
change* did not save him, and after his death in an Inquisition jail his body and
books were burned for heresy (see *The Continuation of our Weekly Newes*,
1 February 1625, p. 1).

205–6. *He . . . him*] William Rowley, who played the Fat Bishop (a satirical
portrait of Spalatro) in Middleton's *A Game at Chess* (1624), died early in
February 1626. See note to I.Int.21–2.

Lickfinger. What news of Gondomar?

Thomas. [*Reading another roll.*]   A second fistula,
     Or an excoriation, at the least,
     For putting the poor English play was writ of him
     To such a sordid use, as is said he did,   210
     Of cleansing his posteriors.

Lickfinger.   Justice! Justice!

Thomas. Since when, he lives condemned to his chair at
          Brussels,
     And there sits filing certain politic hinges
     To hang the States on h'has heaved off the hooks.

Lickfinger. What must you have for these?

P. Junior.   Thou shalt pay
          nothing,   215
     But reckon 'em in i'the bill. There's twenty pieces

---

208. the least] *F;* least *F3.*   209–12.] *F margin:* Gundomar's *vse of the*
game at Chesse, *or* Play *so called.*   212. chair] *conj. de Winter;* share *F.*

207. *Gondomar*] Diego Sarmiento d'Acuña, Count of Gondomar, Spanish
diplomat who worked toward peace and a royal wedding between England and
Spain. He is satirised as the Black Knight in *A Game at Chess* (Kifer).
     second fistula] This is comic duplication: Gondomar was already famous for
such a complaint. See note to line 212.
     209. *poor . . . play*] *A Game at Chess*, suppressed at Gondomar's insistence
after a record-breaking nine-day run at the Globe in August 1624. The word
poor indicates Jonson's contempt for Middleton and his play (see *Conv. Drum.*,
168); *English* is the Staple's clever pretence that this is a foreign report.
     210. *sordid use*] adapted from Rabelais, *Pantagruel*, Bk. IV, 52, where Friar
John is similarly afflicted for thus 'bewraying that sacred book which you
ought rather to have kissed and adored . . . an effect of divine justice!' (II.208)
(*H.&S.*).
     212. *chair*] Gondomar had a special chair to accommodate his fistula. *F*'s
share was probably caught from line 206, where the same word occupies a
similar position in the line. In *A Game at Chess*, IV.ii.3, the Black Knight
refers to 'my chair of ease, my chair of cozenage' (Bullen VII.94). The chair
and a horse-borne litter are both represented on the title-page of Thomas
Scott's anti-Gondomar pamphlet, *Vox Populi* (1624).
     213. *filing . . . hinges*] devising political strategies.
     214. *States*] the States General of the United Provinces, or the Protestant
Netherlands.
     216.] Gifford was the first to mark an exit for Lickfinger in this line, and
subsequent editors who print a modernised text have followed him, failing to
notice that Lickfinger is still on stage at line 285. At that point P. Junior recalls
him to his cooking duties in terms which imply that meanwhile he has been
pumping the Staple clerks for news at the prodigal's expense.

Her grace bestows upon the Office, Tom.
He gives twenty pieces to the Office.
[Lickfinger keeps the clerks busy reading news.]
Write thou that down for news.
Register.   We may well do't:
We have not many such.
P. Junior.   There's twenty more
If you say so. (*Doubles it.*) My princess is a princess!   220
And put that too under the Office seal.

Cymbal takes Pecunia aside [and] courts and woos her to
the Office. [Fitton courts her women.]

Cymbal. If it will please your grace to sojourn here
And take my roof for covert, you shall know
The rites belonging to your blood and birth,
Which few can apprehend. These sordid servants,   225
Which rather are your keepers than attendants,
Should not come near your presence. I would have
You waited on by ladies, and your train
Borne up by persons of quality and honour.
Your meat should be served in with curious dances,   230
And set upon the board with virgin hands
Tuned to their voices, not a dish removed
But to the music, nor a drop of wine
Mixed with his water without harmony.
Pecunia. You are a courtier, sir, or somewhat more,   235
That have this tempting language.
Cymbal.   I'm your servant,
Excellent princess, and would ha' you appear

217.2.] *This ed.*

223. *covert*] shelter and protection; the word also implies jurisdiction and control.

230-4. *Your ... harmony*] These lines invoke the voluptuous appeal to the senses that banquets represent in one allegorical tradition (as in *Temp.*, III.ii, and *Paradise Reg.*, II.337-91). See Introduction, p. 37. In Jonson's hospitable ethos, the obsession with gratification and externals transgresses the important ritual of the meal. Cf. *Ep.* 101, 'Inviting a Friend to Supper', and the debate in *N.I.*, III.ii.

That which you are. Come forth, state and wonder
Of these our times, dazzle the vulgar eyes
And strike the people blind with admiration.   240
P. Canter. [*Aside.*] Why, that's the end of wealth! Thrust
    riches outward
And remain beggars within; contemplate nothing
But the vile sordid things of time, place, money,
And let the noble and the precious go.
Virtue and honesty, hang 'em; poor thin membranes   245
Of honour, who respects them? O, the Fates!
How hath all just, true reputation fall'n
Since money, this base money 'gan to have any!

    Fitton hath been courting the waiting-women this while, and
      is jeered by them.
Band. Pity the gentleman is not immortal –
Wax. As he gives out, the place is, by description –   250
Fitton. A very paradise, if you saw all, lady.
Wax. I am the chambermaid, sir, you mistake:
    My lady may see all.
Fitton. Sweet Mistress Statute, gentle Mistress Band,
    And Mother Mortgage, do but get her grace   255
    To sojourn here.
Picklock.   I thank you, gentle Wax.
Mortgage. If it were a chattel, I would try my credit.
Picklock. So it is; for term of life, we count it so.
Statute. She means inheritance to him and his heirs,
    Or that he could assure a state of years;   260

---

238. state] *F* (*State*,); the state *Whalley*.

238. *state*] 'person of standing, importance or high rank' (*O.E.D.* 24).
Edd. since Whalley have needlessly expanded to 'the state'; Pecunia is being
addressed directly, and the absence of a weak stress in the fourth foot creates
an effective rhetorical pause and emphasis upon *state*.
239–48. *dazzle ... any*] a versification of *Disc.*, 1375–80 & 1448–9,
passages taken from Jonson's own translation of Seneca's *Epistles* 115 & 119
(*H.&S.*).
251. *if ... all*] if you could see the whole place.
257. *chattel*] moveable possession; property other than real estate.
259. *him*] i.e. Fitton.
260. *state of years*] estate or title to property, granted for a set number of
years, as opposed to an estate for life or freehold.

I'll be his Statute-Staple, Statute-Merchant,
  Or what he please.
Picklock.   He can expect no more.
Band. His cousin, Alderman Security,
  That he did talk of so e'en now –
Statute.   Who is
  The very brooch o'the bench, gem o'the City –   265
Band. He and his deputy but assure his life
  For one seven years.
Statute.   And see what we'll do for him
  Upon his scarlet motion –
Band.   And old chain,
  That draws the City ears –
Wax.   When he says nothing
  But twirls it thus.
Statute.   A moving oratory!   270
Band. Dumb rhetoric and silent eloquence,
  As the fine poet says.
Fitton.   Come, they all scorn us,
  Do you not see't? The family of scorn!
Broker. [*To the women.*] Do not believe him. – Gentle Master
    Picklock,
  They understood you not. The gentlewomen,   275
  They thought you would ha' my lady sojourn with you,

---

261. *Statute . . . Merchant*] 'bonds of record acknowledged before the mayor
of the Staple and the chief magistrate of a trading town, respectively, that gave
to the obligee power of seizure of the land of the obligor if he failed to pay his
debt at the appointed time' (Kifer).

265.] a conventional compliment; *H.&S.* compare *Ham.*, IV.vii.92–3: 'the
brooch indeed / And gem of all the nation'. Pecunia's women enjoy an almost
aristocratic sense of superiority to the money-seekers and bureaucrats of the
City.

266. *He*] i.e. let him (Ald. Security).

268. *scarlet*] colour of an alderman's gown.

chain] the ceremonial chain worn by an alderman.

271–2. *Dumb . . . says*] a 'sneering allusion' (Whalley) to Samuel Daniel's
lines, 'Sweet silent rethorique of perswading eyes / Dombe eloquence, whose
powre doth move the blood' (*The Complaint of Rosamund*, 121–2). Jonson had
earlier satirised the lines in *E.M.O.*, III.iii.24–5.

273. *family of scorn*] alluding to The Family of Love, another Protestant sect
originating in Amsterdam.

276. *with you*] i.e. at the Staple.

And you desire but now and then a visit.

Picklock. Yes, if she pleased, sir, it would much advance
   Unto the Office, her continual residence! –
   I speak but as a member.

Broker.   'Tis enough.   280
   [*Aside to Picklock*.] I apprehend you. And it shall go hard,
   But I'll so work as somebody shall work her.

Picklock. [*Aside to Broker*.] Pray you, change with our master
   but a word about it.

P. Junior. Well, Lickfinger, see that our meat be ready;
   Thou hast news enough.

Lickfinger.   Something of Bethlem Gabor,   285
   And then I'm gone.

Thomas. [*Reading*.]   We hear he has devised
   A drum, to fill all Christendom with the sound,
   But that he cannot draw his forces near it
   To march yet, for the violence of the noise.
   And therefore he is fain by a design   290
   To carry 'em in the air, and at some distance,
   Till he be married; then they shall appear.

Lickfinger. Or never. Well, God b'wi'you. [*Leaving*.]

   [*Enter two more* Customers.]   Stay, who's here?

---

283. Pray] *Whalley;* 'pray *F.*   287–8.] *F margin:* Bethlem Gabors *Drum.*

---

277. *And*] whereas.

281–2.] Broker intimates that, while he understands Picklock's real intentions concerning Pecunia, her investment in the news office will have to be secured more discreetly so as not to antagonise her attendants.

285. *Bethlem Gabor*] Gabriel Bethlen, Prince of Transylvania. He sought to marry the sister of the Elector of Brandenburg in return for aiding the Protestant cause; though a Calvinist, he switched allegiances more than once during the war, and used foreign quarrels to maintain political stability at home (C. V. Wedgwood, *The Thirty Years War*, p. 94).

290–1. *by ... air*] parodying frequent reports like that in *The Continuation of the Weekly Newes*, 5 October 1624, of 'A Strange Apparition at *Rome*' in which 'there were seene ... two fearefull and terrible Armies in the skie [which] being ordered in battell ray, fought many houres together ... till at length one ... vanished; and the other was converted into a most fearefull storme, and terrifying tempest' (pp. 1–2). Reports of Gabor's formidable army and campaigns were a staple of the newsbooks, and were frequently couched in apocalyptic terms, as in the claim that 'the Prince of *Transilvania* hath in a manner darkned the former Sunne' (*The Newes and Affaires of Europe*, 7 January 1624, p. 2).

[*To Nathaniel.*] A little of the Duke of Bavier, and then –
Nathaniel. [*Reading.*] H'has taken a grey habit and is turned   295
    The Church's miller, grinds the Catholic grist
    With every wind, and Tilly takes the toll.
4 Customer. Ha' you any news o'the pageants to send down
    Into the several counties? All the country
    Expected from the city most brave speeches   300
    Now, at the coronation.
Lickfinger.   It expected
    More than it understood, for they stand mute,
    Poor innocent dumb things. They are but wood,
    As is the bench and blocks they were wrought on; yet
    If May Day come and the sun shine, perhaps   305
    They'll sing like Memnon's statue and be vocal.
5 Customer. Ha' you any forest news?
Thomas.   None very wild, sir.
    Some tame there is, out o'the forest of fools.
    A new park is a-making there, to sever

294–5.] *F margin: The* Duke *of* Bauier.   298.] *F margin:* 4 *Cust.*
299–300.] *F margin: The Pageants.*   307.] *F margin:* 5. *Cust.*   308–11.]
F margin: The new Parke *in the* Forrest *of* Fooles.

---

294. *Bavier*] Bavaria. See note to line 32. Lickfinger starts to exit on the
previous line, meets the incoming customers (*Stay, who's here?*), and uses this
as an excuse to tarry for further news.
    298–301. *pageants ... coronation*] Charles I was crowned on 2 February
1626. The occasion had been delayed by a severe plague the previous year,
and since London had even now barely recovered from its effects, Charles's
coronation was a muted affair, without pageantry.
    301–2. *expected ... understood*] Cf. Induction, 31–2 and note.
    302–3. *they ... wood*] Cf. George Wither, *Britain's Remembrancer* (1628),
Canto 4, on the 'halfe-built *Pageants*' intended for Charles's coronation, whose
'unpolisht forme, did make them fit / For direfull *Showes*: yea, DEATH
on them did sit' (Spenser Soc., vol. 28–9, p. 220). Since the Lord Mayor's
pageant for 1625 had also been cancelled, owing to the death of James I,
London's streets had not heard *brave speeches* for some time. But Jonson may
also intend a hit at pageants that are all spectacle and no eloquence.
    306. *Memnon's statue*] the statue of Amenhotep III at Karnak in Egypt; after
it was damaged in an earthquake the stone responded to the sun's rays by
giving off a twanging sound. It was a popular image with writers, and had a
topical appeal at this time: in 1613, Cornelius Drebbel wrote a letter to James
I in which he claimed to 'have the skill to construct all kinds of musical instruments which will play themselves by the rays of the sun' (quoted by Harris,
The Two Netherlanders, p. 146).
    307–9. *forest ... park*] The Staple's news-telling concludes on a whimsi-

Cuckolds of antler from the rascals. Such   310
Whose wives are dead, and have since cast their heads,
Shall remain cuckolds pollard.
Lickfinger.   I'll ha' that news.
Dopper. And I.
2 Customer.   And I.
3 Customer.   And I.
4 Customer.   And I.
5 Customer.   And I.

Pennyboy [Junior] would invite the Master of the Office [to dine].
Cymbal. Sir, I desire to be excused; and madam,
I cannot leave my Office the first day.   315
My cousin Fitton here shall wait upon you,
And emissary Picklock.
P. Junior.   And Tom *Clericus?*
Cymbal. I cannot spare him yet, but he shall follow you
When they have ordered the rolls.
                    [*To the clerks.*] Shut up th'Office
When you ha' done, till two o'clock.   320
                    [*Exeunt all but Thomas and Nathaniel.*]

ACT III SCENE iii
[*Enter*] SHUNFIELD, ALMANAC [*and*] MADRIGAL.

[*Shunfield.*] By your leave, clerks,
Where shall we dine today? Do you know?

313. S.H. *Dopper*] This ed.; CVS. *I. F.*   III.iii.0.1.] *Gifford;* SHVNFIELD.
ALMANACK. MADRI-/GAL. CEERKES. *F.*

---

cal note; there seems to be little satirical point to this, although *forest of fools* sounds aphoristic or proverbial. The basic distinction between tame and wild seems to follow that expressed by Coke in 1628: 'A Forest and Chase are not but a Parke must bee enclosed' (quoted in *O.E.D.*). Forests were crown land.
310. *rascals*] inferior deer.
311. *heads*] antlers.
312. *pollard*] without horns. The same joke is found in *The London Chanticleers*, Sc. 13: 'she cuckold him the first night, and clap a pair of horns upon his head, that will confine him to his chamber till rutting time come, and he shed 'um' (Dodsley 12.353).
III.iii.1.] This line was probably intended to complete line 320 at the end of

Thomas. [*To Nathaniel.*]   The jeerers!
Almanac. Where's my fellow Fitton?
Thomas.   New gone forth.
Shunfield. Cannot your Office tell us what brave fellows
    Do eat together today in town, and where?   5
Thomas. Yes, there's a gentleman, the brave heir, young
        Pennyboy,
    Dines in Apollo.
Madrigal.   Come, let's thither then.
    I ha' supped in Apollo.
Almanac.   With the Muses?
Madrigal.   No,
    But with two gentlewomen called the Graces.
Almanac. They were ever three in poetry.
Madrigal.   This was truth, sir.   10
Thomas. Sir, Master Fitton's there too.
Shunfield.   All the better.
Almanac. We may have a jeer, perhaps.
Shunfield.   Yes, you'll drink, doctor,
    (If there be any good meat) as much good wine now
    As would lay up a Dutch ambassador.
Thomas. If he dine there, he's sure to have good meat,   15
    For Lickfinger provides the dinner.
Almanac.   Who?

---

2. S.H. *Thomas*] *H.&S.; F gives whole of line 2 to Shunfield; Nath. Gifford.*
10. They were] They'were *F.*

---

the previous scene, but to avoid problems of lineation I have not combined
them as a single pentameter.
    7. *Apollo*] See note to II.v.127.
    9. *gentlewomen*] Gifford refers to the *Leges Conviviales*, Rule 4: 'Nec lectae
fœminae repudiantur', and cites Shakerley Marmion's reference in *A Fine
Companion* (1633), D3v, to the 'tempting beauties' to be seen at Apollo gather-
ings. No record of individual women who attended has survived, however.
The classical frame of reference he uses here is anticipated, as *H.&S.* point
out, in Drayton's poem 'The Sacrifice to Apollo' (written before the construction of the Apollo room): 'Where be the Graces, where be those fayre Three? /
In any hand They may not absent bee' (*Poems*, 1619, p. 290, lines 17–18).
    13–14. *as ... ambassador*] Dutch fondness for drink was proverbial;
H.&S. compare Chamberlain's letter to Carleton (9 March 1622) about a
Shrove Tuesday feast whose inhabitants, including 'The States Ambassadors
... came all sober away, as having had but six healths that went round'.

The glory o'the kitchen, that holds cookery
A trade from Adam, quotes his broths and salads,
And swears he's not dead yet, but translated
In some immortal crust, the paste of almonds?   20
Madrigal. The same. He holds no man can be a poet
That is not a good cook, to know the palates
And several tastes o'the time. He draws all arts
Out of the kitchen but the art of poetry,
Which he concludes the same with cookery.   25
Shunfield. Tut, he maintains more heresies than that.
He'll draw the magisterium from a minced pie,
And prefer jellies to your juleps, doctor.
Almanac. I was at an *olla podrida* of his making,
Was a brave piece of cookery, at a funeral.   30
But opening the pot-lid, he made us laugh
Who'd wept all day, and sent us such a tickling

17–18. *that . . . Adam*] perhaps anticipating the alchemical reference in line
27 (see note): compare Mammon's claim in *Alch.*, II.i.83–4 (Revels) to own 'a
treatise penn'd by Adam . . . / O'the philosopher's stone, and in High Dutch'.

21–5. *He . . . cookery*] adapted from *N.T.*, 65–72.

24. *but*] i.e. but especially, above all.

27. *magisterium*] philosopher's stone. Cf. Overbury's *Characters*, 'A French
Cooke': 'the Lord calles him his Alchymist that can extract gold out of hearbs,
rootes, mushromes or any thing' (Lucas IV.41).

minced pie] 'not the modern dessert but a substantial baked meat of minced
flesh, fowl, or fish' (Kifer).

28. *juleps*] medicinal drinks sweetened to disguise the taste; alluding to the
Horatian formula for poetry as seen in the play's epigraph: 'mixing sweet, and
fit, teach life the right'. The cook's comprehensive skills derive ultimately
from Athenaeus, *Deipnosophistae*, a work of which Jonson makes more extensive use in IV.ii (see notes).

29. olla podrida] a sumptuous dish of Iberian origin; the spirit of Lickfinger's creation is caught in the dinner served to Queen Whims in Rabelais'
Pantagruel, Bk. V, 23: 'The olla consisted of several sorts of pottages, salads,
fricasees, saugrenees, cabirotadoes, roast and boiled meat, carbonadoes,
swingeing pieces of powdered beef, good old hams, dainty deifical somates,
cakes, tarts, a world of curds after the Moorish way, fresh cheese, jellies, and
fruit of all sorts' (II.305). Sp. *podrido* = rotten; cf. the antimasque in *N.T.*,
240f, where the *olla* consists of various figures including newsmongers 'comming out of the pot' (331). The connection between news and feasting is less
explicit in the play.

30–34. *Was . . . dinner*] from Athenaeus' fragment of Hegesippus, *The
Brothers*, in *Deipnosophistae* (Gulick ed., III.303). See Appendix A.

Into our nostrils as the funeral feast
Had been a wedding dinner.
Shunfield.   Gi' him allowance,
And that but moderate, he will make a Siren   35
Sing i'the kettle, send in an Arion,
In a brave broth and of a wat'ry green
Just the sea colour, mounted on the back
Of a grown conger, but in such a posture
As all the world would take him for a dolphin.   40
Madrigal. He's a rare fellow, without question. But
He holds some paradoxes.
Almanac.   Ay, and pseudodoxes.
Marry, for most he's orthodox i'the kitchen.
Madrigal. And knows the clergy's taste.
Almanac.   Ay, and the laity's.
Shunfield. You think not o'your time. We'll come too late 45
If we go not presently.
Madrigal.   Away then.
Shunfield. [*To the clerks.*]   Sirs,
You must get o'this news to store your Office:
Who dines and sups i'the town, where, and with whom;
'Twill be beneficial. When you are stored
And as we like our fare, we shall reward you.   50
Nathaniel. A hungry trade 'twill be.
Thomas.   Much like Duke Humphrey's;

---

32. Who'd] who'had *F.*

35–40. *he . . . dolphin*] adapted from *N.T.*, 185–91. Arion is the legendary
Greek singer thrown overboard by sailors and rescued by a dolphin. What
Shunfield describes is a 'subtilty' or 'soteltie', a dish elaborately wrought after
some theme and designed to serve as ornament to the table before being eaten.
They occur in Petronius, *Satyricon*, 69–70, and were popular in the fifteenth &
sixteenth centuries, their introduction on platters or trolleys often serving as a
distinct stage or *entremet* in the evening's entertainment (see Enid Welsford,
The Court Masque, pp. 44–7). The Arion theme was clearly popular with
cooks; cf. Fletcher, *Rollo Duke of Normandy*, II.i.20–2: 'For Fish ile make ye
a standing lake of White-broth, / . . . Arion on a Dolphin playing Lachrimae.'
  42. *pseudodoxes*] false opinions. Cf. *O.E.D.*'s 1631 example: 'One Proposition, truely Orthodox (though . . . it seeme a Paradox, or Pseudodox)'.
  46. *presently*] immediately.
  51. *Duke Humphrey's*] The proverbial expression 'To dine with Duke
Humphrey', meaning to go hungry (Tilley D63), derives according to Stow

But now and then, as th'wholesome proverb says,
'Twill *obsonare famem ambulando.*
Nathaniel. Shut up the office, gentle brother Thomas.
Thomas. Brother Nathaniel, I ha' the wine for you.   55
     I hope to see us, one day, emissaries.
Nathaniel. Why not? 'Slid, I despair not to be Master!
                                   [*Exeunt.*]

ACT III   SCENE iv

[*Enter*] PENNYBOY SE[NIOR *and*] BROKER [*at different doors*].

[*P. Senior.*] How now? (*He is started with Broker's coming back.*)
                    I think I was born under Hercules' star!
Nothing but trouble and tumult to oppress me.
Why come you back? Where is your charge?
Broker.   I ha' brought
     A gentleman to speak with you.
P. Senior.   To speak with me?
You know 'tis death for me to speak with any man.   5
What is he? Set me a chair.
Broker. [*Bringing a chair.*]   He's the Master

III.iv.0.1.] *Gifford;* PENI-BOY. SE. BROKER. CYMBAL. *F.*

from dinnerless gallants spending the dinner hour in Duke Humphrey's Walk
in St Paul's (Stow's *Survey*, 1618 ed., p. 642) (*H.&S.*).
     53. obsonare ... ambulando] to provide an appetite by walking (Cicero,
Tusculan Disputations, V.97) (*H.&S.*).
     55. *I ... you*] Let me buy you a drink. Clearly a standard expression,
though not recorded as such; *H.&S.* compare *Ratseis Ghost* (1605), sig. E, and
it also appears in Robert Greene's *Notable Discovery of Coosnage* (1591), ed.
G. B. Harrison (Bodley Head Quartos I), p. 19. Cf. *E.M.I.*, IV.vi.67–8.
     57.] See notes to I.iv.13 and I.v.120–1.

     III.iv.0.1.] The shift of location to the miser's house might be effected on
the Blackfriars stage by closing the curtains in front of the centre doorway (or
booth), perhaps moving the table, and having Broker and P. Senior enter
through the doors on either side.
     III.iv.1. started] startled.
     Hercules' star] Ptolemy associated the fixed star of Hercules in the sign of
Gemini with the planet Mars, which causes 'intestine divisions ... insurrec-
tions ... and all kinds of violence' (Johnstone Parr in *M.L.N.*, 60 (1945),
117).
     3. *your charge*] i.e. Pecunia. Broker is acting on his promise to Picklock at
III.ii.281–2.

Of the great Office.
P. Senior.   What?
Broker.   The Staple of News,
   A mighty thing. They talk six thousand a year.
P. Senior. [*Sits.*] Well, bring your six in. Where ha' you left
   Pecunia?
Broker. Sir, in Apollo. They are scarce set.
P. Senior.   Bring six.   10

   [*Broker exits and returns with Cymbal.*]

Broker. Here is the gentleman.
P. Senior.   He must pardon me:
   I cannot rise, a diseased man.
Cymbal.   By no means, sir.
   Respect your health and ease.
P. Senior.   It is no pride in me,
   But pain, pain. What's your errand, sir, to me? –
   Broker, return to your charge. Be Argus-eyed,   15
   Awake to the affair you have in hand.
   Serve in Apollo but take heed of Bacchus. [*Exit* BROKER.]
   Go on, sir.
Cymbal.   I am come to speak with you.
P. Senior. 'Tis pain for me to speak, a very death,
   But I will hear you.
Cymbal.   Sir you have a lady   20
   That sojourns with you.
P. Senior.   Ha! I am somewhat short
   In my sense too –   (*He pretends infirmity.*)
Cymbal.   Pecunia.
P. Senior. [*Pointing to his other ear.*] O'that side:
   Very imperfect on –
Cymbal. [*Moving round.*] Whom I would draw
   Oft'ner to a poor office I am Master of –
P. Senior. My hearing is very dead; you must speak quicker.   25
Cymbal. Or, if it please you, sir, to let her sojourn

14–16.] *F margin: Hee sends* Broker *backe.*   22, 23. S.D.s] *This ed.*

_____

8. *talk ... year*] an expressive idiom underlining the fact that the Staple
deals in expensive rumour.

> In part with me, I have a moiety
> We will divide, half of the profits.
>
> *P. Senior.*   Ha!
> I hear you better now. How come they in?
> Is it a certain business, or a casual?   30
> For I am loath to seek out doubtful courses,
> Run any hazardous paths. I love straight ways:
> A just and upright man! Now all trade totters.
> The trade of money is fall'n two i'the hundred.
> That was a certain trade while th'age was thrifty   35
> And men good husbands, looked unto their stocks,
> Had their minds bounded. (*He talks vehemently and aloud.*)
>   Now the public riot
> Prostitutes all, scatters away in coaches,
> In footmen's coats and waiting-women's gowns.
> They must have velvet haunches – with a pox –   40
> Now taken up, and yet not pay the use.
> Bate of the use! I am mad with this time's manners.
>
> *Cymbal.* You said e'en now it was death for you to speak.
> *P. Senior.* Ay, but an anger, a just anger as this is,

---

32. paths.] *Kifer; paths, F.*

33–4. *Now ... hundred*] See notes to I.iii.47 and II.i.4.
36. *husbands*] managers of their affairs.
37. *bounded*] occupied within their proper limits.
38. *coaches*] See note to 'Prologue for the Stage', 14.
40. *haunches*] tight-fitting garment designed to improve the body's shape; cf. *B.F.*, IV.v.65–6 (Revels), where Alice accuses Mistress Overdo of stealing the trade of common whores with her 'tuft taffeta haunches'.
   with a pox] Eugene Waith suggests that this is emphatic, an exclamation like 'for God's sake'; E. B. Partridge interprets more elaborately, suggesting that the phrase refers ambiguously to both 'waiting women and "velvet ha[u]nches," each of which seems to have enough life to be diseased' ('The Symbolism of Clothes in Jonson's Last Plays', *J.E.G.P.*, 56 (1957), 399).
41. *taken up*] borrowed.
   use] interest.
42. *Bate of*] reduce.
   mad] furious – as in modern American usage. Cf. V.vi.14.
44. *just anger*] 'moderate and sanctified anger is so farre from hurting and hindering the judgement of Reason, that it rather serviceably aydeth and supporteth it, by inciting and incouraging it couragiously to execute that which Reason hath justly decreed and resolved' (John Downame, *A Treatise of Anger* (1609), p. 7). But P. Senior fails to observe 'this generall rule ... that we use moderation, least we mingle therewith our corrupt & carnall anger, and so it degenerates into fleshly anger, and from that to fury' (p. 15).

Puts life in man. Who can endure to see   45
The fury of men's gullets and their groins?
What fires, what cooks, what kitchens might be spared?
                        [*He*] *is moved more and more.*
What stews, ponds, parks, coops, garners, magazines,
What velvets, tissues, scarfs, embroideries
And laces they might lack? They covet things   50
Superfluous still, when it were much more honour
They could want necessary. What need hath Nature
Of silver dishes or gold chamber pots,
Of perfumed napkins, or a numerous family
To see her eat? Poor and wise, she requires   55
Meat only; hunger is not ambitious.
Say that you were the emperor of pleasures,
The great dictator of fashions for all Europe,
And had the pomp of all the courts and kingdoms
Laid forth unto the show, to make yourself   60
Gazed and admired at? You must go to bed
And take your natural rest; then all this vanisheth.
Your bravery was but shown; 'twas not possessed:
While it did boast itself, it was then perishing.

---

55. Poor and wise, she] *Whalley (subst.); Poore, and wise she, F, F3.*

45–68.] a verse paraphrase of Jonson's translation in *Disc.*, 1387–1412, of
Seneca's *Epistles* 110 & 119 (cf. III.ii.239–48). *H.&S.* comment that it is a
'curious thing' that the passage presented in *Disc.* 'as Jonson's own reflection
is in the play put on the lips of the contemptible miser' (XI 255); but in this
context it takes on an appearance of tactless and inappropriate generalisation.
See note to line 53.
    48. *stews*] tanks or ponds in which fish were kept for the table.
    49. *tissues*] rich fabrics of silk and precious metals combined in twisted
threads (Linthicum, pp. 117–18).
    53. *gold . . . pots*] a detail added to the Seneca transcription from Martial,
Epigrams, 37: 'Ventris onus misero, nec te pudet, excipis auro' (*H.&S.*). But
no doubt Jonson is also aware here (as he seems to be in *E.H.*, III.iii.26,
Revels) of More's use of this image in *Utopia*, Bk. II (*Works*, IV.153), to
illustrate the utopians' admirable contempt for gold. The miser is thus seen not
so much to be raging at tangible follies of the day as missing the point of an
established satire on the love of money. Jonson's art of literary allusion is at its
most subtle here, serving to undermine the authority of P. Senior's 'complaint'.
    54. *napkins*] handkerchiefs, 'costly accessories [which] were usually carried
in the hand to show their richness' (Linthicum, p. 270).
    61. *admired*] wondered.
    63. *bravery*] finery.

Cymbal. [*Aside.*] This man has healthful lungs.

P. Senior.   All that excess   65
      Appeared as little yours as the spectators'.
      It scarce fills up the expectation
      Of a few hours that entertains men's lives.

Cymbal. [*Aside.*] He has the monopoly of sole speaking.
      – Why, good sir, you talk all.

P. Senior. (*He is angry.*)   Why should I not?   70
      Is it not under mine own roof, my ceiling?

Cymbal. But I came here to talk with you.

P. Senior.   Why, an' I will not
      Talk with you, sir? You are answered. Who sent for you?

Cymbal. Nobody sent for me –

P. Senior.   But you came. Why, then
      Go as you came. Here's no man holds you. There,   75
      There lies your way. You see the door.

Cymbal.   This's strange!

P. Senior. 'Tis my civility when I do not relish
      The party or his business. Pray you be gone, sir.
      I'll ha' no venture in your ship, the Office,
      Your bark of six, if 'twere sixteen, good sir.   80

Cymbal. You are a rogue!

P. Senior.   I think I am, sir, truly.

Cymbal. A rascal and a money-bawd!

P. Senior.   My surnames.

Cymbal. A wretched rascal!

P. Senior.   You will overflow,
      And spill all.

Cymbal.   Caterpillar, moth,
      Horse-leech, and dung-worm –

P. Senior.   Still you lose your labour.   85
      I am a broken vessel, all runs out:
      A shrunk old dry-fat. Fare you well, good six!

                              [*Exeunt at different doors.*]

74–5.] F *margin: Bids him get out of his house.*   81–3.] F *margin:* Cymbal
railes at him.   84–5.] F *margin: He ieeres him.*   87.1.] *This ed.; Exeunt*
Gifford.

_____

   79–80.] P. Senior seems to compare the Staple venture to the speculative voyages of the day, which attracted investment with the promise of rich
returns.
   87. *dry-fat*] barrel in which dry goods were contained.

The third Intermean after the third Act.

Censure. A notable tough rascal, this old Pennyboy! Right
    City-bred!

Mirth. In Silver Street, the region of money, a good seat for a
    usurer.

Tattle. He has rich ingredients in him, I warrant you, if they   5
    were extracted; a true receipt to make an alderman an' he
    were well wrought upon, according to art.

Expectation. I would fain see an alderman in *chimia*; that is, a
    treatise of aldermanity truly written.

Censure. To show how much it differs from urbanity.   10

Mirth. Ay, or humanity. Either would appear in this Penny-
    boy, an' he were rightly distilled. But how like you the
    news? You are gone from that.

Censure. O, they are monstrous! Scurvy and stale! And too
    exotic; ill cooked, and ill dished!   15

Exception. They were as good yet as Butter could make them.

Tattle. In a word, they were beastly buttered! He shall never

---

1–56.] *Italic in F.*

III.Int.3. *Silver Street*] Stow, *Survey*, 1618 ed., p. 540: 'Downe lower in
Woodstreet is Silver street, (I thinke of Silver-Smithes dwelling there) in
which be divers faire houses' (*H.&S.*).

5–7. *He ... art*] Cf. Chapman, *The Memorable Masque* (1613), where
Capriccio enters the domain of Plutus carrying a lump of gold: 'A man must
be a second *Proteus*, and turne himselfe into all shapes ... There are manie
shapes to perish in, but one to live in, and that's an Aldermans' (23–4, 28–9;
Holaday, p. 572).

8. *in* chimia] i.e. subjected to alchemical analysis.

10–11. *To ... humanity*] Jonson's general view of officialdom is clear
throughout his work, and crystallises in *Disc.*, 2432–4: 'Every beggerly Corporation affoords the State a *Major*, or two *Bailiffs*, yearly: but, *solus Rex, aut
Poeta, non quotannis nascitur.*'

15. *exotic*] outlandish. Jonson was apparently the first to use the word, in
E.M.O., IV.iii.29–30: 'magicke, witchcraft, or other such exoticke artes';
he may have found it in Rabelais, as did Cotgrave: '*Exotique*: ... Strange,
forreine, outlandish: *Rab.*'. *O.E.D.*'s examples show that the word became
fashionable in the 1620s, and it is used in a Butter newsbook in 1623: 'the
sentences here extended, shall neither receive exoticke interpretation, nor bee
carryed with any wanton hand from the true meaning' (*A True Relation of ...
the great Spanish fleet*, A2).

16–17. *They ... buttered*] See note to I.iv.13, and cf. Dekker, *The Noble
Spanish Soldier*, IV.ii.55–6: 'Woo't not trust an Almanacke? Nor a Coranta
neither, tho it were seal'd with Butter' (Bowers IV.279).

come o'my bread more, nor in my mouth, if I can help it. I
have had better news from the bake-house by ten thousand
parts, in a morning, or the conduits in Westminster; all   20
the news of Tuttle Street, and both the Alm'ries, the two
Sanctuaries, long and round Woolstaple, with King's
Street and Cannon Row to boot!

Mirth. Ay, my gossip Tattle knew what fine slips grew in
Gardiner's Lane, who kissed the butcher's wife with the   25
cow's breath, what matches were made in the Bowling
Alley, and what bets won and lost; how much grist went to
the mill, and what besides. Who conjured in Tuttle Fields,

19–20. *bake-house ... conduits*] natural places of gossip; Dekker in *The
Belman of London* makes his point about another kind of gathering by saying:
'such a noise made they ... that the scolding at ten conduits, and the gossip-
ings of fifteene bake-houses was delicate musicke of it' (Grosart III.87). Conduits were the fountains at central points which provided the city's water.

21. *Tuttle Street*] Tothill Street. All the locations mentioned by the gossips
are in Westminster, where Jonson spent his youth and where he lodged in his
last years (see *H.&S.*, XI 576).

both ... Alm'ries] Almshouses for poor men and women built by Henry VII,
to the west of Westminster Abbey. According to Stow, the Little Almonry was
turned into lodgings for the Abbey choristers, and Caxton's printing press had
been set up there (Chalfant, *Ben Jonson's London*, p. 29).

21–2. *the two Sanctuaries*] precincts on the north and west sides of Westminster. The sanctuary privileges afforded by the Abbey precincts tended to
draw disreputable types to the area, and so presumably helped to turn it into a
hive of gossip. See Chalfant, p. 193.

22. *long ... Woolstaple*] the two parts of the central Woolstaple for England,
where wool was registered for export and the necessary duty paid (Chalfant,
p. 203).

22–3. *King's Street*] King Street, at this time the main thoroughfare from
the court at Whitehall to Westminster; many public figures lived on it, and
Tattle presumably sees it as a place of political gossip.

23. *Cannon Row*] otherwise known as St Stephen's Alley; 'there lodged ...
divers Noblemen and Gentlemen' (Stow) (*H.&S.*).

24. *slips*] youngsters. The word can mean 'counterfeits' (thus, here, illegiti-
mate children) and Jonson puns on this sense in *E.M.I.*, II.v.145–6. But the
pun on 'cuttings' is what preoccupies him here (so Kifer).

25. *Gardiner's Lane*] a thoroughfare once extending from King St to Delahay
St; Chalfant notes that all these streets have now disappeared.

26–7. *Bowling Alley*] possibly located on what is now Bowling St, leading
from Dean's Yard to Tufton Street (*H.&S.*). Chalfant notes that James I
issued licences for twenty-four bowling alleys in the City and Westminster
(p. 46).

28. *mill*] a water-mill belonging to the Abbot of Westminster, turned by a
stream running down what is now College St (H.&S.).

and how many, when they never came there; and which
boy rode upon Doctor Lamb, in the likeness of a roaring   30
lion, that run away with him in his teeth and has not de-
voured him yet.

Tattle. Why, I had it from my maid Joan Hearsay, and she had
it from a limb o'the school, she says, a little limb of nine
year old, who told her the master left out his conjuring   35
book one day and he found it; and so the fable came about.
But whether it were true or no, we gossips are bound to
believe it an't be once out and afoot. How should we entertain the time else, or find ourselves in fashionable discourse for all companies, if we do not credit all and make   40
more of it in the reporting?

Censure. For my part, I believe it. An' there were no wiser than
I, I would have ne'er a cunning schoolmaster in England. I
mean a cunning man, a schoolmaster, that is a conjurer or
a poet or that had any acquaintance with a poet. They   45
make all their scholars playboys! Is't not a fine sight to see
all our children made interluders? Do we pay our money
for this? We send them to learn their grammar and their

---

42. An'] *1716; And* F.

Tuttle Fields] Tothill Fields, open land south of Tothill Street. Apparently
punishments for witchcraft and necromancy were carried out there (Chalfant,
p. 186).

30. *Doctor Lamb*] See note to I.Int.47. Mirth is probably alluding to the
pamphlet literature that must have proliferated on Lamb's exploits.

34. *limb*] deriving from 'limb of Satan', a young imp or rascal (*O.E.D.* 3c,
citing this example).

44. *cunning man*] the common term for faith-healers, diviners etc.: the
Elizabethan equivalent of the witch-doctor. See Keith Thomas, *Religion and
the Decline of Magic* (1971), Chs. 7 & 8. The absurd association of the cunning
man with teachers and poets slyly reinforces Jonson's emphasis in Act III upon
the confusion of false oracles for the voice of genuine authority.

45–6. *They . . . playboys*] Edd. detect an allusion to the annual performances of Latin plays at Westminster School, and *H.&S.* also cite a complaint
from Elizabethan days about the commercial exploitation of boy-actors. Censure's indignation echoes a larger polemic against the stage: Prynne declared in
Histriomastix (1633) that 'Stage-playes' are performed and frequented by '*such
who make* Pauls *their* Westminster; *a Play-house . . . their Study*' (p. 504).
This ironic analogy had been popular since Gosson's condemnation of the
theatres in *The School of Abuse* (1579), and in a sequel to that volume Anthony
Munday deplored the fate of 'yong boies . . . to be brought up by these Schoole-
masters in bawderie, and in idlenes' (*A . . . blast of retrait from plaies and Theaters*
(1586), pp. 110–11).

Terence, and they learn their play-books. Well, they talk
we shall have no more Parliaments (God bless us), but   50
an' we have, I hope Zeal-of-the-Land Busy and my gossip
Rabbi Troubletruth will start up, and see we shall have
painful good ministers to keep school and catechise our
youth, and not teach 'em to speak plays and act fables of
false news in this manner, to the super-vexation of town   55
and country, with a wanion.

49–50. *they . . . Parliaments*] Charles I had dissolved Parliament in August
1625, after bitter dissension over the Crown's request for subsidies to make
war on Spain. It was recalled shortly after the coronation, in February 1626
(only days before the play's first performance), but conflict between King and
Parliament intensified and led to a second dissolution in June of that year.
    51. *Zeal . . . Busy*] the Puritan 'Banbury man' of *B.F.*
    56. *with a wanion*] with a vengeance.

Act IV

ACT IV SCENE i

[*Enter*] PENNYBOY JU[NIOR], FITTON, SHUNFIELD, ALMANAC,
MADRIGAL, [PENNYBOY] CANTER [*and*] PICKLOCK.

[*P. Junior.*] Come, gentlemen, let's breathe from healths
    awhile.
This Lickfinger has made us a good dinner
For our Pecunia. What shall's do with ourselves
While the women water and the fiddlers eat?
Fitton. Let's jeer a little.
P. Junior.   Jeer? What's that?
Shunfield.   Expect, sir.   5
Almanac. We first begin with ourselves, and then at you.
Shunfield. A game we use.
Madrigal.   We jeer all kind of persons
We meet withal, of any rank or quality,
And if we cannot jeer them, we jeer ourselves.
P. Canter. A pretty sweet society, and a grateful!   10

IV.i.o.1. *Enter*] This ed.; *discovered at table Gifford, Kifer (subst.)*.

IV.i.o.1.] Gifford (followed by Kifer) has the characters 'discovered at
table', but it is more likely that the men enter from an inner room where they
have just finished dining (see lines 17, 37–40). The initial feeling of relaxation
quickly hardens into organised conflict, as the knaves channel their pent-up
aggression towards Canter into a parody of formal conversation.
   2. *dinner*] the chief meal of the day, served at noon.
   4. *water*] *O.E.D.* cites this as a rare usage in the sense of 'urinate'; the verb
may have been a euphemism for ladies' ablutions on social occasions, deriving
possibly from the use of 'sweet water' (early concoctions of toilet water) to
freshen hands and clothes.
   5. *Jeer ... that?*] The word was fairly well established by this date, but P.
Junior reacts to the suggestion of an unfamiliar social ritual. (According to
O.E.D. Jonson is the first to use it as a noun, in line 16.) Edd. have been content to repeat Gifford's assertion that Jonson merely reproduces an 'odious'
game then in vogue, which has 'scarcely more to interest the reader than the
vapouring in *Bartholomew Fair*'. But it would seem that the jeering game (like
the vapours episode) is a formal comment on social tendencies rather than a
simple imitation of them, and it clearly has a moral and theatrical, not a documentary function.
   Expect] wait and see.

Picklock. Pray, let's see some.
Shunfield.   Have at you then, lawyer.
 They say there was one of your coat in Bedlam lately.
Almanac. I wonder all his clients were not there.
Madrigal. They were the madder sort.
Picklock.   Except, sir, one
 Like you, and he made verses.
Fitton.   Madrigal,   15
 A jeer.
Madrigal. I know.
Shunfield.   But what did you do, lawyer,
 When you made love to Mistress Band at dinner?
Madrigal. Why, of an advocate, he grew the client.
P. Junior. Well played, my poet.
Madrigal.   And showed the law of nature
 Was there above the common law.
Shunfield.   Quit, quit.   20
P. Junior. Call you this jeering? I can play at this;
 'Tis like a ball at tennis.
Fitton.   Very like,
 But we were not well in.
Almanac.   'Tis indeed, sir,
 When we do speak at volley all the ill
 We can one of another.
Shunfield.   As this morning   25
 (I would you had heard us) of the rogue your uncle.
Almanac. That money-bawd.
Madrigal.   We called him a coat-card
 O'the last order.

---

 12. *Bedlam*] St Mary of Bethlehem's hospital in Bishopsgate, used as a mad-house (Kifer).

 14. *They ... sort*] Madrigal attempts feebly to build on Almanac's taunt, and opens himself to an exemplary jeer.

 18. *of*] from being.

 24. *at volley*] wildly, at random (cf. Cotgrave, 'A la volée. Rashly ... in-considerately; at randome ... at all adventures') – and continuing the tennis figure of 21–2. Cf. *N.I.*, I.vi.62 (Revels).

 27. *coat-card*] now known as *court* card: a playing card with a coated figure, in this case the knave or jack. See note to II.Int.16.

P. Junior.   What's that? A knave?

Madrigal. Some readings have it so. My manuscript
Doth speak it varlet.

P. Canter.   And yourself a fool   30
O'the first rank, and one shall have the leading
O'the right-hand file under this brave commander.

P. Junior. What sayst thou, Canter?

P. Canter.   Sir, I say this is
A very wholesome exercise and comely,
Like lepers showing one another their scabs,   35
Or flies feeding on ulcers.

P. Junior. [*Changing the subject.*] What news, gentlemen?
Ha' you any news for after dinner? Methinks
We should not spend our time unprofitably.

P. Canter. They never lie, sir, between meals; 'gainst supper
You may have a bale or two brought in.

Fitton. [*Aside to the other jeerers.*]   This Canter   40
Is an old envious knave.

Almanac.   A very rascal!

Fitton. I ha' marked him all this meal. He has done nothing
But mock with scurvy faces all we said.

Almanac. A supercilious rogue! He looks as if
He were the patrico –

Madrigal.   Or arch-priest o'canters.   45

Shunfield. He's some primate metropolitan rascal,

---

28. O'the ... What's] *F;* Of the ... What is *Gifford.*

30. *Doth ... varlet*] calls the knave a varlet. The latter term by this date
means simply a rogue or menial, but in its older sense denoted a knight's
attendant, so *varlet* might be taken as a possible equivalent term for the knave
or jack who on playing cards is associated with figures of rank. The readings to
which Madrigal refers, and claims to make his own contribution, seem to
belong to the kind of pamphlet literature discussed in the note to II.Int.16.

31–2. *have ... file*] take precedence (*H.&S.*).

39. *They ... meals*] (1) they never give out news (i.e. tell lies) between
meals; (2) they never rest (from gathering lies); for the pun, see I.v.20–1 note.

45. *patrico*] 'a Patrico ... amongst *Beggers* is their priest; every hedge
beeing his parish, every wandring harlot and *Rogue* his parishioners, the
service he sayes, is onely the marrying of couples, which he does in a wood
under a tree, or in the open field' (Dekker, *The Belman of London*; Grosart
III.104).

46. *primate ... rascal*] leader of some city gang (as opposed to a mere hedge-
priest – with a pun on the ecclesiastical sense of *primate*).

Our shot-clog makes so much of him.
Almanac.   The Law
And he does govern him.
P. Junior.   What say you, gentlemen?
Fitton. We say we wonder not your man o'law
Should be so gracious wi'you, but how it comes   50
This rogue, this canter –
P. Junior.   O, good words!
Fitton.   A fellow
That speaks no language –
Almanac.   But what jingling gypsies
And peddlers trade in –
Fitton.   And no honest Christian
Can understand –
P. Canter.   Why, by that argument,
You all are canters – you, and you, and you,   55
All the whole world are canters; I will prove it
In your professions.
P. Junior.   I would fain hear this.
But stay, my princess comes; provide the while,
I'll call for't anon.

55–7.] *F margin: He speakes to all the* Ieerers.   59. S.D.] *After IV.ii in F;*
placed here by Gifford.   and MORTGAGE] *Gifford.*

47. *shot-clog*] i.e. P. Junior: 'One who was tolerated because he paid the
shot, or reckoning, for the rest' (Nares); cf. *E.H.*, I.i.136: 'thou common shot-
clog, gull of all companies' (Revels).
    The Law] i.e. Picklock.
    50. *gracious . . . you*] enjoy your favour.
    52–4. *speaks . . . understand*] Cf. Dekker, *Lanthorne & Candle-Light*: 'It was
necessary, that a people (so fast increasing, & so daily practising new & strange
Villanies), should borrow to themselves a speech, which (so neere as they
could) none but themselves should understand; & for that cause was this
Language (which some call *Pedlers French*,) Invented' (Grosart III.194). The
existence of a canting language outside the writings of men like Dekker has
however been questioned by historians: see A. L. Beier, 'Social Problems in
Elizabethan London', *J.I.H.*, 9 (1978), 203–21.
    52. *jingling gypsies*] *H.&S.* compare *The Gypsies Metamorphos'd*, 735–8,
where 'the finest olive-colourd sprites . . . should be Morris dancers by theire
gingle'.
    58.] P. Junior's line is cued by the sound of Pecunia's approach; Gifford's
placing of the S.D. seems correct. The entry of new characters delays Canter's
lecture until the main action of Act IV is complete, and as a result we remain
subliminally aware throughout of a waiting judgement, ripened and vindicated
by the parade of exquisite pretension that ensues.

[*Enter*] LICKFINGER, PECUNIA, STATUTE, BAND, WAX
[*and* MORTGAGE] *to them.*
                                How fares your grace?

ACT IV   SCENE ii

[*Lickfinger.*] I hope the fare was good.
Pecunia.   Yes, Lickfinger,
And we shall thank you for't and reward you.

Pennyboy [Junior] is courting his princess all the while
Lickfinger is challenged by Madrigal of an argument.

Madrigal. Nay, I'll not lose my argument, Lickfinger.
Before these gentlewomen, I affirm
The perfect and true strain of poetry   5
Is rather to be given the quick cellar
Than the fat kitchen.

IV.II.2.1–2.] *Two F margin entries conflated here: 42–5, Pennyboy ... while (so*
Kifer); 2–5, Lickfinger ... argument.   4. gentlewomen] *Gifford;* Gentlemen
F.

IV.ii.3. *my argument*] Madrigal's combative opening emphasises that the
two men resume an old disagreement (cf. III.iii.21–5); but the ceremony of
Pecunia's arrival and reception by P. Junior will probably take enough stage
time to allow Madrigal and Lickfinger some preliminary conversation.

4. *gentlewomen*] Gifford's emendation both restores the metre and reinforces
the point that the battle between cook and poet must be fought in the presence
of Pecunia, whom each serves through banquet and encomium respectively.
Madrigal was previously attentive to the ladies in II.iv (see line 127), and
supped with gentlewomen in Apollo (III.iii.8–9).

5–40.] taken almost verbatim from *N.T.*, 70–112, which lines in turn
derive largely from Jonson's reading of Athenaeus, *Deipnosophistae* (The
Sophists at Dinner), a lengthy dialogue on cooks and cooking which dates from
the 2nd–3rd century A.D. and is heavily influenced by the classical *symposium.*
See next note.

5–7. *The ... kitchen*] an argument which refers back ultimately to rival
classical notions of educated conviviality. For Plato and Xenophon the *sym-*
posium, the occasion of cultured discourse, is not a meal but the drinking time
which follows it; but Athenaeus tends to conflate the two in his dialogue, 'in
order to find occasion for discussing food as well as drink' (Gulick ed., I.x),
and thus provides a congenial source for Lickfinger's argument.

6. *quick*] animating, lively – as in Falstaff's tribute to a 'good sherris-sack':
'It ascends me into the brain ... makes it apprehensive, quick, forgetive, full
of nimble, fiery, and delectable shapes, which delivered o'er to the voice, the
tongue, which is the birth, becomes excellent wit' (*2H4*, IV.iii.94–100).

7. *fat*] greasy. The word could mean simply 'stuffy, overheated', as in *1H4*,

Lickfinger.   Heretic, I see
Thou art for the vain oracle of the bottle.
The hogshead, Trismegistus, is thy Pegasus.
Thence flows thy Muse's spring, from that hard hoof.   10
Seducèd poet, I do say to thee,
A boiler, range and dresser were the fountains
Of all the knowledge in the universe.
And they're the kitchens, where the master cook
(Thou dost not know the man, nor canst thou know him,   15
Till thou hast served some years in that deep school
That's both the nurse and mother of the arts,

---

14. they're] they'are *F*.

II.iv.1, where the tavern parlour is 'that fat room'. But de Winter is probably
right to suppose that Jonson got the phrase *fat kitchen* from current Italian
proverbs, e.g. Florio, *Second Frutes* (1591), p. 109: *Grassa cucina, magro
testamento* – a rich diet [will lead to] a meagre legacy. It. *cucina* (= kitchen) was
according to Florio 'Used also for dressing or rosting of meate'; Jonson's literal
rendering of the phrase only faintly echoes the cautionary note of the proverb.
     8. *oracle ... bottle*] Cf. *N.T.*, 77, where Jonson adds a marginal note *Vid.
Rabl. lib. 5*. In *Pantagruel*, Bk. V, 34, the seekers of the oracle approach the
Temple of the Holy Bottle through a vineyard stacked with drinking vessels
and 'other bacchic artillery' (II.335).
     9. *The ... Trismegistus*] In *Pantagruel*, Bk. V, 44, the 'epileny' Panurge
sings, 'Speak, so may the liquid mine / Of rubies or of diamonds, shine', is
answered by the single word TRINC from the 'trimegistian [thrice-greatest]
bottle'; the priestess Bacbuc glosses with the comment that 'drinking is the
distinguishing character of man ... by wine we become divine' (Ch. 45). In
the next chapter Panurge is taken with a fit of rhyming, and the Friar curses
'that damned empty food'; but he then finds himself afflicted: 'the spirit of
fustian possesses us all ... I will poetise, since everybody does; I find it coming' (II.355–9). Trismegistus was the mythical Egyptian priest supposedly
responsible for the Hermetic books, thought to predate Plato and the Bible and
to lay the foundations of human knowledge.
     9–10. *Pegasus ... hoof*] Cf. the inscription over the door to the Apollo
Room: 'Wine it is the Milk of Venus, / And the Poets' Horse accounted. / Ply
it, and you all are mounted' (lines 12–14; see *H.&S.* VIII 657). The poets'
spring was Hippocrene, which rose from the spot where Mount Helicon was
struck by Pegasus' hoof.
     11–13. *I ... universe*] Northrop Frye comments that in Greek Middle
Comedy (many fragments of which are preserved by Athenaeus) the cook is a
conventional buffoon figure, closely associated with the parasite, who 'breaks
into comedies to bustle and order about and make long speeches about the
mysteries of cooking. [He is] something ... like a master of ceremonies, a
center for the comic mood' (*Anatomy of Criticism*, p. 175).

And hearst him read, interpret and demonstrate!) –
A master cook! Why, he's the man o'men
For a professor. He designs, he draws,   20
He paints, he carves, he builds, he fortifies,
Makes citadels of curious fowl and fish;
Some he dry-ditches, some moats round with broths.
Mounts marrowbones, cuts fifty-angled custards,
Rears bulwark pies; and for his outerworks   25
He raiseth ramparts of immortal crust,
And teacheth all the tactics at one dinner:
What ranks, what files to put his dishes in,

23. dry-ditches] *H.&S.; dry-dishes F.*   24. fifty-angled] *Gifford;* fifty
angled *F.*

19–20. *he's ... professor*] Jonson uses the cooking metaphor to guide our
response to another set of allusions in this speech, to the maxims of Vitruvius
in his *De Architectura*, Ch. 1, on the education of the architect: 'The architect
should be equipped with knowledge of many branches of study, and varied
kinds of learning, for it is by his judgement that all work done by the other arts
is put to test' (transl. M. H. Morgan, Harvard, 1914, p. 5). See Introduction,
p. 39.
    20–6. *He ... crust*] English cooks were famous for elaborate dishes (see
note to III.iii.35–40); cf. Earle, *Microcosmographie*, 'A Cook': 'His cunning is
not small in Architecture, for he builds strange Fabricks in Paste, Towres and
Castles, which are offered to the assault of valiant teeth' (sig. M). Allusions to
'fortifications in the pastrie', as Massinger calls them (*A New Way to Pay Old
Debts*, I.ii.25) are common in contemporary writing, and sustain the Athenaean
emphasis on cooking as a civilised art.
    23. *dry-ditches*] See collation. *H.&S.* adopt the reading of *N.T.*, 92 at this
point. *F*'s -*dishes* may be a compositorial misreading, though on the evidence
of Jonson's script in the *Masque of Queens* holograph, it is difficult to see how
anyone could confuse his elegant long *s* with his bold and definite *t*. More likely
an authorial slip.
    24. *Mounts marrowbones*] i.e. as cannon. Cf. Fletcher, *Rollo Duke of
Normandy*, II.ii.16–19, where the cook boasts that 'I have fram'd a fortification, / Out of Rye past, which is impregnable, / And against that for two
long houres together, / Two dozen of maribones shall play continually' (ed.
J. D. Jump, London, 1948).
    27–9. *And ... military*] Athenaeus cites Nichomachus, *Eileithyia*: 'it is a
matter of military tactics ... this use of reason and harmony, the knowing just
where in cookery each unit is to be posted in number and quantity' (vii.291;
Gulick ed., III.309). Cf. the passage from Poseidippus reproduced in Appendix A (*H.&S.* give both in the original Greek). *H.&S.* also compare the
military dinner served up in Cartwright's *The Ordinary*, II.i.556f., 'All must
be Souldier-like; / No dish but must present Artilery' (*Plays & Poems*, ed.
Blakemore Evans, p. 290).

The whole art military. Then, he knows
The influence of the stars upon his meats,   30
And all their seasons, tempers, qualities,
And so to fit his relishes and sauces,
He has Nature in a pot 'bove all the chemists
Or airy brethren of the Rosy Cross.
He is an architect, an engineer,   35
A soldier, a physician, a philosopher,
A general mathematician.

Madrigal.   It is granted.

Lickfinger. And that you may not doubt him for a poet –

Almanac. This fury shows, if there were nothing else!
And 'tis divine. I shall forever hereafter   40
Admire the wisdom of a cook.

Band.   And we, sir!

---

33. He has] *F;* He'has *conj. this ed.*   chemists] *Chymists F.*
35. engineer] *F3; Inginer F.*

29–31. *Then . . . qualities*] Cf. Athenaeus (ix.378), quoting Sosipater, *The False Accuser*: 'The cook must know . . . all about the heavenly bodies, the setting of the stars, their risings . . . For all our dishes and foods virtually take on a flavour that is different at different times, in the revolution of the universal system' (Gulick, IV.213).

33.] Cf. *The Fortunate Isles*, 151–2, where the Rosicrucian Mere-Foole is told that his Order's founder 'has left you the inheritance, / Here in a pot'. See note to III.ii.99. The Rosicrucian movement had a strongly alchemical flavour.

chemists] alchemists. The word 'chemist' was just beginning to be used in its modern sense at this date, but Jonson's *Chymists* clearly refers to more traditional and arcane practices. Cf. Donne, 'Love's Alchemy', 7–8: 'as no chymic yet the Elixar got / But glorifies his pregnant pot' (*Songs and Sonets*, ed. T. Redpath, p. 62).

34. *airy . . . Cross*] Jonson substitutes *airy* for *bare-breechd* in *N.T.*, 103; in *The Fortunate Isles*, 38, the Rosicrucians are 'that aerie order'.

39–40. *This . . . divine*] In Rabelais the revelation of 'the goddess Bottle' immediately provokes in Panurge a rhyming 'poetic fury' (see note to line 9); but Almanac claims this inspiration, the essential *furor poeticus*, for the kitchen.

42–7. *O . . . you*] The casting of Pecunia in the role of Siren has some classical precedent; in Plato's *Cratylus*, 403, Socrates argues that Plutus the god of wealth is a figure of such compelling virtue that even 'the Sirens, like all the rest of the world, have been laid under his spells' (*Dialogues of Plato*, ed. Jowett, I.346). The identification is more generally explicable in terms of Money's universal power to attract; but her role is much more than that of temptress, and there is considerable irony in the way the prodigal's misleadings are projected on to the stately and passive Pecunia at this moment.

P. Junior. O, how my princess draws me with her looks
        And hales me in, as eddies draw in boats
        Or strong Charybdis ships that sail too near
        The shelves of love! The tides of your two eyes,   45
        Wind of your breath, are such as suck in all
        That do approach you.
Pecunia.   Who hath changed my servant?
P. Junior. Yourself, who drink my blood up with your beams
        As doth the sun, the sea! Pecunia shines
        More in the world than he, and makes it spring   50
        Where'er she favours. Please her but to show
        Her melting wrists or bare her ivory hands,
        She catches still! Her smiles, they are love's fetters!
        Her breasts his apples! Her teats strawberries!
        Where Cupid, were he present now, would cry,   55
        Farewell my mother's milk, here's sweeter nectar!
        Help me to praise Pecunia, gentlemen.
        She's your princess: lend your wits.
            They all begin the encomium of Pecunia.
Fitton.   A lady
        The Graces taught to move!
Almanac.   The Hours did nurse!
Fitton. Whose lips are the instructions of all lovers!   60
Almanac. Her eyes their lights, and rivals to the stars!
Fitton. A voice as if that Harmony still spake!
Almanac. And polished skin, whiter than Venus' foot –
Fitton. Young Hebe's neck, or Juno's arms!

---

51. Please] 'please *F.*

---

50. *he*] i.e. the sun. Pecunia's association with the sun is transformed through
hyperbole into an image of pastoral fecundity (*makes it spring*), one which allies
her with such mythological figures as Demeter, who in many versions is the
mother of Plutus, god of riches under the earth and thus also symbolic of the
coming crop. See Robert Graves, *The Greek Myths*, I.89, II.198.
    52. *melting*] delicately moulded.
    53. *catches*] ensnares, captivates.
    55. *Where Cupid*] Cupid traditionally reposes in Venus' cleavage: 'And
between each rising breast / Lies the valley called my nest' (*Und.*, 2.v.33–4).
    59.] Cf. Milton's *Comus*, 986–8: 'The Graces and the rosy-bosomed Hours /
Thither all their bounties bring, / That there eternal summer dwells'. The
pastoral motif of line 50 is sustained.
    62. *Harmony*] the music of the spheres, inaudible to fallen ears.

Almanac.   An air
    Large as the morning's, and her breath as sweet   65
    As meadows after rain and but new-mown!
Fitton. Leda might yield unto her for a face –
Almanac. Hermione for breasts –
Fitton.   Flora for cheeks –
Almanac. And Helen for a mouth!
P. Junior.   Kiss, kiss 'em, princess.
                                              She kisseth them.
Fitton. The pearl doth strive in whiteness with her neck –   70
Almanac. But loseth by it. Here the snow thaws snow;
    One frost resolves another!
Fitton.   O, she has
    A front too slippery to be looked upon.
Almanac. And glances that beguile the seer's eyes.
P. Junior. Kiss, kiss again. [*She kisseth them*] *again.*
                            What says my man o'war?   75
Shunfield. I say she's more than fame can promise of her,

64. An air] *H.&S.;* A haire *F.*

---

64. *Hebe*] goddess of youth, and cupbearer to the gods.
Juno's arms] *H.&S.* compare 'white-armed Hera' in the *Iliad*, I.595. The
comparison is conventional in descriptions of Lady Money (cf. *The Trial of
Treasure*, Dodsley III.289), but Jonson might also have had in mind the fact
that during the Empire the Roman mint was housed in the temple of Juno
Moneta, whence derives the word 'money'.
    An air] *H.&S.* justify their emendation by comparing *Und.*, 42, 14–15: 'No
face, no hand, proportion, line, or air / Of beauty'. *F*'s reading is excessively
clumsy, although the idea itself is not uncommon; compare James Howell's
declaration, 'One hair of a woman can draw more than a hundred pair of oxen'
(*Familiar Letters*, II.5); and the famous moment in the *Greek Anthology*, 230:
'Doris pulled one thread from her golden hair and bound my hands with it, as
if I were her prisoner ... now most ill-fated of men, I am hung on a hair'
(transl. W. R. Paton, I.243–4). But the comparison with *morning* in line 65 is
tenuous and strained, whereas 'air' fits the context naturally, and associates
Pecunia with Aurora, goddess of dawn. Cf. *C.R.*, II.iii.168–9, on Argurion:
'you shall have her looke as cleere and fresh as the morning'.
    65–6. *her ... new-mown*] Cf. *Und.*, 2.v.27–8, where Venus' lips are
'Ripened with a breath more sweet, / Than when flowers and west winds
meet'.
    68. *Hermione*] the daughter of Helen and Menelaus.
    72. *resolves*] dissolves.
    73. *slippery*] dangerous. The line is adapted from Horace, *Odes*, I.xix.8:
'vultus nimium lubricus aspici' (*H.&S.*). Jonson also uses it in *S.S.*, II.i.26,
and *Gypsies Metamorphos'd*, 506.

A theme that's overcome with her own matter!
Praise is struck blind and deaf and dumb with her:
She doth astonish commendation!
P. Junior. Well pumped i'faith, old sailor. – Kiss him too,   80
Though he be a slug. (*She kisseth Captain Shunfield.*)
                    What says my poet-sucker?
He's chewing his Muse's cud, I do see by him.
Madrigal. I have almost done. I want but e'en to finish.
Fitton. That's the ill luck of all his works still.
P. Junior.   What?
Fitton. To begin many works but finish none.   85
P. Junior. How does he do his mistress' work?
Fitton.   Imperfect.
Almanac. I cannot think he finisheth that.
P. Junior. [*To Madrigal.*]   Let's hear.
Madrigal. It is a madrigal. I affect that kind
    Of poem much.
P. Junior.   And thence you ha' the name.
Fitton. It is his rose. He can make nothing else.   90
Madrigal. I made it to the tune the fiddlers played
    That we all liked so well.
P. Junior.   Good: read it, read it.
Madrigal. The sun is father of all metals, you know,
    Silver and gold.
P. Junior.   Ay, leave your prologues. Say!

---

84. the ill] the'ill *F*.

---

81. *slug*] sluggard.
poet-sucker] would-be or budding poet (literally, one that is unweaned).
84. *ill*] See collation. *H.&S.* speculate that Jonson thought 'ill' to be a
clipped form of 'evil', but as far as I know he does not elsewhere use this
contracted form. Cf., however, *Cat.*, III.859: 'The'evill we doe, untill we
suffer it', where the metrical apostrophe achieves a similar compression.
88. *affect*] like.
90.] Cf. *Conv. Drum.*, 490–2, where Jonson defends the painter 'who could
paint nothing but a Rose' because 'a Rose was above them all' (*H.&S.*).
93–4. *The . . . gold*] Cf. Bernardo Davanzati, *A Discourse upon Coins* (1588,
transl. 1696), p. 7: 'The Sun and Internal Heat do separate, as it were by Distillation, the best Juices and Substances in the Bowels of the Earth; which
being percolated into proper Veins and Mines, and there congeal'd, grown
solid, and ripen'd, they are in time made *Mettals*: whereof the most rare and
perfect are *Gold* and *Silver*, resembling the two great Luminaries of the World
in Splendor and Colour.'

SONG.

Madrigal. As bright as is the Sun her sire,   95
    Or Earth, her mother, in her best attire,
    Or Mint, the midwife, with her fire,
    Comes forth her grace!
(P. Junior. That 'Mint the midwife' does well.)
    The splendour of the wealthiest mines,   100
    The stamp and strength of all imperial lines,
    Both majesty and beauty shines
(Fitton. That's fairly said of money.)
    In her sweet face!
    Look how a torch, of taper light,   105
    Or of that torch's flame, a beacon bright –
(P. Junior. Good!)
    Now there, I want a line to finish, sir.
P. Junior. [Considers for a moment.]
    Or of that beacon's fire, moonlight –
Madrigal. So takes she place!   110
(Fitton. 'Tis good.)
Madrigal. And then I've a saraband –
    She makes good cheer, she keeps full boards,
    She holds a fair of knights and lords,
    A market of all offices   115

99.] Opposite 98–100 in F.   103.] Opposite 102–4 in F.   107.] Opposite
106 in F.   111.] Opposite 110 in F.   112. I've] I'have F.

95–8. As … grace] On the genesis of mineral wealth, see note to II.Int.29.
Madrigal invokes a controversy in his praise of coining that is dealt with by
Patrick Scot in his The Tillage of Light (1623), where he attacks the idea that
'Mineralls removeed from their naturall places, may by art bee brought to
multiply in a greater perfection, then by nature in the wombe of the earth,
where the sunne applieth his force' (p. 8). But others were prepared to argue
(often in defending usury, the 'breeding' of money) that 'The Earth it self
without labour of him that useth it will yeelde in all small gaine' (J. Spottiswood,
The Execution of Neschech (1616), p. 33); and in 1626 Sir Robert Cotton, in a
speech to the Privy Council 'touching the Alteration of Coin', described the
Royal Mint as 'the Pulse of the Common-wealth' (Scarce and Valuable Tracts on
Money, p. 131).
    105. light] lit: the obsolete past participle form (see Partridge, Accidence,
p. 184).
    110. place] precedence.
    112. saraband] See note to line 137.
    113. keeps … boards] provides abundant food.

And shops of honour more or less.
According to Pecunia's grace,
The bride hath beauty, blood and place,
The bridegroom virtue, valour, wit,
And wisdom, as he stands for it.   120
P. *Junior.* Call in the fiddlers.

[*Enter Fiddlers and Boy Singer.*]

                                        Nick the boy shall sing it;
Sweet princess, kiss him. Kiss 'em all, dear madam,
And at the close, vouchsafe to call them cousins.
Pecunia. [*Kissing them in turn.*] Sweet cousin Madrigal, and
    cousin Fitton,
My cousin Shunfield, and my learned cousin –   125
Picklock. Al-manach, though they call him Almanac.
P. *Canter.* [*Aside.*] Why, here's the prodigal prostitutes his
    mistress!
P. *Junior.* And Picklock, he must be a kinsman too.
My man o'law will teach us all to win
And keep our own. Old Founder –
P. *Canter.*   Nothing, I, sir.   130
I am a wretch, a beggar. She the fortunate
Can want no kindred, we the poor know none.

---

116. *honour*] F; Honours *1716.*   *more or less.*] F; more and less *conj. de*
Winter.   121. S.H. P. *Junior.*] *1716;* PIC. F.   121–3.] F *margin: He*
vrgeth her to kisse them all.   126. S.H.] *Gifford;* P.CA. F.   127. S.H.]
Gifford; P.IV. F; PIC. *1716.*   130. I, sir.] I sir? F.

116. more or less] De Winter's conjecture 'more *and* less' (meaning great
and small) is attractive. But we should probably not try to improve Madrigal's
verses.
    123. *cousins*] kin. To 'call cousin' is to claim kinship with someone (*O.E.D.*
call, v.17b). Here the ritual has something of the decadent formality of Cres-
sida's introduction to the Greek camp in *Troil.,* IV.v.
    126. *Al-manach*] the French spelling, as in Cotgrave; but with an insistence
that the accent falls on the second syllable. Jonson may have thought that the
word derived from Lat. *manacus,* meaning a zodiac circle, or perhaps knew the
Spanish Arabic form *al-manakh.* See *O.E.D.*
    132. *want*] lack. Cf. Barnfield's lines on the deposition of Honesty by Riches:
'now *Pecunia* on his Seate is mounted; / Since Honestie in great Disgrace did
fall. / No state, no Calling now, doeth him esteeme; / . . . In Countinance so
changde, that none can know him' (*Encomion,* p. 89). Jonson avoids casting

Fitton. Nor none shall know by my consent.
Almanac.   Nor mine.
P. Junior. Sing, boy; stand here.

[*Music.*] *The boy sings the song.*

P. Canter. [*Aside.*]   Look, look how all their eyes
          Dance i'their heads – observe! – scattered with lust   135
          At sight o'their brave idol. How they are tickled
          With a light air, the bawdy saraband!
          They are a kind of dancing engines all,
          And set by nature, thus to run alone
          To every sound! All things within, without them   140
          Move, but their brain, and that stands still: mere monsters
          Here in a chamber, of most subtle feet!
          And make their legs in tune, passing the streets!
          These are the gallant spirits o'the age,
          The miracles o'the time, that can cry up   145
          And down men's wits, and set what rate on things

Canter as moral opponent to Pecunia but underscores the visual contrast
between her splendour and his ragged appearance.

135. *scattered*] distracted, crazed.

137. *the ... saraband*] i.e. music composed in the rhythm of a saraband,
a slow Spanish dance in triple time. It attracted the regular disapproval of
moralists. Wittipol's catalogue of vanities in *D.A.*, IV.iv.164–6 includes to
'Coach it to *Pimlico*; daunce the *Saraband*; / Heare, and talke bawdy; laugh as
loud, as a larum; / Squeake, spring, do any thing'.

138–41. *engines ... monsters*] The characteristic Jonsonian critique of
mechanical fashion, life reduced to a 'motion', blends here with suggestions of
the ape-dance, a trope made famous by Lucian in *Piscator*, and which in the
Christian tradition becomes a figure for the vanity of worldly pleasure (H. W.
Janson, *Apes and Ape Lore in the ... Renaissance*, p. 171). Richard Brathwaite
cautions gentlemen that they should not 'in their *Dancing* use those mimicke
trickes which our apish Professants use ... so supple and pliable in their
joynts, as you would take them to be some Tumblers; but what are these but
Jacke-an-Apes in gay cloathes?' (*The English Gentleman*, p. 204).

143. *make ... legs*] The phrase 'make a leg' usually means to show obei-
sance, but Jonson is using it in a more general sense of elegant comportment.
Cf. Selden's *Table-Talk*, 'Poetry': 'As 'tis good to learn to dance, a man may
learn his Leg, learn to go handsomly, but 'tis ridiculous for him to dance,
when he should go' (Arber ed., p. 85).

passing] perambulating.

145–6. *cry ... down*] extol and denigrate.

Their half-brained fancies please. Now pox upon 'em!
[*Indicating P. Junior.*] See how solicitously he learns the
    jig,
As if it were a mystery of his faith!
Shunfield. A dainty ditty.
Fitton.   O, he's a dainty poet   150
    When he sets to't.
P. Junior.   And a dainty scholar.
Almanac. No, no great scholar; he writes like a gentleman.
Shunfield. Pox o'your scholar!
P. Canter. [*Aside.*]   Pox o'your distinction! –
    As if a scholar were no gentleman.
    With these, to write like a gentleman will in time   155
    Become all one as to write like an ass.
    These gentlemen? These rascals! I am sick
    Of indignation at 'em.
P. Junior.   How do you like't, sir?
Fitton. 'Tis excellent.
Almanac.   'Twas excellently sung.
Fitton. A dainty air.
P. Junior.   What says my Lickfinger?   160
Lickfinger. I am telling Mistress Band and Mistress Statute
    What a brave gentleman you are, and Wax here!
    How much 'twere better that my lady's grace

151. to't] *F;* to it *Whalley.*   151–2.] *F margin: They are all struck with
admiration.*

148. *jig*] applied to a number of lively dances.
149. *mystery*] holy rite.
151. *scholar*] 'often applied to one who had studied at the university, and
who, not having entered any of the learned professions or obtained any fixed
employment, sought to gain a living by literary work' (*O.E.D.*).
152.] De Winter detects a further satire (see note to I.vi.81–4) on George
Wither, who several times in his *Juvenilia* alludes to his gentle status and signs
himself 'Gentleman' on two title-pages. But the personal taunt is only glancing, and makes way for a wider attack on the lightweight refinement of much
contemporary writing, and what Jonson saw as the decay of learning and
serious literary purpose in his society. Cf. the dialogue on Scogan in *The
Fortunate Isles*, 289–94: 'But, wrote he like a Gentleman? / In rime! fine tinck-
ling rime! and flowand verse! / With now & then some sense! & he was paid for
it, / Regarded, and rewarded: which few *Poets* / Are now adaies.'
158. *How ... sir?*] perhaps addressed to Canter, whose stony silence is
broken by the tinkling praise of the jeerers.

Would here take up, sir, and keep house with you.
P. Junior. What say they?
Statute.   We could consent, sir, willingly.   165
Band. Ay, if we knew her grace had the least liking.
Wax. We must obey her grace's will and pleasure.
P. Junior. I thank you, gentlewomen. [*Aside.*] Ply 'em,
        Lickfinger.
    Give Mother Mortgage there –
Lickfinger.   Her dose of sack.
    I have it for her, and her distance of hum.   170
                The gallants are all about Pecunia.
Pecunia. Indeed, therein I must confess, dear cousin,
    I am a most unfortunate princess.
Almanac.   And
    You still will be so when your grace may help it?
Madrigal. Who'd lie in a room with a close-stool and garlic
    And kennel with his dogs, that had a prince   175
    Like this young Pennyboy to sojourn with?
Shunfield. He'll let you ha' your liberty –
Almanac.   Go forth
    Whither you please, and to what company –
Madrigal. Scatter yourself amongst us –
P. Junior. [*To Madrigal.*]   Hope of Parnassus!
    Thy ivy shall not wither, nor thy bays.   180
    Thou shalt be had into her grace's cellar
    And there know sack and claret all December.
    Thy vein is rich, and we must cherish it.
    Poets and bees swarm nowadays, but yet

---

164. *take up*] lodge.
170. *distance*] quantity measured by the mark or peg in a drinking vessel
(*H.&S.*).
    hum] Gifford understands this to be 'an infusion of spirits in ale or beer', but
it may be simply a strong traditional ale.
174. *close-stool*] chamber pot enclosed in a stool or box. Garlic was presumably used to ward off infection, as it was during a plague.
179. *Scatter*] The word retains its overtones of dissipation from line 135.
180.] *H.&S.* compare *Poet.*, apologeticall Dialogue, 235: 'To come forth
worth the ivy, or the bayes'; but Jonson's original in Juvenal, *Satires*, vii.28–9,
has none of P. Junior's facile optimism: 'you that are inditing lofty strains in a
tiny garret, that you may come forth worthy of a scraggy bust wreathed with
ivy!' (Loeb ed., p. 139).

There are not those good taverns for the one sort   185
As there are flow'ry fields to feed the other.
Though bees be pleased with dew – ask little Wax,
That brings the honey to her lady's hive –
The poet must have wine. And he shall have it.

ACT IV SCENE iii
[*Enter*] PENNYBOY SE[NIOR *hastily*].

[*P. Senior.*] Broker, what, Broker!
P. Junior.   Who's that? My uncle!
P. Senior. I am abused. Where is my knave, my broker?
Lickfinger. Your broker is laid out upon a bench yonder.
    Sack hath seized on him in the shape of sleep.
Picklock. He hath been dead to us almost this hour.   5
P. Senior. This hour?
P. Canter.   Why sigh you, sir? 'Cause he's at rest?
P. Senior. It breeds my unrest.
Lickfinger.   Will you take a cup
    And try if you can sleep?
P. Senior.   No, cogging Jack,
    Thou and thy cups too, perish!
        He strikes the sack out of his hand.

187–8. dew – . . . hive –] *This ed.; dew, . . . hive: F.*   IV.iii.o.1.] *Gifford;*
PENI-BOY. SE. PENY-BOY. IV. / LICKFINGER.&C..

---

189. *The . . . wine*] Cf. Thomas Gainsford, *The Rich Cabinet* (1616): 'Poetry must take vigor and spirit from *Bacchus* company . . . a wearied wit is refreshed with a little wine, and the verses slip more easily out, being washed over with that pleasant and lively liquor' (fol. 112*v*–113).

IV.iii.o.1.] The entry of P. Senior brings an interlude in the praise of Pecunia, reserving Piedmantle's triumphant entry with her pedigree until her freedom from the usurer's grip is confirmed. The scene functions as an antimasque, anatomising the conditions that frustrate Pecunia's apotheosis, and concluding with a ritual expulsion of her jailor.
    3. *laid . . . yonder*] P. Senior had sent Broker to 'Serve in Apollo but take heed of Bacchus' at III.iv.17; it is therefore possible that as Act IV opens he is lying on a bench to the side in full view of the audience. But it is more probable that Broker remains off-stage since *F* provides no entry for him, either here or at IV.i, and if he were visible here it would be odd if P. Senior did not attempt to shake him awake.

Shunfield.   O, the sack!

Madrigal. The sack, the sack!

P. Canter.   A madrigal on sack!   10

Picklock. Or rather an elegy, for the sack is gone.

Pecunia. Why do you this, sir? Spill the wine and rave
    For Broker's sleeping?

P. Senior.   What through sleep and sack
    My trust is wronged, but I am still awake
    To wait upon your grace. Please you to quit   15
    This strange, lewd company; they are not for you.

Pecunia. No, guardian, I do like them very well.

P. Senior. Your grace's pleasure be observed; but you,
    Statute and Band and Wax, will go with me.

Statute. Truly we will not.

Band.   We will stay and wait here   20
    Upon her grace, and this your noble kinsman.

P. Senior. Noble? How, noble? Who hath made him noble?

P. Junior. Why, my most noble money hath, or shall;
    My princess here. She that had you but kept
    And treated kindly would have made you noble,   25
    And wise too. Nay, perhaps have done that for you
    An Act of Parliament could not, made you honest.
    The truth is, uncle, that her grace dislikes
    Her entertainment, specially her lodging.

15–20.] *F margin: Hee would haue* Pecunia *home. But shee refuseth. And her*
Traine.   22.   How, noble?] how noble! *F.*

---

13. *For*] just because.

17. *I . . . well*] Cf. *The Contention between Liberality and Prodigality*, II.iv,
where Money, after being given by Fortune to Prodigality, declares 'I am,
where I like' (Dodsley 8.349).

23–5.] The satirical proposition that nobility can be bought (common
enough in James's reign when peerages and knighthoods were sold in great
numbers) moves under the pressure of Jonson's thought to the more serious
idea that the right use of riches is a sign of personal worth and substance. It is
an elevated thought for P. Junior, but at this stage he is being prepared for his
reformation.

27.] Cf. Jonson's attack on Inigo Jones, 'Whom not ten fires nor a parliament can, / With all remonstrance, make an honest man' ('An Expostulation',
U.V., 34, lines 103–4). Jonson seems to have been partial to this figure of
speech, which I have not found elsewhere.

29. *entertainment*] treatment; but in this context the word also has the force
of 'conditions of employment' (see *O.E.D.* 2). The usurer puts money to
work.

Pecunia. Nay, say her jail. Never unfortunate princess   30
    Was used so by a jailor. Ask my women:
    Band, you can tell, and Statute, how he has used me,
    Kept me close prisoner, under twenty bolts –
Statute. And forty padlocks –
Band.   All malicious engines
    A wicked smith could forge out of his iron,   35
    As locks and keys, shackles and manacles,
    To torture a great lady.
Statute.   H'has abused
    Your grace's body.
Pecunia.   No, he would ha' done;
    That lay not in his power. He had the use
    Of your bodies, Band and Wax, and sometimes Statute's.   40
    But once he would ha' smothered me in a chest
    And strangled me in leather, but that you
    Came to my rescue then and gave me air.
Statute. For which he crammed us up in a close box,
    All three together, where we saw no sun   45
    In one six-months.
Wax.   A cruel man he is!
Band. H'has left my fellow Wax out i'the cold –
Statute. Till she was stiff as any frost, and crumbled
    Away to dust and almost lost her form.

---

40. Of your] *H.&S.*; O'your *conj. S.T. Coleridge, cit. Cunningham;* Of our *F.*

30–45.] Gifford points out a parallel with Aristophanes' *Ploutos*, 234–5: 'If
I went / Into a miser's house he'd bury me / In a flash' (Oxford ed., transl. P.
Dickinson), and de Winter a more substantial one with Zeus' speech to Wealth
in Lucian's *Timon*, 13, about how the rich 'locked you up so tightly with bolts,
bars, and seals you couldn't see a ray of light' (*Selected Satires*, transl. L.
Casson, p. 244). Jonson probably had both passages in mind, but the idea is a
commonplace in his day; cf. John Taylor, 'The Travels of Twelve-Pence',
where the old miser is 'so Jealous day and night, / He would not suffer her goe
out of sight . . . Old men within Doores would ever worr'y her' (*Workes* 1630,
sig. H).
    40. *your bodies*] Coleridge's emendation (*Literary Remains*, II.286) is clear-
ly essential unless we assume a confident use of the royal possessive 'we',
referring to 'our minions'. As before, Jonson touches on but does not fully
exploit the idea of 'the two usuries', linking copulation and interest, as Dekker
has it: 'the Usurer lives by the lechery of mony' (Grosart II.28); cf. Overbury's
Characters, 'A Divellish Usurer': 'He puts his money to the unnaturall Act of
generation; and his Scrivener is the supervisor Bawd to't' (Lucas IV.36).

Wax. Much ado to recover me.
P. Senior.   Women jeerers!   50
   Have you learned too the subtle faculty?
   Come, I'll show you the way home, if drink
   Or too full diet have disguised you.
Band.   Troth,
   We have not any mind, sir, of return –
Statute. To be bound back to back –
Band.   And have our legs   55
   Turned in or writhed about –
Wax.   · Or else displayed –
Statute. Be lodged with dust and fleas as we were wont –
Band. And dieted with dogs' dung.
P. Senior.   Why, you whores,
   My bawds, my instruments, what should I call you
   Man may think base enough for you?
P. Junior.   Hear you, uncle.   60
   I must not hear this of my princess' servants,
   And in Apollo, in Pecunia's room.
   Go, get you down the stairs, home to your kennel
   As swiftly as you can. Consult your dogs,
   The *lares* of your family, or, believe it,   65
   The fury of a footman and a drawer
   Hangs over you.
Shunfield.   Cudgel and pot do threaten
   A kind of vengeance.   (*They all threaten [him].*)
Madrigal.   Barbers are at hand.
Almanac. Washing and shaving will ensue.
Fitton.   The pump

---

   53. *disguised you*] made you drunk. A proverbial usage (Tilley D362).
   56. *displayed*] in both the allegorical and physical senses: (i) spread open (as documents); (ii) lying supine with the limbs extended (*O.E.D.* 1.c).
   59. *instruments*] For the pun, cf. Subtle's complaint about Face: 'the slave will run a-wiving, Doll, / Against the instrument that was drawn between us' – where Doll is the *instrument* the two men share (*Alch.*, V.iv.80–1, Revels).
   62. *Apollo . . . room*] Apollo as sun-god is the alchemical symbol for gold.
   63. *down . . . stairs*] Apollo is thought of as an upstairs room (like the prodigal's lodgings in Act I; see I.ii.4), but suggestions that this scene was played in the gallery above the Blackfriars main stage can be discounted. P. Senior is ejected through one of the tiring-house doors.
   69. *pump*] i.e. at a well or conduit.

Is not far off. If 'twere, the sink is near,   70
Or a good jordan.
Madrigal.   You have now no money –
Shunfield. But are a rascal.
P. Senior.   I am cheated, robbed,
Jeered by confederacy.
Fitton.   No, you are kicked
And used kindly, as you should be.
Shunfield.   Spurned
From all commerce of men, who are a cur.   75
Almanac. A stinking dog in a doublet, with foul linen.
Madrigal. A snarling rascal. Hence!
Shunfield.   Out!
P. Senior. [Retreating.]   Well, remember
I am cozened by my cousin and his whore.
Bane o'these meetings in Apollo!
Lickfinger. [Trying to lead him away.] Go, sir;
You will be tossed like Block in a blanket else.   80
P. Junior. Down with him, Lickfinger.
P. Senior. [Shaking him off.]   Saucy Jack, away.
Pecunia is a whore.   [*Exit, followed by* LICKFINGER.]
P. Junior.   Play him down, fiddlers,
And drown his noise.

73–4.] *F margin: And spurne him.*   76.] *F margin: Kicke him out.*   77–8.]
F margin: Hee exclaimes.   80.] *F margin: One of his Dogges.*

---

70. *sink*] cesspool.
71. *jordan*] chamberpot.
74. *kindly*] fittingly, in kind.
76. *dog . . . doublet*] proverbial (Tilley D452) for pride. Tilley cites Dekker,
The Shoemaker's Holiday, vii.113–14: 'My master will be as proud as a dog in a
doublet, all in beaten damask and velvet' (Revels). As so often, Jonson gives
a twist to a familiar phrase, linking P. Senior's arrogant avariciousness to a
festering self-absorption.
78. *cozened . . . cousin*] proverbial (Tilley C739).
80. *Block . . . blanket*] The marginal note (see collation) explains the reference; dogs as well as people were tossed in this way as a punishment; but that
Block is the name of P. Senior's own dog is made clear only at V.iii.42–3.
82. *Pecunia . . . whore*] a conventional judgement, here perceived as a reduction; cf. *D.A.*, II.i.1–2: 'Sir, money's a whore, a bawd, a drudge; / Fit to
runne out on errands: Let her goe.'

[*Enter*] PIEDMANTLE *to them* [*carrying a scroll*]

Who's this?

Fitton.   O, Master Piedmantle!

ACT IV   SCENE iv
Piedmantle brings the Lady Pecunia her pedigree.

[*Piedmantle.*] By your leave, gentlemen.
Fitton.   Her grace's herald.
Almanac. No herald yet; a heraldet.
P. Junior.   What's that?
P. Canter. A canter.
P. Junior.   O, thou saidst thou'dst prove us all so!
P. Canter. Sir, here is one will prove himself so, straight.
    So shall the rest in time.
Pecunia. [*To Piedmantle.*]   My pedigree?   5
    I tell you, friend, he must be a good scholar
    Can my descent. I am of princely race,
    And as good blood as any is i'the mines
    Runs through my veins. I am every limb a princess!
    Duchess o' Mines was my great grandmother,   10
    And by the father's side I come from Sol.

---

83. S.D.] *After IV.iv in F.*

IV.iv.2. *heraldet*] petty herald. But in the next line Canter interprets the
term as a diminishment of heraldry itself.
    7. *Can*] knows.
    8. *blood . . . mines*] Cf. Davanzati, *A Discourse upon Coins*, p. 18: 'For as
Blood, which is the Juice and Substance of Meat in the natural Body, does by
circulating out of the greater into the lesser Vessels, moisten all the Flesh . . .
In like manner, Money . . . preserves alive the *Civil Body* of the Commonwealth.' See note to IV.ii.93–4.
    9. *veins . . . limb*] Cf. J. de Acosta, *The Naturall and Morall History of the
Indies* (1604): 'Mettalls are (as plants,) hidden and buried in the bowels of the
earth, which have some conformitie in themselves, in the forme and maner of
their production; for that wee see and discover even in them, branches, and as
it were a bodie, from whence they grow and proceede, which are the greater
veines and the lesse, so as they have a knitting in themselves' (pp. 203–4).
    11–12. *Sol . . . Or*] Nason, *Heralds and Heraldry*, p. 116: 'blazoning tinc-
tures . . . by the name of planets . . . was usually reserved for . . . the arms of
kings and princes.' *Sol* is therefore 'the *royal* term for gold', whereas *Or* reflects
the more usual designation by names of metals and colours.

My grandfather was Duke of Or, and matched
In the blood royal of Ophir.
Piedmantle. [Pointing.]   Here's his coat.
Pecunia. I know it if I hear the blazon.
Piedmantle.   He bears
In a field azure, a sun proper, beamy,   15
Twelve of the second.
P. Canter.   How far's this from canting?
P. Junior. Her grace doth understand it.
P. Canter.   She can cant, sir.
Pecunia. What be these? Besants?
Piedmantle.   Yes, an't please your grace.
Pecunia. That is our coat too, as we come from Or.
What line's this?
Piedmantle.   The rich mines of Potosi,   20
The Spanish mines i'the West Indies.
Pecunia.   This?
Piedmantle. The mines o'Hungary; this, of Barbary.
Pecunia. But this, this little branch?

20. line's] *F;* line is *Whalley, Gifford.*

---

13. *blood ... Ophir*] The legend of Ophir (see I.vi.42–4 note) was given a
fresh infusion in the sixteenth century with the discovery of mineral wealth in
the Americas, combined with the Renaissance passion for correspondences:
'there are many ... which affirme that our *Peru* is *Ophir*, deriving one name
from another ... grounding it upon that which the holy scripture saith, that
they brought from *Ophir* pure gold, precious stones, and wood which was rare
and goodly: which things abound in Peru' (de Acosta, *History*, pp. 41–2).
  coat] coat of arms.
  14. *blazon*] 'Blazon is the description of Armes, and their appurtenances, by
the received termes' (Bolton, *Elements of Armories*, p. 63).
  15. *field azure*] blue background. The *field* is the surface of an heraldic shield
(Nason, p. 117).
  a ... beamy] a sun represented as a human face surrounded by rays, in its
natural (*proper*) colour of gold (*ibid.*).
  16. *Twelve ... second*] twelve beams of the second tincture named, i.e. Or.
  18. *Besants*] small gold circles; originally large gold pieces or talents used as
currency.
  20. *Potosi*] The wealth flowing from the silver mine at Mount Potosì in
Bolivia was legendary at this time; e.g. John Taylor, *The Travels of Twelve-
Pence*: 'the Potent King of Spaine, / ... from Pottozzy Mines he daily had /
Three hundred thirty thousand Ryals made' (*Workes*, 1630, Hv).
  23. *Welsh mine*] A 'Proclamation concerning Royall Mynes', 10 July 1624,
announced that the King had 'received advertisement of great probabilities,
and assured hopes of finding within ... the Dominion of Wales, many rich

Piedmantle.   The Welsh mine that.
Pecunia. I ha' Welsh blood in me too. Blaze, sir, that coat.
Piedmantle. She bears (an't please you) argent, three leeks vert   25
   In canton or, and tasseled of the first.
P. Canter. Is not this canting? Do you understand him?
P. Junior. Not I. But it sounds well, and the whole thing
   Is rarely painted. I will have such a scroll
   Whate'er it cost me.
Pecunia.   Well, at better leisure   30
   We'll take a view of it, and so reward you.
P. Junior. Kiss him, sweet princess, and style him a cousin.
Pecunia. I will, if you will have it. (*She kisseth* [*him*].)
                       Cousin Piedmantle.
P. Junior. I love all men of virtue, from my princess
   Unto my beggar here, old Canter. On,   35
   On to thy proof. Whom prove you the next canter?
P. Canter. The doctor here. I will proceed with the learned.
   When he discourseth of dissection
   Or any point of anatomy, that he tells you

38–73, 104–8. dissection *etc.*] *This and subseq. canting terms italic in* F.

Mynes of Silver and other Metalls, having in them Silver and Gold' (*Stuart Royal Proclamations*, ed. J. F. Larkin, no. 254, I.595).

24. *Welsh blood*] perhaps also derived from her ancestor *Duchess O' Mines* (line 10), recalling Pecunia's Cornish extraction (I.vi.39) and Drayton's derivation of that county's name: 'The whole name is, as if you should say *Cornewales*; for hither in the *Saxon* conquest the *British* called *Welsh* ... made transmigration' (*Polyolbion*, 1622, p. 21).

25. *bears*] is entitled to display heraldically (Kifer).

25–6. *argent* ... *or*] breaking the heraldic rule against placing metal on metal (Nason, p. 115). Traditionally, the leek was the Welsh national badge (as Fluellen explains in *H5*, IV.vii.100f); its connotations are notably unheraldic. The *canton* is a square division less than a quarter, occupying the upper (usually dexter) corner of the shield (*O.E.D.*).

26. *of the first*] i.e. argent, the tincture of the 'field'.

38. *dissection*] *O.E.D.*'s examples suggest that, although dissections had been carried out in England since the 1540s, the term only really came into medical vogue in the seventeenth century. (Brainworm's remark in *E.M.I.*, IV.vi.36–7, 'they must ha' dissected, and made an *Anatomie* o'me' appears only in the 1616 version of the play.) Canter's point is that terminology is used to mystify, and perhaps he stresses the word *discourseth*; at this date it was still common for medical professors to lecture on anatomy without performing operations, and students continued to go abroad, especially to Italy, for practical experience of dissection.

Of *vena cava* and of *vena porta*,   40
The meseraics and the *mesenterium*,
What does he else but cant? Or if he run
To his judicial astrology
And trowl the trine, the quartile and the sextile,
Platic aspect and partile, with his hyleg   45
Or alchochoden, cusps and horoscope,
Does not he cant? Who here does understand him?

---

40. vena cava] one of the main veins opening into the right atrium of the
heart. Harvey's work on the veins, which contributed to his (as yet unpublished) discovery of the circulation of the blood, was doubtless discussed
amongst educated men of the time. But the term had long been familiar usage.

vena porta] believed by Galen and Renaissance doctors to carry *chyle* (a
white milky fluid) from the upper intestine to the liver where it was turned
into blood and other humours.

41.] Both terms refer to the mesentery, the double layer of peritoneal mem-
brane which supports the small intestine (so Kifer).

42. cant] to use the special jargon of a particular class or subject (*O.E.D.* v³
3). Dekker had used the word of vagabond 'language' in 1609 (*Lanthorne &
Candle-Light*), and since the mid sixteenth century it had been defined as 'to
beg'. *O.E.D.* suggests that Jonson is the only pre-Restoration user in this
sense, although there are signs of its being applied to the growing problem of
jargon and linguistic pretension in other writings of the period (e.g. Massinger's
The Picture, II.ii.46–8).

43. judicial astrology] astrology as we understand it today; in the seventeenth
century distinguished from natural astrology, the calculation of dates and
natural phenomena (tides, the calendar, etc.). There were numerous attacks
on judicial astrology at this time, in the form of mock-prognostications like
Vox Graculi and *A New and Merry Prognostication* (1623), and also serious
polemics such as J. Chamber's *A Treatise against Judicial Astrology* (1601).
These do not however concern themselves with the problem of linguistic
mystification.

44. trowl] variant form of 'troll' (usually meaning 'sing', as in *Temp.*,
III.ii.115, 'troll the catch'). Here it means 'to recite in a full rolling voice'
(*O.E.D.* IV.12), with a suggestion of jargon mechanically produced like the
repetitions of a catch or round.

trine ... sextile] Planets 120 degrees, 90 degrees and 60 degrees distant from
one another are said to be in trine, quartile and sextile aspects respectively (so
Kifer, following W. Lilly, *Christian Astrology* (1647), cited by *H.&S.*).

45. Platic ... partile] Two opposite aspects of rays cast from one planet to
another (Lilly, pp. 106–7). *partile* = exact to the same degree and minute;
Platic = not within a degree, but within the orbit of its own light (*H.&S.*).

hyleg] ruling planet of a nativity.

46. alchochoden] planet which indicates by its position the length of life
(Kifer).

cusps] The cusp is the entrance of an astrological house.

Almanac. This is no canter, though!

P. Canter.   Or when my muster-master
Talks of his tactics, and his ranks and files,
His bringers up, his leaders on, and cries   50
'Faces about to the right hand', 'the left';
Now, 'as you were'; then tells you of redoubts,
Of cats and cortines, doth he not cant?

P. Junior.   Yes, faith.

P. Canter. My egg-chinned laureate here, when he comes forth
With dimeters and trimeters, tetrameters,   55
Pentameters, hexameters, catalectics,
His hyper- and his brachy-catalectics,
His pyrrhics, epitrites and choriambics,
What is all this but canting?

Madrigal.   A rare fellow!

Shunfield. Some begging scholar.

Fitton.   A decayed doctor at least!   60

P. Junior. Nay, I do cherish virtue though in rags.

---

53. faith] 'faith *F.*   57. hyper-] *Kifer; Hyper, F.*

---

50. *bringers up*] *H.&S.* compare Sir Thomas Browne's words in *Religio
Medici*, i.58: 'my desires onely are . . . to be but the last man, and bring up the
Rere in Heaven' (*Works*, ed. Keynes, I.68).

53. *cats*] from Lat. *cattus*: moveable enclosures used by besiegers to protect
themselves in approaching a fortification. Jonson might have remembered
them from his soldiering days.

cortines] variant form of 'curtain', used of the plain wall connecting two
towers, bastions, etc., of a fortification (*O.E.D.*).

54. *egg-chinned*] smooth-chinned (*H.&S.*). Madrigal's youth and naivety
have been stressed from his first appearance.

55–8.] The effect of this catalogue is similar to the litany of trivial literary
forms in 'An Execration upon Vulcan', 33–41, which Jonson claims he would
happily have lost to the flames: 'those hard trifles, anagrams, / Or eteostics
. . .' (35–6). But here his target is the name and not the thing; cf. Horace's
judgement on Virgil in *Poet.*, V.i.129–30: 'His learning labours not the schoole-
like glosse, / That most consists in *ecchoing* wordes, and termes'. See also *The
Art of Poetrie*, 65–103.

56. *catalectics*] verses lacking a syllable in the last foot.

57. *hyper-*] having one or two syllables after the last foot.

brachy-] lacking two syllables in the last foot.

58. *epitrites*] metrical feet made up of three long and one short syllable, in
any order.

choriambics] feet of four syllables, long-short-short-long.

60.] See note to IV.ii.151.

P. Canter. And you, Mas Courtier.
P. Junior. [*To Fitton.*]   Now he treats of you:
    Stand forth to him fair.
P. Canter.   With all your fly-blown projects
    And looks-out of the politics, your shut-faces
    And reserved questions, and answers that you game with,
    as –   65
    'Is't a clear business? Will it manage well?
    My name must not be used else.' 'Here 'twill dash.'
    'Your business has received a taint; give off,
    I may not prostitute myself.' 'Tut, tut,
    That little dust I can blow off at pleasure.   70
    Here's no such mountain yet i'the whole work
    But a light purse may level.' 'I will tide
    This affair for you, give it freight and passage' –
    And such mint-phrase, as 'tis the worst of canting
    By how much it affects the sense it has not.   75
Fitton. This is some other than he seems.
P. Junior.   How like you him?
Fitton. This cannot be a canter.
P. Junior.   But he is, sir,
    And shall be still, and so shall you be too.
    We'll all be canters. Now I think of it,

64. looks-out] *Gifford;* lookes out *F.*

---

63. *fly-blown*] corrupt.
64. *looks-out*] i.e. look-outs: emissaries or observers; not recorded by
O.E.D. before 1699.
    shut-faces] mysterious airs.
67. *dash*] founder. The usual word for the rejection of a bill in Parliament at
this time.
68. *give off*] leave off (cf. modern English north-country usage 'give over').
F italicises only *off*, but Jonson probably intends to satirise a currently fashionable phrase at court.
72. *But . . . may*] that a little money won't.
    tide] carry through. *O.E.D.*'s only pre-nineteenth-century example.
73. *freight and passage*] This phrase appears to be an example of hendiadys,
meaning roughly 'I'll smooth the way with a little financial persuasion'. The
word *freight* at this time means 'passage money'; and for the sense of *passage*
meaning 'general currency or acceptance', *O.E.D.*, compares a reference in
Bacon's *Advancement* (1605).
74. *mint-phrase*] *O.E.D.* glosses 'a phrase coined for a purpose', citing this
example; but Jonson also means, more simply, 'fancy new phrases'.
75. *affects . . . not*] pretends to meaning where there isn't any.

A noble whimsy's come into my brain!   80
I'll build a college, I and my Pecunia,
And call it Canters' College. Sounds it well?
Almanac. Excellent!
P. Junior.   And here stands my Father Rector.
And you, professors: you shall all profess
Something, and live there with her grace and me,   85
Your founders. I'll endow't with lands and means,
And Lickfinger shall be my master-cook.
What, is he gone?
P. Canter.   And a professor.
P. Junior.   Yes.
P. Canter. And read Apicius *De re culinaria*
To your brave doxy and you.
P. Junior.   You, cousin Fitton,   90
Shall, as a courtier, read the politics;
Doctor Almanac, he shall read astrology.
Shunfield shall read the military arts.

81–4.] *F margin:* Canters-Colledge, *begun to be erected.*

82. *Canters' College*] This is a fairly common figure in contemporary writing, in which an incongruous or bathetic subject is satirically endowed with
pretensions of organised learning. Nashe declares that 'A great office is not so
gainefull as the principalship of a Colledge of Curtizans' (*Christs Teares over
Jerusalem*, McKerrow, II.151), and Jonson in *Poet.* savagely denounces his
public as 'the barking students of Beares-Colledge' who 'swallow up the gar-
badge of the time' (apologeticall Dialogue, 45–6). But here he turns a familiar
idea to more serious use, implying a close link between his imagined structure
of Canters' College and developments in education in Jacobean England. See
Introduction, p. 47.
89. *read*] in its obsolete sense of teach or profess; cf. the academic rank of
'reader'.
De re culinaria] 'Of Cooking', a collection of recipes dating from the third
century A.D. which became attributed (wrongly) to the famous Roman gour-
mand H. Gabius Apicius. In *Alch.*, II.ii.75–7 (Revels), Mammon gets inspiration from Apicius for his own extravagances: 'tongues of carps, dormice, and
camels' heels', etc. (*H.&S.*).
90. *doxy*] whore. The word originally described a vagabond's mistress (see
Dekker, *The Belman of London*, Grosart III.107), but came to have a looser
application; Canter uses it in uncharacteristically savage fashion here.
91. *politics*] The elevation of Fitton from court gossip to one who pro-
fesses the science and art of government is the most blatant of P. Junior's
appointments.

P. Canter. As carving, and assaulting the cold custard.
P. Junior. And Horace here, the art of poetry,   95
    His lyrics and his madrigals, fine songs,
    Which we will have at dinner, steeped in claret,
    And against supper, soused in sack.
Madrigal.   In troth,
    A divine whimsy!
Shunfield.   And a worthy work,
    Fit for a chronicle.
P. Junior.   Is't not?
Shunfield.   To all ages.   100
P. Junior. And Piedmantle shall give us all our arms.
    But Picklock, what wouldst thou be? Thou canst cant too.
Picklock. In all the languages in Westminster Hall,
    Pleas, Bench or Chancery; fee-farm, fee-tail,
    Tenant in dower, 'at will', 'for term of life',   105
    'By copy of court roll', knights' service, homage,
    Fealty, escuage, soccage or frank almoigne,

94–5.] *F margin: That's* Madrigall.   98. soused] sowc't *F.*

---

94. *As*] such as. Canter's chilly sarcasm remains focused (as in line 88) on
the decadence of the Lickfinger ethic. See notes to IV.ii. 20–9. Here it provides an apt gloss on Shunfield's name.
    98. *against*] in preparation for.
    101.] In his *Annals* (1615 ed.) Stow reviews the professions and describes the
arms of each (chapters 38–48).
    102. *But Picklock*] Picklock's exclusion from Canter's roll-call of linguis-
tic abuse is explained by their alliance in the play (see lines 128–9); but the
voluntary demonstration of cant he proceeds to offer is neat proof of his
untrustworthiness.
    104. *fee-farm*] land held in perpetuity subject to a fixed rent, without other
services required (*O.E.D.*).
    fee-tail] an inheritable estate which can descend to certain classes of heirs
only (so Kifer).
    105. *Tenant in dower*] a widow who holds for life a portion of her dead
husband's estate.
    at will] an estate held during the owner's pleasure.
    106. *court roll*] the records in a manor, in which names, rents and services
of tenants were enrolled.
    107. *Fealty*] the oath of fidelity by a feudal tenant to his lord.
    escuage] the principal form of feudal tenure (literally 'shield service'), per-
sonal service in the field for a period of forty days in each year (*O.E.D.*). It
could also mean a money payment in lieu of military service (the tenant's
customary obligation to serve his lord in war).

Grand sergeanty, or burgage.
P. Junior.   Thou appearst
Κατ ἐξοχὴυ a canter. Thou shalt read
All Littleton's *Tenures* to me, and indeed   110
All my conveyances.
Picklock.   And make 'em too, sir!
Keep all your courts, be steward o'your lands,
Let all your leases, keep your evidences.
But first, I must procure and pass your mortmain.
You must have licence from above, sir.
P. Junior.   Fear not,   115
Pecunia's friends shall do it.

*Here his father [throws off his patched cloak and] discovers
    himself.*
P. Canter.   But I shall stop it!
Your worship's loving and obedient father,
Your painful steward, and lost officer,
Who have done this to try how you would use
Pecunia when you had her. Which since I see,   120
I will take home the lady to my charge,
And these her servants, and leave you my cloak

---

soccage] tenure of lands by performing certain agricultural services (Kifer).
frank almoigne] free alms: tenure granted by gift of charity. In practice, tenure of lands by a religious organisation or community in return for divine service or related duties performed.
108. *Grand sergeanty*] O.E.D. cites Sir Henry Finch's *Law* (1636 ed., p. 154): 'every grand Serjeanty is a tenure in chiefe, being of none but of the King, to do unto him a more especiall service . . . as to beare his Banner or Lance, to lead his horse, to carry his sword before him at this coronation'.
burgage] tenure 'proper to *Boroughs*, whereby the Inhabitants . . . hold their Lands or Tenements of the King, or other Lord of the *Borough*, at a certain yearly Rent' (Cowell's *Law Dictionary* (1727). cited by *H.&S.*).
109. Κατ ἐξοχὴυ] par excellence.
110. *Littleton's* Tenures] fifteenth century treatise on land law, which had gone through over sixty editions by 1627.
114–15. *mortmain . . . licence*] Property in mortmain is held inalienably by a corporation ('dead hand' being metaphorical for impersonal ownership) and can only be sold or transferred by special permission of the Crown (*O.E.D.*).
118. *painful*] painstaking.
officer] the word used by the son of his father at I.vi.20.

To travel in to Beggars' Bush. A seat
Is built already, furnished too, worth twenty
Of your imagined structures, Canters' College.   125
Fitton. 'Tis his father!
Madrigal.   He's alive methinks.
Almanac. I knew he was no rogue.
P. Canter.   Thou prodigal,
Was I so careful for thee, to procure
And plot wi' my learn'd counsel, Master Picklock,
This noble match for thee? And dost thou prostitute,   130
Scatter thy mistress' favours, throw away
Her bounties as they were red-burning coals
Too hot for thee to handle, on such rascals
Who are the scum and excrements of men?
If thou hadst sought out good and virtuous persons   135
Of these professions, I had loved thee and them.
For these shall never have that plea 'gainst me,
Or colour of advantage, that I hate
Their callings, but their manners and their vices.
A worthy courtier is the ornament   140
Of a king's palace, his great master's honour.
[*Points to Fitton.*] This is a moth, a rascal, a court rat
That gnaws the commonwealth with broking suits
And eating grievances! So, a true soldier,
He is his country's strength, his sovereign's safety, 145

---

129. wi' my learn'd] *F;* with my learn'd *Gifford.*   136. I had] I'had *F.*

---

123. *Beggars' Bush*] 'This is the way to Beggars' Bush' was proverbial for
falling into poverty – 'being a tree notoriously known, on the ... London
road' which acted as a rendezvous for beggars (Fuller's *Worthies,* cited in
Oxford Dict. of Proverbs, ed. F. P. Wilson, 3rd ed., W165).
    128. *careful*] solicitous.
    129. *wi' my learn'd*] See collation. The Gifford emendation ('with') is part of
his effort to regularise Jonson's metre, and possesses no intrinsic merit. However, retention of the light syllable *wi'* will inevitably encourage an actor to
discard Jonson's *learn'd* and give the word its modern disyllabic pronunciation.
    138. *Or ... advantage*] or the opportunity of claiming.
    142. *court rat*] *H.&S.* compare *Sej.,* I.427, 'Palace-rattes', where Jonson's
marginalia indicate ancient Roman inspiration for the phrase. Cf. *Poet.,*
IV.vii.44–53.
    143. *broking*] unscrupulous, wheedling.
    144–8. *So ... hazards*] Cf. A. Gardyne, *Characters and Essayes* (1625), 'A
Worthie Souldier': 'Hee is the Peace, Preserver, and a Shield, / Unto his king

And to secure his peace, he makes himself
The heir of danger, nay, the subject of it,
And runs those virtuous hazards that this scarecrow
Cannot endure to hear of.
Shunfield.   You are pleasant, sir.
P. Canter. With you I dare be! Here is Piedmantle: 150
'Cause he's an ass, do not I love a herald
Who is the pure preserver of descents,
The keeper fair of all nobility,
Without which all would run into confusion?
Were he a learned herald, I would tell him   155
He can give arms and marks; he cannot honour,
No more than money can make noble. It may
Give place and rank, but it can give no virtue.
And he would thank me for this truth. [*Points to Almanac.*]
    This dog-leech,
You style him Doctor, 'cause he can compile   160
An almanac, perhaps erect a scheme
For my great madam's monkey when't has ta'en
A glister, and berayed the ephemerides.
Do I despise a learn'd physician,
In calling him a quacksalver? – Or blast   165
The ever-living garland, always green,

---

166. garland] *1716; ghirlond* F.

---

and Countrey in the Field . . . / And to no Fortune stoups, nor perill spares'
(p. 30). H.&S. compare *Ep.* 108, 'To True Soldiers'.
    151–4.] Jonson probably had in mind here his old teacher William Camden,
who had been Clarenceux king-of-arms until his death in 1623, and whom he
had praised in *Ep.* 14 for his 'sight in searching the most antique springs' (line
8).
    156–8.] Cf. *E.M.O.*, III.ii.28–30, on Sogliardo's pretensions to gentility:
'has he purchast armes, then? / I, and rare ones too: of as many colours, as e're
you saw any fooles coat in your life.' And Cicero's separation of virtue from
'dustie moniments; / . . . broken images of ancestors, / Wanting an eare, or
nose; . . . forged tables / Of long descents; to boast false honors from' (*Cat.*,
III.14–17).
    161. *scheme*] horoscope.
    163. *glister*] enema.
    berayed] befouled. *O.E.D.* notes that *F*'s *bewrai'd* is a common misspelling,
born of confusion with 'bewray' meaning to disclose.
    165–8. *Or . . . flowers*] Cf. William Hawkins's play *Apollo Shroving* (1626),
p. 17: 'what wast hath beene made of the trees in Parnassus grove with crop-
ping off laurell garlands to adorn the light head of every ballad belching Poet.'

Of a good poet, [*Points to Madrigal.*] when I say his
    wreath
Is pieced and patched of dirty, withered flowers?
Away; I am impatient of these ulcers
(That I not call you worse). There is no sore   170
Or plague but you to infect the times. I abhor
Your very scent. Come, lady; since my prodigal
Knew not to entertain you to your worth,
I'll see if I have learned how to receive you
With more respect to you and your fair train here.   175
Farewell, my beggar in velvet, for today.
    He points him to his patched cloak thrown off.
Tomorrow you may put on that grave robe
And enter your great work of Canters' College,
Your work, and worthy of a chronicle.
        [*He leads Pecunia off. The others follow.*]

The fourth Intermean after the fourth Act.

Tattle. Why, this was the worst of all, the catastrophe!
Censure. The matter began to be good but now, and he has
    spoiled it all with his beggar there.
Mirth. A beggarly Jack it is, I warrant him, and akin to the
    poet.   5
Tattle. Like enough, for he had the chiefest part in his play, if
    you mark it.
Expectation. Absurdity on him, for a huge overgrown play-

---

169. *ulcers*] rarely used of people; cf. Marston, *Antonio's Revenge*, I.iv.21
(Revels): 'Yon putrid ulcer of my royal blood.'
176. *beggar in velvet*] See note to I.Int.11.

IV.Int.1. *catastrophe*] Tattle appears to misinterpret the play's *catastasis* (or
extra complication in the plot) for its *catastrophe* or resolution. Cf. Damplay in
the Chorus following Act IV of *M.L.*: 'Why, here his *Play* might have ended,
if hee would ha' let it, and have spar'd us the vexation of a *fift Act* yet to come'.
To which he receives the reply: 'Stay and see his last *Act*, his *Catastrophe*, how
hee will perplexe that, or spring some fresh cheat, to entertain the *Spectators*
... till some unexpected, and new encounter breake out to rectifie all, and
make good the *Conclusion*' (lines 21–31). Jonson renews the action of *Staple* in
a similar way; but see Introduction, p. 48.

maker! Why should he make him live again, when they
and we all thought him dead? If he had left him to his rags,   10
there had been an end of him.

Tattle. Ay, but set a beggar on horseback, he'll never lin till he
be a-gallop.

Censure. The young heir grew a fine gentleman in this last Act.

Expectation. So he did, gossip, and kept the best company.   15

Censure. And feasted 'em and his mistress.

Tattle. And showed her to 'em all, was not jealous –

Mirth. But very communicative and liberal, and began to be
magnificent if the churl his father would have let him
alone.   20

Censure. It was spitefully done o'the poet, to make the chuff
take him off in his height, when he was going to do all his
brave deeds.

Expectation. To found an academy!

Tattle. Erect a college!   25

Expectation. Plant his professors, and water his lectures –

Mirth. With wine, gossips, as he meant to do; and then to
defraud his purposes!

Expectation. Kill the hopes of so many towardly young spirits!

Tattle. As the doctor's –   30

Censure. And the courtier's! I protest, I was in love with
Master Fitton. He did wear all he had, from the hat-band
to the shoe-tie, so politically, and would stoop, and leer –

---

17. jealous –] *Kifer; iealous! F.*

12–13. *set ... a-gallop*] proverbial (Tilley B238). An alternative form of the
adage, quoted by Tilley from *3H6*, I.iv.127: 'beggars mounted run their horse
to death', more forcibly conveys Tattle's sense that the play has been am-
bushed. *lin* = cease.

17–18. *showed ... liberal*] the natural generosity of the prodigal, affirmed
by Aristotle in the *Ethics*, ch. 4. Jonson seems both to mock the gossips' inference and to endorse P. Junior's capacity for reformation.

21. *chuff*] churlish fellow.

26. *Plant ... lec⸱ ⸱s*] Cf. Bacon, *The Advancement of Learning*, II.9:
'founders of colleg s do plant, and founders of lectures do water' (ed. A.
Johnston, p. 63).

29. *towardly*] promising.

32–3. *hat-band ... shoe-tie*] both articles of considerable display at this time
(see Linthicum, pp. 221, 243).

33. *politically*] in stylish fashion. The adverbial form is apparently rare at
this date.

Mirth. And lie so, in wait for a piece of wit, like a mousetrap!

Expectation. Indeed, gossip, so would the little doctor: all his   35
behaviour was mere glister! O'my conscience, he would
make any party's physic i'the world work with his
discourse.

Mirth. I wonder they would suffer it, a foolish old fornicating
father to ravish away his son's mistress.   40

Censure. And all her women at once, as he did!

Tattle. I would ha' flyen in his gypsy's face, i'faith.

Mirth. It was a plain piece of political incest, and worthy to be
brought afore the high commission of wit. Suppose we
were to censure him. You are the youngest voice, gossip   45
Tattle, begin.

Tattle. Marry, I would ha' the old cony-catcher cozened of all

---

42. flyen] *F;* flown *F3;* flien *Kifer.*

leer] look invitingly, without the modern suggestion of prurience; Falstaff
plans to 'leer upon' the newly-crowned Hal (*2H4*, V.v.6), and *O.E.D.* cites
Dryden, *The Spanish Friar*, I.177–8: 'the arts of court, / To guild a face with
smiles, and leer a man to ruin.' But these examples and Jonson's use show the
word starting to gather unpleasant associations.

34. *lie so*] For the pun, cf. I.v.20, and on its aptness to Fitton, I.v.122.

36. *glister*] (1) lustre, (2 clyster or enema. The further implication, of which
Expectation is comically unaware, is that the doctor's professional manner is
entirely specious.

36–8. *he ... discourse*] the usual facility of the quacksalver. In *Volp.*,
II.ii.13 (Revels), Peregrine describes the Venetian mountebanks as 'The only
languaged men of all the world!'

42. *gypsy's*] roguish. The word was used loosely of outlaws and vagrants in
general, although Dekker insisted on the difference between 'one of these
counterfeit Egiptians and a true English Beggar' (*Lanthorne & Candle-Light*,
Grosart III.259).

43. *political*] scheming.

44. *high ... wit*] a common term for the audience, especially in epilogues
where the dramatist refers his play for judgement. Cf. the preface by Heminge
and Condell to the 1623 Folio of Shakespeare's *Works*: 'though you be a
Magistrate of wit, and sit on the Stage at *Black-Friers*, or the *Cock-pit*, to
arraigne Playes dailie, know, these Playes have had their triall alreadie, and
stood out all Appeales' (A3). Jonson manages some of this genial wit in the
present instance, but there is also a touch of his 'just indignation at the ...
malicious spectators' of *N.I.* three years later: 'Let their fastidious, vain /
Commission of the brain / Run on and rage, sweat, censure, and condemn'
(Revels ed., p. 205).

47. *cony-catcher*] trickster.

he has, i'the young heir's defence, by his learn'd counsel,
Master Picklock.

Censure. I would rather the courtier had found out some trick   50
to beg him from his estate.

Expectation. Or the captain had courage enough to beat him.

Censure. Or the fine madrigal-man in rhyme to have run him
out o'the country like an Irish rat.

Tattle. No, I would have Master Piedmantle, her grace's   55
herald, to pluck down his hatchments, reverse his coat
armour, and nullify him for no gentleman.

Expectation. Nay, then let Master Doctor dissect him, have
him opened, and his tripes translated to Lickfinger to
make a probation dish of.   60

Censure & Tattle. Agreed! Agreed!

Mirth. Faith, I would have him flat disinherited by a decree of
court, bound to make restitution of the Lady Pecunia and
the use of her body to his son.

---

51. *beg ... estate*] i.e. as a reward for informing on him. Gifford cites *Jacke
Drums Entertainment*, sig. CI: 'I have followed Ordinaries this twelve-month,
onely to find a Foole that had landes, or a fellow that would talke treason, that
I might beg him' (see *H.&S.* IX 572). The practice was common among
courtiers on the make.

53–4.] alluding to the Irish belief that rats could be killed by incantation;
H.&S. compare *Poet.*, 'To the Reader', 161–4: 'write *Iambicks*, / ... Rime
'hem to death, as they doe Irish rats / In drumming tunes.' 'Rat-rime' was also
a common term for doggerel.

56–7.] Nason, *Heralds & Heraldry*, pp. 122–3, notes an 'instance of de-
gradation' of this kind that took place in 1621. 'The sentence was read by a
pursuivant; then the culprit's spurs were hacked from his heels, his sword was
broken over his head, and [he was] pronounced ... no longer a knight but a
knave.'

56. *hatchments*] escutcheons or ensigns armorial; since they often took the
form of a tablet showing the arms of a deceased person and were displayed at
his funeral or former home, Tattle may presume a breach of privilege by the
'resurrected' Canter. (See Nason, p. 123.)

56–7. *coat armour*] originally, arms emblazoned upon a surcoat to be worn
over armour; later, simply the display of arms on a shield. At one time they
were drawn or painted in reverse to signify disgrace (Nason, p. 122).

57. *nullify ... gentleman*] Nason compares Bolingbroke's complaint in *R2*,
III.i.24–7, that the King has 'From my own windows torn my household coat,
/ Rac'd out my imprese, leaving me no sign ... To show the world I am a
gentleman'.

60. *probation dish*] essay in cookery, masterpiece (cf. I.v.102).

62. *disinherited*] i.e. deprived of his estate. As *H.&S.* point out, the word is
better suited to the son than to the father.

Expectation. And her train, to the gentlemen.   65
Censure. And both the poet and himself to ask them all for-
   giveness!
Tattle. And us too.
Censure. In two large sheets of paper –
Expectation. Or to stand in a skin of parchment; which the   70
   court please.
Censure. And those filled with news –
Mirth. And dedicated to the sustaining of the Staple –
Expectation. Which their poet hath let fall most abruptly.
Mirth. Bankruptly, indeed!   75
Censure. You say wittily, gossip; and therefore let a protest go
   out against him –
Mirth. A mournival of protests, or a gleek at least!
Expectation. In all our names –
Censure. For a decayed wit –   80
Expectation. Broken –
Tattle. Nonsolvent –
Censure. And forever forfeit –
Mirth. To scorn. Of Mirth –
Censure. Censure –   85
Expectation. Expectation –
Tattle. Subsigned, Tattle. Stay, they come again.

74. abruptly.] *F3; abruptly? F.*

___

70. *stand*] i.e. in the pillory, wearing a parchment costume as penance.
skin] piece.
78. *mournival*] four aces or 'coat' cards; thus, four of anything.
gleek] (1) three of the above, similarly generalised; (2) gibe, taunt. Perhaps
Mirth is encouraging Tattle, who is temporarily silent, to pull her weight in
the indictment.

Act V

[*Enter*] PENNYBOY JU[NIOR]. *He comes out in the patched cloak his father left him.*

[*P. Junior. Indicating his clothes.*] Nay, they are fit as they had
    been made for me,
  And I am now a thing worth looking at,
  The same I said I would be in the morning.
  No rogue at a *comitia* of the canters
  Did ever there become his parent's robes   5
  Better than I do these. Great fool and beggar!
  Why do not all that are of those societies
  Come forth and gratulate me one of theirs?
  Methinks I should be on every side saluted,
  Dauphin of Beggars! Prince of Prodigals!   10
  That have so fall'n under the ears and eyes
  And tongues of all, the fable o'the time,
  Matter of scorn and mark of reprehension!
  I now begin to see my vanity

V.i.0.1–2] PENY-BOY. IV. {*to him* THO. BARBER. / {*after*, PICKLOCKE. F.
9. be on] be, on F; be'on *conj. this ed.*   12. o'the] F; of the F3.

V.i.0.1–2. He . . . him] The prodigal as beggar was a common theme in the iconography and drama of the period (see Young, *Prodigal Son Plays*, pp. 48, 310–13). Cf. Dekker's *If This Be Not A Good Play*, IV.ii, where Scumbroth enters 'like a begger' (Bowers III.179), and *The London Prodigal*, V.i.22–3, where Flowerdale tries to cadge 'so much as will pay for my supper' (*Shakespeare Apocrypha*, ed. Tucker Brooke, p. 213).

4. comitia . . . canters] assembly of beggars. H.&S. point out that *comitia* was the name of the assembly in ancient Rome which elected magistrates. The exalted term permits Jonson to recall the inflation of Canters' College and align it with the congregation of ragged vagrants.

8. *gratulate*] welcome.

10. *Dauphin*] Prince. Strictly, the title of the heir to the French throne; probably pronounced 'dorfin' by English speakers at this date.

14–15.] recalling his opening speech (I.i.4–9): having solicited the audience's admiring gaze, he now finds in its scrutiny only a judgement on his foolishness. Alternatively, the *glass* is his beggar's cloak, which is set off by the *foil* of the extravagant attire he still wears beneath.

Shine in this glass, reflected by the foil.   15
Where is my fashioner, my featherman,
My linener, perfumer, barber, all
That tail of riot followed me this morning?
Not one! – but a dark solitude about me,
Worthy my cloak and patches, as I had   20
The epidemical disease upon me;
And I'll sit down with it.   [*He sits on the floor.*]

[*Enter* THOMAS BARBER.]

Thomas.   My master! Maker!
How do you? Why do you sit thus o'the ground, sir?
Hear you the news?
P. Junior.   No, nor I care to hear none.
Would I could here sit still and slip away   25
The other one and twenty, to have this
Forgotten and the day razed out, expunged
In every ephemerides or almanac.
Or if it must be in, that Time and Nature
Have decreed – still, let it be a day   30
Of tickling prodigals about the gills,
Deluding gaping heirs, loosing their loves
And their discretions, falling from the favours
Of their best friends and parents, their own hopes,

---

27. razed] *F3;* rac'd *F;* ras'd *Kifer.*   32. loosing] *F;* losing *F3.*

21. *epidemical*] The severe plague of 1625 was a very recent memory at the play's first performance.

22. *sit down*] Pennyboy could in fact kneel; *O.E.D.* 21.b shows the phrase 'sit down upon her knees' in use in 1626, and Young, *Prodigal Son Plays,* p. 48, points out that in many visual representations of the prodigal story he 'is shown kneeling or with his knees partly bent in the pose associated iconographically with contrition'. See Dürer's etching of 'Prodigal with Swine' (1498) and Rubens's 1618 painting of the same title.

27. *razed*] *F*'s 'rac'd' is a common spelling at this time, as in *R2*, III.i.25, quoted in the note to IV.Int.57 above. Kifer proposes 'rased', but it is doubtful whether this form is in use today (as distinct from 'erased'), although *O.E.D.* does not describe it as obsolete. In a modernised text it seems safest to follow *F3* and read *razed.*

29–35.] Pennyboy invokes the play's theme of festivity, but from his present perspective holiday is a matter of atonement rather than an occasion for mirth and release. See Introduction, p. 43.

32. *loosing*] *F*'s spelling alerts us to the sense (not retained by the more

And ent'ring the society of canters.   35
Thomas. A doleful day it is, and dismal times
   Are come upon us. I am clear undone.
P. Junior. How, Tom?
Thomas.   Why, broke, broke, wretchedly broke.
P. Junior.   Ha!
Thomas. Our Staple is all to pieces, quite dissolved.
P. Junior.   Ha!
Thomas. Shivered, as in an earthquake! Heard you not   40
   The crack and ruins? We are all blown up!
   Soon as they heard th'Infanta was got from them,
   Whom they had so devourèd i'their hopes
   To be their patroness and sojourn with 'em,
   Our emissaries, Register, Examiner   45
   Flew into vapour; our grave governor
   Into a subtler air, and is returned
   (As we do hear) grand-captain of the jeerers.
   I and my fellow melted into butter
   And spoiled our ink, and so the Office vanished.   50
   The last hum that it made was that your father
   And Picklock are fall'n out, the man o'law.
P. Junior. How? This awakes me from my lethargy.
                              He starts up at this.
Thomas. And a great suit is like to be between 'em.
   Picklock denies the feoffment and the trust   55

---

43. i'their] *F;* in their *Gifford.*

passive 'losing') of something freely but unwisely dispensed. Cf. *Temp.*,
II.i.119–21, on the marriage of Alonso's daughter: 'you may thank yourself
for this great loss, / That would ... rather loose her to an African'.
    40–6. *Shivered ... vapour*] Cf. the disaster in *Alch.*, IV.v.57–8: 'All the
works / Are flown *in fumo*: every glass is burst' (Revels). F. H. Mares compares
Scot, *The Discoverie of Witchcraft*: 'As for all their gold, it is resolved *In primam
materiam*, ... into a light smoke, or fumigation of vapours.' The cracking of
both worlds, laboratory and news office, is a dramatic metaphor as well as a
theatrical event.
    47. *is returned*] has reverted to being. But there is also a sense of a process
being completed: Cymbal is finally transformed into what he really is.
    49. *fellow ... butter*] The clerk's ambitions at III.iii.57 are buried with this
final sneer at Nathaniel Butter.
    51. *hum*] the 'buzz' of rumour.
    55. *feoffment*] endowment.

Your father says he made of the whole estate
Unto him, as respecting his mortality,
When he first laid this late device to try you.
P. Junior. Has Picklock then a trust?
Thomas.   I cannot tell.
[*Looks out.*] Here comes the worshipful –

[*P. Junior makes a sign to Tom, who conceals himself.
He then resumes his attitude of despair as*]
                PICKLOCK *enters.*

Picklock.   What, my velvet heir   60
Turned beggar in mind as robes?
P. Junior.   You see what case
Your and my father's plots have brought me to.
Picklock. Your father's you may say indeed, not mine.
He's a hard-hearted gentleman! I am sorry
To see his rigid resolution.   65
That any man should so put off affection
And human nature to destroy his own,
And triumph in a victory so cruel.
He's fall'n out with me for being yours
And calls me knave, and traitor to his trust,   70
Says he will have me thrown over the bar –
P. Junior. Ha' you deserved it?
Picklock.   O, good heaven knows
My conscience and the silly latitude of it!

---

60. S.D. *P. Junior ... himself*] *Gifford subst.   He ... as*] *This ed.*
70. traitor] *F3;* Traytors *F;* trait'rous *conj. this ed.*

57. *as respecting*] in the event of.
60. *velvet*] foppish.
61. *case*] (1) condition; (2) dress; with a pun on Picklock's legal machinations.
71. *thrown ... bar*] disbarred.
72–3. *O ... it!*] The compression of this creates ambiguity: Picklock begins with a simple exclamation of feigned surprise, as if to say 'my conscience is clear', but then takes *conscience* in the looser sense of 'mental capacity (for mischief)'.
73. *silly*] meagre.

A narrow-minded man, my thoughts do dwell
All in a lane or line indeed, no turning   75
Nor scarce obliquity in them. I still look
Right forward to th'intent and scope of that
Which he would go from now.
P. Junior.   Had you a trust, then?
Picklock. Sir, I had somewhat will keep you still lord
Of all the estate, if I be honest as   80
I hope I shall. My tender scrupulous breast
Will not permit me see the heir defrauded
And, like an alien, thrust out of the blood.
The laws forbid that I should give consent
To such a civil slaughter of a son.   85
P. Junior. Where is the deed? Hast thou it with thee?
Picklock.   No,
It is a thing of greater consequence
Than to be borne about in a black box
Like a Low Country *vorloffe* or Welsh brief.
It is at Lickfinger's, under lock and key.   90
P. Junior. O, fetch it hither.
Picklock.   I have bid him bring it
That you might see it.
P. Junior. [*Casually.*]   Knows he what he brings?
Picklock. No more than a gardener's ass what roots he carries.
P. Junior. I was a-sending my father, like an ass,
A penitent epistle, but I am glad   95
I did not now.

92. what he brings] *F3;* what brings *F.*

---

74. *narrow-minded*] not devious. Kifer points out that *O.E.D.* mistakenly
uses this as an example of the sense 'illiberal, bigoted'.
  85. *civil*] legal as opposed to natural (de Winter).
  89. vorloffe] leave of absence, furlough (Dutch *forlov*) (*H.&S.*).
  Welsh brief] On the Welsh reputation for litigiousness, *H.&S.* cite Harrison,
The Description of England, I.206: 'But in this toie our Welshmen doo exceed
of all that ever I heard, for you shall here and there have some one od poore
David of them given so much to contention and strife, that without all respect
of charges he will up to London, though he go bare legged by the waie' (ed.
Furnivall).
  92. *Knows . . . brings?*] The question is deliberately casual, as a scheme for
outwitting Picklock begins to form in P. Junior's mind.
  94. *like an ass*] Pennyboy's use of Picklock's word in the previous line shows
his usual clumsiness with language, but here it is excused by the fact that he is
rapidly improvising a deception.

Picklock.   Hang him, an austere grape
That has no juice but what is verjuice in him.
P. Junior. I'll show you my letter!   [*Exit.*]
Picklock.   Show me a defiance!
If I can now commit father and son
And make my profits out of both; commence   100
A suit with the old man for his whole state
And go to law with the son's credit, undo
Both, both with their own money, it were a piece
Worthy my nightcap and the gown I wear,
A picklock's name in law. [*Calls.*] Where are you, sir?   105
What do you do so long?   [*P. Junior returns.*]
P. Junior.   I cannot find
Where I have laid it, but I have laid it safe.
Picklock. No matter, sir; trust you unto my trust.
'Tis that that shall secure you, an absolute deed.
And I confess, it was in trust for you,   110
Lest anything might have happened mortal to him.
But there must be a gratitude thought on,
And aid, sir, for the charges of the suit,

98–101.] F *margin:* Peny-boy *runnes out to fetch his letter.*   107. but I havc]
F; but I've *Whalley.*   111. happened] hapned F.

---

97. *verjuice*] juice of unripe grapes or crab apples used like a mild vinegar in cooking (Kifer).
98. P. Junior ... *letter!*] See collation. 'This is merely a pretence. He runs out to dispatch a ticket-porter to meet Lickfinger, and take the deed of trust from him' (Gifford).
defiance] challenge.
101. *state*] estate; right or title to property.
103. *piece*] masterpiece, in its more usual sense of 'supreme accomplishment'. Cf. *Volp.*, V.ii.13–14 (Revels), where Mosca measures the achievement of their villainy: 'This is our masterpiece; / We cannot think to go beyond this.' In both cases, though, the overreacher spoils the perfections of intrigue.
104. *nightcap*] i.e. the white skull-cap of lawn or silk worn by senior lawyers. In *Appius & Virginia*, IV.i.121, an advocate is described as 'the fellow i'th'nightcap' (Lucas III.202), and Mosca refers to Voltore's 'biggen' (*Volp.*, I.ix.5, Revels).
105. *picklock's ... law*] Kifer compares Dekker, *The Belman of London*, 'the *Trade* of *Lock-picking* may well be called the *Black-Art*, for none study it, but those that for other mens goods have sold their verie soules to the Divell' (Grosart III.138).
112. *gratitude*] gratuity. Jonson uses the modern form at V.ii.77, where it fits the metre.

Which will be great, 'gainst such a mighty man
As is our father, and a man possessed   115
Of so much land, Pecunia and her friends.
I am not able to wage law with him,
Yet must maintain the thing as mine own right –
Still for your good – and therefore must be bold
To use your credit for monies.
P. Junior.   What thou wilt,   120
So we be safe, and the trust bear it.
Picklock.   Fear not;
'Tis he must pay arrearages in the end.
We'll milk him and Pecunia, draw their cream down
Before he get the deed into his hands.
My name is Picklock, but he'll find me a padlock.   125

ACT V   SCENE ii
[*Enter*] PENNYBOY CAN[TER].

[*P. Canter.*] How now? Conferring wi' your learned counsel
Upo' the cheat? Are you o'the plot to cozen me?
P. Junior. What plot?
P. Canter.   Your counsel knows there, Master Picklock:
Will you restore the trust yet?
Picklock.   Sir, take patience
And memory unto you, and bethink you,   5
What trust? Where does't appear? I have your deed.
Doth your deed specify any trust? Is't not
A perfect act, and absolute in law,
Sealed and delivered before witnesses,
The day and date emergent?
P. Canter.   But what conference,   10
What oaths and vows preceded?
Picklock.   I will tell you, sir,

---

115. our] *F*; your *Whalley.*   V.ii.0.1.] *Gifford*; PENY-BOY. CAN. PENY-
BOY. IV. / PICKLOCK. THO. BARBAR. *F.*   1. wi'] *F*; with *Gifford.*

115. *our*] See collation. This may be an error like 'our bodies' at IV.iii.40,
but *our* is consistent with Picklock adopting an intimate, conspiratorial tone,
identifying himself with Pennyboy's interests.
117. *wage law*] go to law. (Technically an incorrect usage, according to
H.&S.).

Since I am urged, of those. As I remember,
You told me you had got a grown estate
By griping means, sinisterly,
(*P. Canter.*   How!)
                              and were
Ev'n weary of it. If the parties lived   15
From whom you had wrested it,
(*P. Canter.*   Ha!)
                            you could be glad
To part with all for satisfaction.
But since they'd yielded to humanity,
And that just heaven had sent you for a punishment –
You did acknowledge it – this riotous heir,   20
That would bring all to beggary in the end
And daily sowed consumption where he went –
P. Canter. You'd cozen both, then? Your confederate too?
Picklock. After a long, mature deliberation
You could not think where better how to place it –   25
P. Canter. Than on you, rascal?
Picklock.   What you please i'your passion.
But with your reason, you will come about
And think a faithful and a frugal friend
To be preferred.
P. Canter.   Before a son?
Picklock.   A prodigal,
A tub without a bottom, as you termed him.   30
For which I might return you a vow or two
And seal it with an oath of thankfulness;
I not repent it, neither have I cause. Yet –
P. Canter. Forehead of steel and mouth of brass! Hath

---

3. S.H. *P. Canter.*] *1716*; P.SE. *F.*   there, Master Picklock:] there, Mr
Picklock, *F.*   6. does't] *1716*; dost *F*; dos't *F3*.   18. they'd] they'had
F.   23. You'd] You'old *F.*

V.ii.10. *emergent*] unspecified. Picklock denies the provision of V.i.57, 'as
respecting his mortality'.
    13. *grown*] huge.
    14. *sinisterly*] dishonestly; with the accent on the second syllable.
    30. *tub . . . bottom*] adapting the proverb 'every tub must stand on its own
bottom' (Tilley T596) to a sharp comment on the nature of prodigality.
    34. *Forehead of steel*] i.e. what impudent assurance; cf. *Volp.*, Epistle, 12:
'nor can it with any forehead be opposed' (Revels). Jonson perhaps alludes to

impudence
Polished so gross a lie, and dar'st thou vent it?   35
Engine, composed of all mixed metals! Hence:
I will not change a syllab with thee more
Till I may meet thee at a bar in court
Before thy judges.

[*Enter* Porter. *P. Junior talks to him aside.*]

Picklock.   Thither it must come
Before I part with it to you, or you, sir.   40
P. Canter. I will not hear thee.   (*His son entreats him.*)
P. Junior.   Sir, your ear to me though.
Not that I see through his perplexèd plots
And hidden ends, nor that my parts depend
Upon the unwinding this so knotted skein
Do I beseech your patience. Unto me   45
He hath confessed the trust.
Picklock.   How! I confess it?

---

37. syllab] *F;* syllable *Whalley.*   39. S.D.] *This ed.*

---

the proverbial sentiment of 'Ex fronte perspicere' (Tilley F590), which he
renders in *Cat.*, IV.434–5, as: 'let it be writ in each mans fore-head / What
thoughts he beares the publike.'
    mouth of brass] The learned inspiration for this phrase is the *Iliad*, V.786–7,
recalled more specifically at V.vi.49; in Chapman's rendition, 'Saturnia put on
Stentor's shape, that had a brazen voice / And spake as lowd as fiftie men'
(*Chapman's Homer*, ed. Nicoll, I.132). It serves to remind us of Picklock's
emissary role in the 'sounding brass' of the news trade (see V.vi.7, and note to
III.ii.115).
    36. *mixed*] impure.
    39. Enter . . . aside] The cue for line 41 (*your ear to me*) is presumably P.
Junior's reception of the deed of trust from the porter sometime during the
exchange between his father and Picklock. There is nothing in *F* to indicate
when this occurs, but P. Junior must have the deed by the end of the scene, and
his challenge to Picklock is dramatically stronger if the audience suspects that
he has not one but two cards up his sleeve (the hidden Tom and the deed). An
entry at line 39, or just before, avoids any distraction from the Picklock–Canter
argument and puts the lawyer's next confident declaration in an ironic light.
    42. *Not that*] not simply because.
    perplexèd] intricate, tangled.
    43. *parts*] This appears to mean 'share in the estate', although the plural
form rather suggests 'qualities, attributes'. But P. Junior is hardly in a position
to be speaking of his intrinsic worth.

P. Junior. Ay, thou, false man.
P. Canter.   Stand up to him and confront him.
Picklock. Where? When? To whom?
P. Junior.   To me, even now, and here.
  Canst thou deny it?
Picklock.   Can I eat or drink,
  Sleep, wake, or dream, arise, sit, go, or stand,   50
  Do anything that's natural?
P. Junior.   Yes: lie
  It seems thou canst, and perjure; that is natural!
Picklock. O me! What times are these, of frontless carriage!
  An egg o'the same nest! The father's bird,
  It runs in a blood, I see.
P. Junior.   I'll stop your mouth.   55
Picklock. With what?
P. Junior.   With truth.
Picklock.   With noise! I must have witness.
  Where is your witness? You can produce witness?
P. Junior. As if my testimony were not twenty
  Balanced with thine.
Picklock.   So say all prodigals
  Sick of self-love, but that's not law, young Scattergood.   60
  I live by law.
P. Junior.   Why, if thou hast a conscience,
  That is a thousand witnesses.
Picklock.   No court
  Grants out a writ of summons for the conscience,
  That I know, nor subpoena, nor attachment.
  I must have witness, and of your producing,   65
  Ere this can come to hearing, and it must

---

53. *frontless carriage*] shameless conduct. Cf. *Volp.*, IV.v.31–2 (Revels):
'The most prodigious and most frontless piece / Of solid impudence and
treachery'.
    54. *egg . . . nest*] proverbial (Tilley E81).
    60. *Scattergood*] a traditional name for the spendthrift; it is given to charac-
ters in Cooke's *Greene's Tu Quoque* (1611) and the anonymous *Lady Alimony*
(*c.* 1634).
    61–2. *if . . . witnesses*] proverbial: 'Conscience is a thousand witnesses'
(Tilley C601). *H.&S.* cite Quintilian, V.xi.41, 'Conscientia mille testes', but
Jonson would not have needed his classical learning for the phrase.
    64. *attachment*] arrest.

Be heard on oath and witness.

P. Junior. (*He produceth Tom.*)   Come forth, Tom.
Speak what thou heardst: the truth, and the whole truth,
And nothing but the truth. What said this varlet?

Picklock. A rat behind the hangings!

Thomas.   Sir, he said   70
It was a trust, an act, the which your father
Had will to alter, but his tender breast
Would not permit to see the heir defrauded
And, like an alien, thrust out of the blood.
The laws forbid that he should give consent   75
To such a civil slaughter of a son –

P. Junior. And talked of a gratuity to be given,
And aid unto the charges of the suit,
Which he was to maintain in his own name
But for my use, he said.

P. Canter.   It is enough.   80

Thomas. And he would milk Pecunia and draw down
Her cream before you got the trust again.

P. Canter. Your ears are in my pocket, knave; go shake 'em
The little while you have them.

Picklock.   You do trust
To your great purse.

P. Canter.   I ha' you in a purse-net,   85

---

70. *rat ... hangings*] In the Induction to *B.F.*, 7–8, the Stage-Keeper is
anxious 'lest the poet hear me ... behind the arras' (Revels). The hangings at
the back of the stage were frequently used for purposes of concealment, and
there is no need to refer the phrase back to *Hamlet*, III.iv.23. Yet it is probable
that the killing of Polonius had become a theatrical cliché, and as Harold
Jenkins points out, the 1608 *Hystorie of Hamblet* was influenced by the play
to the extent of having the counsellor 'behind the hangings' and stabbed by
Hamlet crying 'A rat, a rat!' (Arden ed., pp. 89–90).

81–2.] Tom's recital becomes superfluous; Jonson does not forget the barber's characteristic loquacity in working out the rapid intrigue of the play's
denouement.

83. *Your ... pocket*] Ear-cropping often accompanied being placed in the
pillory, as in the case of William Prynne in 1634.

85. *I ... purse-net*] proverbial: 'There I caught a Knave in a purse-net'
(Tilley K138). A purse-net was a bag-shaped net with a draw-string, used to
catch rabbits.

Good Master Picklock, wi' your worming brain
And wriggling engine-head of maintenance,
Which I shall see you hole with very shortly.
A fine round head, when those two lugs are off,
To trundle through a pillory. [*To Thomas.*] You are sure   90
You heard him speak this?
P. Junior.   Ay, and more.
Thomas.   Much more!
Picklock. I'll prove yours maintenance and combination,
And sue you all.
P. Canter.   Do, do, my gownèd vulture,
Crop in reversion. I shall see you quoited
Over the bar as bargemen do their billets.   95
Picklock. This 'tis, when men repent of their good deeds
And would ha' 'em in again. They are almost mad,
But I forgive their *lucida intervalla.*

---

86. wi'] *F;* with *Gifford.*   97. ha' 'em] ha'hem *F;* have 'em *Gifford.*

---

86. *worming brain*] Cf. John Taylor on 'A Corrupted Lawyer': 'Such Law-wormes are the Divels dearest brood, / Who make the common harme their private good' (*Workes* 1630, sig. Bbb).
   87. *engine-head*] snare. Canter's image is of the trapper trapped.
   maintenance] wrongfully aiding and abetting litigation.
   88. *hole*] Cf. the stocking of Wasp in *B.F.*, IV.vi.48–9 (Revels): 'Come put in his leg in the middle roundel, and let him hole there' (*H.&S.*).
   92. *combination*] conspiracy.
   93. *gownèd vulture*] a traditional emblem of the lawyer; Jonson realises it more fully in Voltore, the advocate in *Volp.* See R. B. Parker's note 3 on p. 86 of his Revels ed. of that play, and *Und.*, 33, line 9. Parker points out that legacy-hunters also were commonly called vultures, and this has its appropriateness to Picklock's attempt to deprive P. Junior of his inheritance.
   94. *Crop in reversion*] i.e. crop our ears in turn – if you can.
   quoited] thrown. Canter finds an energetic metaphor for disbarring.
   95. *bargemen . . . billets*] This probably refers to watermen throwing firewood from their barges on to the Thames quays. A *billet* could be a log of wood or a fighting staff; the latter sense is sometimes used in connection with bargemen (e.g. Beaumont & Fletcher, *The Captain*, II.i.214, 'Fighting at single billet with a Barge-man', *B.&F.* I.576), but it does not seem applicable here.
   98. lucida intervalla] i.e. the brief period of 'sanity' in which Canter made his original deal with Picklock. The phrase had its legal uses, and shows Picklock formulating a means of proving his version of events by demonstrating that his opponents are no longer in their right mind. His unctuousness at this point anticipates the methods of Molière's Tartuffe.

[*Enter* LICKFINGER *to them.*]

O Lickfinger! Come hither. [*Aside to him.*] Where's my
  writing?   [*P. Canter and P. Junior talk apart.*]

ACT V SCENE iii

[*Lickfinger.*] I sent it you, together with your keys.
Picklock. How?
Lickfinger.   By the porter that came for it from you,
  And by the token, you had giv'n me the keys,
  And bade me bring it.
Picklock.   And why did you not?
Lickfinger. Why did you send a countermand?
Picklock.   Who, I?   5
Lickfinger. You, or some other you, you put in trust.
Picklock. In trust?
Lickfinger.   Your trust's another self, you know,
  And without trust, and your trust, how should he
  Take notice of your keys, or of my charge?
Picklock. Know you the man?
Lickfinger.   I know he was a porter,   10
  And a sealed porter, for he bore the badge
  On breast, I am sure.
Picklock.   I am lost. A plot! I scent it.
Lickfinger. Why, and I sent it by the man you sent,
  Whom else I had not trusted.
Picklock.   Plague o'your trust.
  I am trussed up among you.

98.1.] *After V.iii in F.*   99. S.D.s] *This ed.;* Pick-lock *spies* Lick-finger, *and
askes him aside for the writing. F (margin).*

V.iii.1–16.] See collation at lines 16–24. Clearly it is during the opening
dialogue that P. Junior reveals to his father that he has outwitted Picklock, and
in this silent conversation he has two props, the keys and the deed itself, with
which to make the accomplishment clear to an audience.

  11. *sealed porter*] member of the Company of Porters. *H.&S.* cite Middleton, *The Family of Love,* IV.iii.46–8, where one of them says: 'Here's my
breastplate; and besides our own arms we have the arms of the city to help us
in our burdens' (Bullen III.81).

  12. *I am ... I am*] The metre requires a double elision here; in performance
it would be almost automatic.

  scent] *F*'s 'sent' is the usual spelling at this time, facilitating Jonson's pun in
the next line.

P. Junior.   Or you may be.   15
Picklock. In mine own halter I have made the noose.
                              PICKLOCK *goes out.*
P. Junior. What was it, Lickfinger?
Lickfinger.   A writing, sir,
    He sent for't by a token. I was bringing it,
    But that he sent a porter, and he seemed
    A man of decent carriage.
P. Canter.   'Twas good fortune.   20
    To cheat the cheater was no cheat but justice.
    Put off your rags and be yourself again;
    This act of piety and good affection
    Hath partly reconciled me to you.
P. Junior.   Sir –
P. Canter. No vows, no promises. Too much protestation   25
    Makes that suspected oft we would persuade.
Lickfinger. Hear you the news?
P. Junior.   The Office is down: how should we?
Lickfinger. But of your uncle?
P. Junior.   No.
Lickfinger.   He's run mad, sir.
P. Canter. How, Lickfinger! ([*He*] *startles at the news.*)
Lickfinger.   Stark staring mad, your brother;
    H'has almost killed his maid –
P. Canter.   Now heaven forbid.   30

16–24.] *F margin: Young* Peny-boy *discouers it, to his Father to be his plot of
sending for it by the* Porter, *and that hee is in possession of the* Deed.
29. S.D. [*He*] *startles*] *Elder* Peny-boy *startles* F (*margin*).

---

15. *trussed up*] ensnared by your efforts. P. Junior immediately makes the
obvious further inference that Picklock might be more radically 'strung up' –
on a gallows.
    20. *A ... carriage*] a familiar joke; *H.&S.* compare *The London Prodigal*,
V.i.6–10: 'I got it at an Ale-house among Porters, such as will beare out a man,
if he have no mony indeed – I mean out of their companyes, for they are men
of good carriage' (*Shakespeare Apocrypha*, ed. Tucker Brooke, p. 213).
    23–4. *This ... you*] Cf. *E.M.I.*, IV.x.63, where Edward Knowell is ac-
knowledged by his father who consents to 'halfe forgive my sonne, for the
device'. But this half-rueful, half-jocular concession has little of the complexity
of Canter's response.
    25–6. *Too ... persuade*] proverbial: 'Too much protesting makes the truth
suspected' (Tilley P614).

Lickfinger. But that she's cat-lived and squirrel-limbed,
   With throwing bed-staves at her. H'has set wide
   His outer doors, and now keeps open house
   For all the passers-by to see his justice.
   First, he has apprehended his two dogs   35
   As being o'the plot to cozen him;
   And there he sits like an old worm of the peace,
   Wrapped up in furs, at a square table, screwing,
   Examining and committing the poor curs
   To two old cases of close-stools, as prisons;   40
   The one of which he calls his Lollard's tower,
   Th'other his Block-house, 'cause his two dogs' names
   Are Block and Lollard.
P. Junior.   This would be brave matter
   Unto the jeerers!
P. Canter.   Ay, if so the subject
   Were not so wretched.
Lickfinger.   Sure, I met them all,   45
   I think, upon that quest.
P. Canter.   Faith, like enough.
   The vicious still are swift to show their natures.
   I'll thither too, but with another aim,
   If all succeed well, and my simples take.   [*Exeunt*.]

36. o'the] *F; of the Gifford*.   46. Faith] 'Faith *F*.

---

32. *bed-staves*] Dr Johnson explained 'bed-staff' as 'a wooden pin stuck
anciently on sides of the bed-stead to hold the cloaths from slipping on either
side'; this is uncorroborated, however. It seems to have been generally regarded as a ready weapon (*O.E.D.*).
   37–8. *like . . . furs*] Jonson makes the same conflation of usurer and judge
that Shakespeare has in *Lear*, IV.vi.165–7: 'The usurer hangs the cozener. /
Thorough tatter'd clothes small vices do appear; / Robes and furr'd gowns hide
all.' That usurers' gowns are trimmed with fur was a well-established tradition,
and some writers ingeniously derived this from the Latin *fur*, meaning thief or
extortioner (C. T. Wright, 'The Usurer in Elizabethan Literature', *Studies in
Philology*, 31 (1934), 189–92).
   38. *screwing*] interrogating.
   40. *old . . . close-stools*] i.e. boxes which formerly contained a chamber-pot.
   41. *Lollard's tower*] after the tower of this name at the west end of old St
Paul's, next to the Bishop of London's palace (*H.&S.*).
   42. *Block-house*] blockhouse, slang term for prison (Kifer).
   47. *still*] invariably.
   49. *simples*] medicines of a single ingredient, usually herbal; here, as often
in Renaissance literature, metaphorical for the curing of folly and excess.

ACT V   SCENE iv

[*Enter*] PENNYBOY SEN[IOR *and a*] Porter. ([PENNYBOY SENIOR] *is
seen sitting at his table with papers before him.*) [*Two boxes are standing
in front of the table.*]

[*P. Senior.*] Where are the prisoners?
Porter.   They are forthcoming, sir,
    Or coming forth at least.
P. Senior. [*Studying him.*]   The rogue is drunk
    Since I committed them to his charge. Come hither,
    Near me – yet nearer; breathe upon me. (*He smells him.*)
    Wine!
    Wine, o'my worship! Sack, canary sack!   5
    Could not your badge ha' been drunk with fulsome ale
    Or beer, the porter's element? But sack!
Porter. I am not drunk. We had, sir, but one pint,
    An honest carrier and myself.
P. Senior.   Who paid for't?
Porter. Sir, I did give it him.
P. Senior.   What, and spend sixpence?   10
    A frock spend sixpence? Sixpence!
Porter.   Once in a year, sir.
P. Senior. In seven years, varlet! Knowst thou what thou hast
    done,

V.iv.0.1. [PENNYBOY SENIOR] *He F* (*margin*).

V.iv.5. *canary sack*] sweet wine from the Canary Isles. Nares quotes an
opinion from 1634: '*Canarie-wine* . . . is of some termed a sacke [i.e. sherry]
. . . but yet very improperly, for it differeth not only from sacke in sweetnesse
and pleasantness of taste, but also in colour and consistence.'
    6. *fulsome*] coarse, foul-smelling.
    7. *beer* . . . *sack!*] Cf. *The London Chanticleers* (*c.* 1636), sc.13: 'men are
grown such dottrels, that they had rather give five or six shillings to be drunk,
like the Spaniard, with canary, or the Frenchman, with claret, than so many
pence to be foxed with their own native beer' (Dodsley, 12.353).
    11. *frock*] a poor man, one who wears a smock-frock (*H.&S.*).
    12–30.] P. Senior's 'advice' takes place against a background of contem-
porary prudential ideas and changing attitudes to usury. On one level, it
subtly distorts the familiar guidance given in a book like William Basse's *The
Countrimans Counsellour* (1621), which after a conventional account of the
fascinating but fickle Lady Pecunia urges the use of thrift: 'A penny is a small
regardlesse somme, / Yet may in some time to some thing come' (p. 260). But
this careful putting away is sharply distinguished from usury, which is seen

What a consumption thou hast made of a state?
It might please heaven, a lusty knave and young,
To let thee live some seventy years longer,   15
Till thou art fourscore and ten, perhaps a hundred.
Say seventy years: how many times seven in seventy?
Why, seven times ten is ten times seven. Mark me,
I will demonstrate to thee on my fingers.
Sixpence in seven year (use upon use)   20
Grows in that first seven year to be a twelvepence.
That, in the next, two shillings; the third, four shillings;
The fourth seven year, eight shillings; the fifth, sixteen;
The sixth, two and thirty; the seventh, three pound four;
The eighth, six pound and eight; the ninth, twelve pound
    sixteen;   25
And the tenth seven, five and twenty pound
Twelve shillings. This thou art fall'n from, by thy riot,
Shouldst thou live seventy years, by spending sixpence
Once i'the seven. But in a day to waste it!
There is a sum that number cannot reach.   · 30
Out o'my house, thou pest o'prodigality,
Seed o'consumption! Hence! A wicked keeper

---

not as a means of investment but as a threat from which savings can protect the common man; the author proceeds to discuss usury with 'her teeth discovered, that the borrower may beware' of thriftlessness and consequent dependence on money-lenders (p. 264). An earlier chart showing how savings can accumulate is set against one illustrating the uncontrollable multiplication of interest upon loans. The reader is warned: 'In 7.yeares, a terme of time but small, / The Interest lookes as bigge as principall' (p. 268). Yet there is an important ambiguity in this undertaking to show 'what the principall, with interest and interest upon interest from many summes amounteth unto ... which for the easinesse thereof, needes no further explication' (p. 267). The chief *practical* argument against usury at this time is that it discourages circulation and enterprise (e.g. Culpeper's *Tract against Usurie*, 1621, p. 1), and while the *moral* argument remained vocal (usury is 'the trayning of men into debt': *Usurie Araigned and Condemned*, 1625, p. 5), it is clear that the prudential ethic is not fundamentally in conflict with the case for usury (as Calvinist arguments had already shown). Jonson glosses this in his own way, demonstrating how easily the case for thrift can be appropriated by the usurer and twisted to serve an avaricious extreme.

20. *use upon use*] at compound interest. *H.&S.* comment: 'apparently of 100 per cent.; Penyboy is delirious', but in fact the figures show him using the old 10 percent rate of interest (see note to II.i.4) in compound form. P. Senior's delirium only increases his obsessive precision in money matters.

Is oft worse than the prisoners. There's thy penny,
Four tokens for thee. [*He pays him.*] Out, away. My
    dogs   [*Exit* Porter.]
May yet be innocent and honest. If not,   35
I have an entrapping question or two more
To put unto 'em, a cross-interr'gatory,
And I shall catch 'em. Lollard!
(*He calls forth Lollard and examines him.*) Peace!
What whisp'ring was that you had with Mortgage
When you last licked her feet? The truth now! Ha,   40
Did you smell she was going? [*To an imaginary clerk.*] Put
    down that. – And not,
Not to return? You are silent? Good. And when
Leaped you on Statute? As she went forth? 'Consent'!
There was consent as she was going forth?
'Twould have been fitter at her coming home,   45
But you knew that she would not –? To your tower.
(*He commits him again.*) You are cunning, are you? I will
    meet your craft.
(*Calls forth Block and examines him.*) Block, show your
    face; leave your caresses. Tell me,
And tell me truly, what affronts do you know
Were done Pecunia that she left my house?   50
None? Say you so? Not that you know, or will know?
I fear me I shall find you an obstinate cur.
Why did your fellow Lollard cry this morning?
'Cause Broker kicked him? Why did Broker kick him?
Because he pissed against my lady's gown?   55

---

41. S.D.] *This ed.*   43. 'Consent'!] *Consent.* F.

---

34. *tokens*] farthings.
38. *Lollard! . . . Peace!*] De Winter supposed that the dogs would be played
by boy-actors, as they apparently were in the scene from Aristophanes' *Wasps*
(891–1008) which Jonson's episode loosely resembles. But animals were
specially trained for the Elizabethan stage (see L. B. Wright in *P.M.L.A.*, 42
(1927), 656–69), and might have been trusted to bark or growl on cue both
here (motivating P. Senior's *Peace!*) and at line 46 in the next scene. The clash
of human delusion and placid canine reality is important to the episode. Samuel
Taylor Coleridge, clearly haunted by echoes of Tray, Blanch and Sweetheart,
commented rather desperately: 'I dare not, will not, think that honest Ben had
Lear in his mind in this mock mad scene' (*Literary Remains*, II.287).
51. *will know*] will admit to knowing.

Why, that was no affront? No? No distaste?
'You knew o'none'. You're a dissembling tyke.
(*Commits him.*) To your hole again, your Block-house.
Lollard, arise.
Where did you lift your leg up last? 'Gainst what?
Are you struck dummerer now, and whine for mercy?   60
Whose kirtle was't you gnawed, too? Mistress Band's?
And Wax's stockings, who? Did Block bescumber
Statute's white suit wi' the parchment lace there,
And Broker's satin doublet? All will out.
They had offence, offence enough to quit me.   65
Appear, Block. – Fough, 'tis manifest. He shows it.
Should he forswear't, make all the affidavits
Against it that he could afore the bench
And twenty juries, he would be convinced.
He bears an air about him doth confess it.   70

Enter the jeerers CYMBAL, FITTON, SHUNFIELD, ALMANAC
[*and*] MADRIGAL.

To prison again, close prison. Not you, Lollard,
You may enjoy the liberty o'the house.
And yet, there is a quirk come into my head,
For which I must commit you too, and close.
Do not repine, it will be better for you.   75

---

57. You're] Yo'are *F.*   59–60.] *F margin*: Lollard *is call'd again.*   62.
who? Did] who did? *F.*   66–7.] *F margin*: Blocke *is summon'd the second
time.*   70–1.] *F margin*: Hee *is remanded.*   70.1–2.] S.D. *placed here by
Gifford; Enter the* Ieerers. *F margin at start of V.v;* CYMBAL ... MADRIGAL
From V.v mass entry (see below).   73–4.] *F margin*: Lollard *has the liberty of
the house.*

---

57. *tyke*] cur.
60. *dummerer*] cant name for a beggar who pretended to be mute; de Winter
compares Dekker, *The Belman of London*, 'A Dummerar ... counterfets
Dumbnes; but let him be whipped well and his tongue ... will walke as fast, as
his handes doe when hee comes where any booty is' (Grosart III.103).
61. *kirtle*] woman's gown or outer petticoat.
62. *bescumber*] befoul.
63. *parchment lace*] 'Lace made of metal thread wound on thin threads of
parchment is extant. The term may also refer to the lace made with needle and
thread over patterns inked in parchment' (Linthicum, p. 134).
69. *convinced*] convicted.
73. *quirk*] sudden turn of thought (*H.&S.*).

ACT V   SCENE V

[*Cymbal.*] This is enough to make the dogs mad too.
  Let's in upon him.
P. Senior.   How now? What's the matter?
  Come you to force the prisoners? Make a rescue?
Fitton. We come to bail your dogs.
P. Senior.   They are not bailable.
  They stand committed without bail or mainprise.   5
  Your bail cannot be taken.
Shunfield.   Then the truth is,
  We come to vex you.
Almanac.   Jeer you.
Madrigal.   Bait you rather.
Cymbal. A baited usurer will be good flesh.
Fitton. And tender, we are told.
P. Senior.   Who is the butcher
  Amongst you that is come to cut my throat?   10
Shunfield. You would die a calf's death fain, but 'tis an ox's
  Is meant you.
Fitton.   To be fairly knocked o'the head –
Shunfield. With a good jeer or two.
P. Senior.   And from your jawbone,
  Don Assinigo?
Cymbal.   Shunfield, a jeer; you have it.
Shunfield. I do confess, a washing blow. But snarl,   15
  You that might play the third dog, for your teeth;
  You ha' no money now.

V.v.] ACT. V. SCENE. II. / CYMBAL. FITTON. SHVNFIELD. ALMA- / NACH.
MADRIGAL. PENY-BOY. SEN. / LICKFINGER. *F.*

V.v.5. *mainprise*] from the French *mainprendre*, to take in the hand; thus,
assume responsibility for, go surety for.
  8. *baited*] (1) tormented (as bulls and bears were by dogs); (2) bated: de-
graded, robbed of his power. Kifer notes the echo of III.iv.42. It was a common
belief (still held in some circles) that baited flesh makes better eating. See note
to line 47.
  13–14. *jawbone ... Assinigo*] Samson slew a thousand Philistines with the
jawbone of an ass (Judges, xv.15–17; so Kifer). The punning name derives
from Sp. *asnico*, meaning a little ass, here roughly 'dolt'; Jonson makes further
play with it in 'An Expostulation with Inigo Jones', 20: 'You would be an
asinigo, by your ears?' (*U.V.* 34). *H.&S.* compare a similar reference in *Troil.*,
II.i.43).
  15. *washing*] obsolete variant of 'swashing'.

Fitton.   No, nor no Mortgage.
Almanac. Nor Band.
Madrigal.   Nor Statute.
Cymbal.   No, nor blushet Wax.
P. Senior. Nor you no Office, as I take it.
Shunfield.   Cymbal,
     A mighty jeer.
Fitton.   Pox o'these true jests, I say.   20
Madrigal. He will turn the better jeerer.
Almanac. [*Rallying his companions.*]   Let's upon him,
     And if we cannot jeer him down in wit –
Madrigal. Let's do't in noise.
Shunfield.   Content.
Madrigal.   Charge, man o'war.
Almanac. Lay him aboard.
Shunfield.   We'll gi' him a broadside first.
Fitton. Where's your venison now?
Cymbal.   Your red-deer pies?   25
Shunfield. Wi' your baked turkeys?
Almanac.   And your partridges?
Madrigal. Your pheasants and fat swans?
P. Senior.   Like you, turned geese.
Madrigal. But such as will not keep your Capitol!
Shunfield. You were wont to ha' your breams –
Almanac.   And trouts sent in –
Cymbal. Fat carps and salmons –
Fitton.   Ay, and now and then,   30
     An emblem o'yourself, an o'ergrown pike.
P. Senior. You are a Jack, sir.

---

21. He will] *F;* He'll *Whalley.*   25. Where's] *F;* Where is *Whalley.*
29–31. in – ... salmons – ... pike.] *Kifer;* in? ... *Salmons? ... Pyke? F.*

---

20. *Pox ... jests*] proverbial: Tilley records this exact form of words (P537), but much more common are the sayings 'true jests are the worst' (J43) and 'the truest jests sound worst in guilty ears' (J44).
22–3. *if ... noise*] the jeerers' ultimate acknowledgement of their own futility.
25–7. *Where's ... swans*] the enticements previously offered to Pecunia's guardian; see II.iii.25–6.
27–8. *geese ... Capitol*] a hackneyed joke, referring to the legend of the geese whose cackling warned Rome of an attack on the Capitol in 390 B.C.
31. *o'ergrown pike*] The pike is notably voracious; see note to III.ii.176–9. De Winter points out that it was sometimes called a *jack*.

Fitton.   You ha' made a shift
    To swallow twenty such poor Jacks ere now.
Almanac. If he should come to feed upon poor John –
Madrigal. Or turn pure Jack-a-Lent after all this –   35
Fitton. Tut, he'll live like a grasshopper –
Madrigal.   On dew.
Shunfield. Or like a bear, with licking his own claws.
Cymbal. Ay, if his dogs were away.
Almanac.   He'll eat them first
    While they are fat.
Fitton.   Faith, and when they are gone,
    Here's nothing to be seen beyond.
Cymbal.   Except   40
    His kindred, spiders, natives o'the soil.
Almanac. Dust he will ha' enough here to breed fleas.
Madrigal. But by that time he'll ha' no blood to rear 'em.
Shunfield. He will be as thin as a lantern; we shall see through
    him –
Almanac. And his gut colon, tell his *intestina* –   45

34–5. John – ... this –] *Iohn?* ... this? *F.*   44. through] thorow *F.*

33–4. *poor Jacks ... poor John*] terms for dried hake.
    35. *Jack-a-Lent*] a stuffed figure set up in Lent to be pelted by children and
finally burned. Cf. *T.T.*, IV.ii.49–50: 'thou didst stand sixe weekes the *Jack*
of *Lent*, / For boyes to hoorle, three throwes a penny, at thee'. But the term
was also used more generally to personify the season of abstinence: John
Taylor affirms that '*Jack a Lent* hath no societie, affinitie or propinquitie with
flesh and blood' (*Workes* 1630, p. 113). Jonson draws on this idea to sharpen
our picture of the unfestive P. Senior but also to suggest the sterility of the
humour which uses the miser as its butt. Cf. Falstaff's remark in *Wiv.*,
V.v.127–9: 'See now how wit may be made a Jack-a-Lent, when 'tis upon ill
employment!'
    36.] Cf. Pliny's *Naturall Historie* (transl. Holland, 1601), p. 325: 'Of all
creatures that are known to live, the Grashoppers alone have no mouth: in
stead whereof, they have a certaine sharpe pointed thing in their breast ...
and with it they sucke and licke in the dew' (Kifer). Jonson may be remember-
ing also, as he does in *N.N.W.*, 202 (referring to those who live 'O'th'deaw
o'th'Moone like Grashoppers'), Lucian's description of Empedocles' 'subsisting
on a diet of dew' in *Icaromenippus* (*Satirical Sketches*, transl. P. Turner,
p. 119).
    37.] Pliny says that hibernating bears 'fall to sucking of their fore-feet, and
this is all their food whereof they live for the time' (p. 216) (Kifer).
    42.] the doctrine of equivocal generation; Pliny examines its various forms
and avers that 'ye shall have others again engendere of filthie drie dust, namely, fleas, which use to skip and hop with their hinder feet lustily' (p. 329).
    45. *colon*] i.e. belly. The word was often used figuratively for appetite, as in

P. Senior. Rogues! Rascals!   (*His dogs bark*: bow wow.)
Fitton.   He calls his dogs to his aid.
Almanac. O, they but rise at mention of his tripes.
Cymbal. Let them alone; they do it not for him.
Madrigal. They bark *se defendendo.*
Shunfield.   Or for custom,
    As commonly curs do, one for another.   50

[*Enter* LICKFINGER.]

Lickfinger. Arm, arm you, gentlemen jeerers, th'old Canter
    Is coming in upon you with his forces;
    The gentleman that was the Canter.
Shunfield.   Hence!
Fitton. Away!
Cymbal.   What is he?
Almanac.   Stay not to ask questions.
Fitton. He's a flame.
Shunfield.   A furnace.
Almanac.   A consumption,   55
    Kills where he goes.   (*They all run away.*)
Lickfinger.   See! The whole covey is scattered.
    'Ware, 'ware the hawk! I love to see him fly.

ACT V   SCENE vi

[*Enter*] PENNYBOY CA[NTER], PENNYBOY JU[NIOR], PECUNIA [*with her attendants* STATUTE, BAND, WAX *and* MORTGAGE].

[*P. Canter.*] You see by this amazement and distraction
    What your companions were, a poor, affrighted

46.] *As Gifford (subst.);* Rascalls (*baw waw) [*In margin:*] **His dogges barke.* F.
57. hawk] *Whalley; Hawkes* F.   V.vi.0.1–2.] PENY-BOY. CA. PENY-BOY.
SE. PENI-BOY. / IV. PECVNIA. TRAINE. *F.*

Middleton's *A Chaste Maid in Cheapside*, II.ii.79 (Revels), where the hungry Allwit exclaims: 'What cares colon here for Lent?' Jonson is of course making the opposite point about P. Senior.
    tell] count. Given Almanac's trade, there may be a reference to fortune-telling by examining the entrails of slaughtered animals.
    47.] Cf. *E.H.*, II.ii.229, where Quicksilver hopes 'to see dog's meat made of the old usurer's flesh' (Revels).
    49. *se defendendo*] in self-defence.
    57. *'Ware* ... *hawk*] proverbial: 'A phrase applied to an officer of the law, who pounced upon criminals' (Tilley H227).

And guilty race of men that dare to stand
No breath of truth, but conscious to themselves
Of their no-wit or honesty, ran routed   5
At every panic terror themselves bred.
Where else, as confident as sounding brass,
Their tinkling captain, Cymbal, and the rest
Dare put on any visor to deride
The wretched, or with buffon licence jest   10
At whatsoe'er is serious, if not sacred.
P. *Senior.* Who's this? My brother, and restored to life?
P. *Canter.* Yes, and sent hither to restore your wits,
If your short madness be not more than anger
Conceivèd for your loss, which I return you.   15
See here, your Mortgage, Statute, Band and Wax,
Without your Broker, come to abide with you
And vindicate the prodigal from stealing
Away the lady. Nay, Pecunia herself
Is come to free him fairly and discharge   20
All ties but those of love unto her person,
To use her like a friend, not like a slave
Or like an idol. Superstition

---

10. buffon] *F;* buffoon *F3.*   12–15.] *F margin:* Peny-boy Se. *acknowl-
edgeth his elder brother.*

V.vi.3. *stand*] face.
6. *panic terror*] Cf. Massinger, *The Duke of Milan,* I.iii.165–7: 'Where
is *Sforza?* / To whom all dangers that fright common men, / Appear'd but
Panicque terrors?' (*E.&G.* I.230). *O.E.D.* glosses out of Holland's translation
of Plutarch (1603): 'sudden foolish frights, without any certeine cause, which
they call *Panique Terrores*'; this is recorded as the first use of 'panic', which
apparently came from the French: Cotgrave finds *'panique* ... Distraught with
causeless fear' in Rabelais.
7–8. *sounding* ... *Cymbal*] See The Persons of the Play, note 4, and
III.ii.115 note.
10. *buffon licence*] (1) the freedom granted to a jester or fool; (2) licentious
buffoonery.
12.] In this line and the marginal note (see collation), Jonson recalls the
spirit of the prodigal son parable whilst modifying some of its details: the
father as well as the son is 'restored', and the casting of Canter as the elder
brother avoids (as it were) the traditional disaffection of that character in the
episode of the prodigal's return.
14. *short* ... *anger*] Horace's 'Ira furor brevis est' (*Epistles,* I.ii.62). See also
note to III.iv.44 (*H.&S.*).
22–3. *To* ... *idol*] Cf. Barnfield, *The Encomion of Lady Pecunia*: 'Yet

Doth violate the deity it worships
No less than scorn doth. And believe it, brother,   25
The use of things is all, and not the store:
Surfeit and fullness have killed more than famine.
The sparrow with his little plumage flies
While the proud peacock, overcharged with pens,
Is fain to sweep the ground with his grown train   30
And load of feathers.
P. Senior.   Wise and honoured brother,
None but a brother and sent from the dead,
As you are to me, could have altered me;
I thank my destiny, that is so gracious.
Are there no pains, no penalties decreed   35
From whence you come, to us that smother money
In chests and strangle her in bags?
P. Canter.   O mighty,
Intolerable fines, and mulcts imposed
(Of which I come to warn you), forfeitures
Of whole estates, if they be known and taken!   40
P. Senior. I thank you, brother, for the light you have given
          me;
I will prevent 'em all. First, free my dogs,
Lest what I ha' done to them (and against law)
Be a praemunire. For, by Magna Carta,

---

44. praemunire] *F3; Premuniri F.*

would I wish, the Wight that loves her so, / ... / To use her wisely, lest she
prove his foe; / ... / She may be kyst; but shee must not be *clypt'* (*Poems*,
p. 92).
    26.] proverbial: 'Use is all' (Tilley U23).
    27.] proverbial: 'More die by food than famine' (Tilley F441), and a host of
related proverbs. Ironically, P. Senior has in one sense lived by this axiom (cf.
II.iii.25f, III.iv.45f), but the statement of the golden mean momentarily
comprehends the kinship of reckless consumption and retentive avarice as
material indulgences.
    29. *pens*] plumes.
    35. *pains*] punishments.
    36. *From ... come*] i.e. beyond the grave. P. Senior's occupation tradi-
tionally assigns him a place in hell.
    38. *mulcts*] fines.
    40. *known and taken*] perhaps a hendiadys: 'known to have been appro-
priated'.
    44. *praemunire*] the offence of taking a case to court outside the jurisdiction
of the Crown, usually punishable by forfeiture (Kifer). Jonson uses the word
more loosely, suggesting merely a violation of legal process.

They could not be committed as close prisoners,   45
My learned counsel tells me here, my cook.
And yet, he showed me the way first.
Lickfinger.   Who did? I?
I trench the liberty o'the subjects?
P. Canter.   Peace.
Picklock your guest, that stentor, hath infected you,
Whom I have safe enough in a wooden collar.   50
P. Senior. Next, I restore these servants to their lady
With freedom, heart of cheer, and countenance.
It is their year and day of jubilee.
Attendants. We thank you, sir.
P. Senior.   And lastly, to my nephew,
I give my house, goods, lands, all but my vices,   55
And those I go to cleanse, kissing this lady
Whom I do give him too, and join their hands.
P. Canter. If the spectators will join theirs, we thank 'em.
P. Junior. And wish they may, as I, enjoy Pecunia.

---

49. guest] Ghest *F.*   54. S.H. *Attendants.*] *This ed.;* TRA. *F; Omnes.*
Gifford.   55–6.] *F margin: Her Traine thanks him.*

44–8. *For . . . subjects*] Kifer shows that these lines were added by Jonson
to the printed text of the play, almost certainly to protect himself against a
charge of libel. (See 'Too Many Cookes . . .', *English Language Notes*, 11
(1974), 264–7.) As Cunningham noted, the passage alludes to the eminent
lawyer Sir Edward Coke (who Kifer argues is the original of P. Senior), and is
apparently designed to identify him with Lickfinger (*my cook*) and thus distract
from his caricature in the shape of the old and unappealing usurer. Not all of
Kifer's parallels between Coke and P. Senior carry conviction, but there can be
no doubt that Jonson refers here to a controversy over civil liberties in the 1628
parliament, and that Coke, who had been out of favour in 1625, had regained
much of his former influence in the years when Jonson was preparing *Staple*
for the press.
49. *guest*] lodger. See II.v.112–13.
stentor] See second note to V.ii.34. De Winter compares *The Gypsies
Metamorphos'd*, 1340: 'a Lawier three parte noise'.
53. *year . . . jubilee*] appropriately for a play completed in 1625; in seventeenth century England a jubilee was celebrated every twenty-five years. But
the phrase *year of jubilee* is of Biblical origin (Leviticus, xxv), and designated a
'year of emancipation and restoration, which . . . was to be kept every fifty
years . . . during it the fields were to be left uncultivated, Hebrew slaves were
to be set free, and lands and houses in the open country or unwalled towns that
had been sold were to revert to their former owners or their heirs' (*O.E.D.*;
so Kifer). Jonson is probably not thinking of such distant precedent with any
precision, but his interest in festivity here goes beyond the familiar calendar to
more radical notions of restitution and release.

Pecunia. And so Pecunia herself doth wish,   60
     That she may still be aid unto their uses,
     Not slave unto their pleasures or a tyrant
     Over their fair desires, but teach them all
     The golden mean: the prodigal how to live,
     The sordid and the covetous how to die;   65
     That, with sound mind; this, safe frugality.

                                        [*Exeunt.*]

                    THE END.

The Epilogue

Thus have you seen the maker's double scope,
To profit and delight; wherein our hope
Is, though the clout we do not always hit,
It will not be imputed to his wit –
A tree so tried and bent as 'twill not start.   5
Nor doth he often crack a string of art,
Though there may other accidents as strange
Happen; the weather of your looks may change,
Or some high wind of misconceit arise
To cause an alteration in our skies.   10
If so, we're sorry that have so misspent
Our time and tackle, yet he's confident,
And vows the next fair day, he'll have us shoot
The same match o'er for him, if you'll come to't.

                                                       [*Exit.*]

1–14.] *Italic in F.*   11. we're] *we'are F; w'are F3.*   12. he's] *he'is F.*

---

3. *clout*] The closing speech renews the archery figure from The Prologue
for the Stage, lines 27–8. 'Clout is merely the French *clou*, the wooden pin by
which the target is fastened to the butt. As the head of this pin was commonly
painted *white*, to hit the *white*, and hit the *clout*, were of course synonymous:
both phrases expressed perfection in art, or success of any kind. In pursuing
his metaphor, Jonson mentions the accidents by which the highest skill in
archery was occasionally defeated; humidity which affected the elasticity of the
string and high winds which diverted the course of the shaft' (Gifford).

4–5.] i.e. that any shortcomings won't be put down to the old author's
waning powers. But the apology is less Jonson's admission of incipient dotage
than, perhaps, an acknowledgement of changing tastes, of the increasing difficulty in reaching his audience with the old truths, and of the likelihood that
his dramatic fable will look old-fashioned, the product of a talent that is *tried
and bent* and easily dismissed as obsolete.

5. *tree*] bow.
start] let fly.
9. *misconceit*] misconception.

255

Jonson and Athenaeus

Athenaeus's *Deipnosophistae* (The Sophists at Dinner), which makes extensive quotation from now lost Greek comedies where cooking was a prominent theme (see notes to IV.ii.5–40, 11–13), is a work which feeds Jonson's satiric imagination at a number of points in the play, allowing him to exploit the metaphor of art as a feast without having to commit himself to a statement about its ultimate validity.

References are to the edition by C. B. Gulick (London, 1927), but I have preferred the translations of these passages by J. M. Edmonds in *The Fragments of Attic Comedy* (Leiden, 1957–61), for which sources are also cited.

(*a*) *The Staple*, III.ii.165–79. Compare Athenion, *The Samothracians*:

Cook. Do you or don't you know that piety
    Owes nearly everything to cookery?
B. Piety?
Cook. Yes, of course, barbarian.
    It turned a treacherous animal into man,
    Stopped cannibalism, started discipline,
    And clothed us in the life we're living in.
                                    (xiv.660; Edmonds, III.253)

(*b*) III.iii.30–4. Compare Hegesippus, *The Brothers*:

Cook.   . . . whenever I apply
    My skill to a funeral feast, the folks in black
    Who've gone to the burying are no sooner back
    Than off my lid goes, and the mourners smile;
    Their insides tickle so, in a little while
    You'd think it was a wedding.
                                    (vii.290; Edmonds, III.257)

(*c*) IV.ii.20–9. Compare an unnamed play by Poseidippus:

Seuthes (a cook, speaking of his own profession).
    He might be a fine general ... Here the enemy's
    The whole array of guests, an army corps;
    They move in force, they've had a week or more
    Of waiting for this meal, and now they're in it;
    They're full of fight and thinking every minute
    They'll be at close quarters. Such a host recalls
    A wave that's gathered force before it falls.
                              (ix.377; Edmonds, III.241)

The Staple and the news syndicate

Our knowledge of the news syndicate formed in 1622 (see Introduction, p. 22) is scanty, but D. F. McKenzie has suggested some possible parallels between this organisation and Jonson's fiction. Linking the names of the six stationers known to have been part of the syndicate with evidence that Captain Thomas Gainsford edited their newsbooks in 1622–23, McKenzie offers, as an appendix to his Sandars Lectures on *The London Book Trade in the Later Seventeenth Century* (Cambridge 1976; unpublished), the following avowedly speculative table:

A.	CYMBAL 'the just moiety'	£700	*Thomas Gainsford*
B.	1. FITTON (Court)	100	Thomas Archer
	2. AMBLER (Paul's)	100	Nicholas Bourne
	3. BUZ (Exchange)	100	Nathaniel Butter
	4. PICKLOCK (Westminster)	100	Bartholomew Downes
	5. REGISTER	100	Nathaniel Newbury
	6. EXAMINER	100	William Sheffard
	7. (*a*) Nathaniel 'A decayed		
	stationer'	50	
	(*b*) Thomas the Barber	50	
		£1,400	

These figures are based on Cymbal's description of the Staple at I.v.106–14, and the fact that Pennyboy Junior buys Tom Barber a half-share for £50 (line 135). The pairing of names in this table is of course merely a convenience. In the play, Nathaniel the 'decayed stationer' is a lampoon of Nathaniel Butter; as McKenzie points out, 'Butter's role is satirically undervalued and there is no way of telling how accurately Jonson has assessed the stock' (p. 6). Furthermore, there is no evidence that Captain Thomas Gainsford was a shareholder in the enterprise, or that one partner dominated the syndicate in this way (though Butter was clearly a leading figure). Despite being modelled in part on Gainsford, Cymbal is very much Jonson's independent creation, an imaginary authority-figure and new broom ('It is not now as when the Captain lived', I.iv.17) who has no exact counterpart in the relatively makeshift world of Jacobean publishing. (For more on Gainsford, see Wayne H. Phelps's profile in *P.B.S.A.*, 73 (1979), 79–85, and Mark Eccles, 'Thomas Gainsford "Captain Pamphlet"', *H.L.Q.*, 45 (1982), 259–70 – though Phelps's assumption that Gainsford edited for Butter until July 1624 is almost certainly incorrect. The Captain's retirement during the previous year appears to be recorded in the letter from Joseph Mead reproduced by L. Hanson in *The Library* (4th series), 18 (1937–38), 382.) It is possible, in fact, that hints of Gainsford's editorial role linger as much in the shadowy figure of the Examiner who 'sits private there within' (I.v.4); if we combine this suggestion with the fact that Newbery dropped out of the syndicate after only a few months, it seems possible that in thinking of a seven-share operation (leaving aside Cymbal with his 'moiety'), Jonson had in mind the five remaining stationers, Gainsford as editor, and a share subdivided – as in the play – between junior associates.

All this, as McKenzie makes clear, is very speculative; by the time the play was performed, in any case, the syndicate had broken up and quite different commercial relations were in force.

Glossarial Index to the Commentary

An asterisk before a word indicates that the annotation contains information regarding meaning, usage or date which supplements that given in the *O.E.D.*

Epil. = Epilogue; Ind. = Induction; Int. = Intermean; Pers. = The Persons of the Play; Prol.Ct. = Prologue for the Court; Prol.St. = Prologue for the Stage; Read. = To the Readers (preface to Act III).